THE TRUTH, THE WAY, THE LIFE

CHRISTIAN COMMENTARY ON THE THREE HOLY MANTRAS OF THE ŚRĪVAIṢṆAVA HINDUS

CHRISTIAN COMMENTARIES ON NON-CHRISTIAN SACRED TEXTS

GENERAL EDITOR

Catherine Cornille

EDITORIAL BOARD

David Burrell, Francis Clooney, Paul Griffiths,
James Heisig

EDITORIAL ADVISORS

Daniel Joslyn-Siemiatkoski, Daniel Madigan, Joseph O'Leary,
Nicolas Standaert, Paul Swanson, Elliot Wolfson

The series "Christian Commentaries on Non-Christian Sacred Texts" provides a forum for Christian reflection on the meaning and importance of sacred texts (scriptures and religious classics) of other religious traditions for Christian faith and practice.

THE TRUTH, THE WAY, THE LIFE

CHRISTIAN COMMENTARY ON THE THREE HOLY MANTRAS OF THE ŚRĪVAIṢṆAVA HINDUS

BY

FRANCIS X. CLOONEY, S.J.

PEETERS
LEUVEN – PARIS – DUDLEY, MA

WILLIAM B. EERDMANS PUBLISHING COMPANY
GRAND RAPIDS, MICHIGAN/CAMBRIDGE, U.K.

2008

Published jointly 2008
in Belgium by
Peeters Publishers
Bondgenotenlaan 153
3000 Leuven
and in the United States of America by
Wm. B. Eerdmans Publishing Company
2140 Oak Industrial Dr. N.E., Grand Rapids, Michigan 49505 /
P.O. Box 163 Cambridge CB3 9PU U.K.
www.eerdmans.com

Manufactured in Belgium

12 11 10 09 08 5 4 3 2 1

A catalogue record for this book is available from the Library of Congress.

Eerdmans ISBN 978-0-8028-6413-0
Peeters ISBN 978-90-429-2047-7
D. 2008/0602/43

In gratitude to the great commentators of the
Vaṭakalai Śrīvaiṣṇava tradition
from Śrī Uttamūr T. Vīrarāghavācārya
back to Śrī Vedānta Deśika
and his own teachers as well:
by the light of their wisdom and insight
my own small contribution has found its voice

TABLE OF CONTENTS

PREFACE

For more than thirty years I have been reflecting on Hindu religious traditions. As the primary means of that reflection, I have been studying classic Hindu texts and commentaries. Some of my books – *Thinking Ritually* (1990), *Theology after Vedanta* (1993), *Seeing through Texts* (1996) – have been dedicated simply to explicating one or another classic text from the Sanskrit or Tamil traditions. Other projects have been thematic, aimed at clearing a space for thoughtful comparisons with similar ideas in the Catholic tradition. My recent books, for instance – *Hindu God, Christian God* (2001) and *Divine Mother, Blessed Mother* (2005) – were comparative studies that traced, respectively, theological reasoning as a practice common to both the Hindu and Christian traditions (dogmatic differences notwithstanding), and intense contemplation of the supreme female person as a theological topic and spiritual practice shared by some Hindus and Christians, despite evident differences between Mary and the Goddesses. Such studies, even as thematic, clear the mind and, ideally, make it impossible for the thoughtful person to retreat to study that is not comparative.

In *The Truth, the Way, the Life*, I return most directly to the practice that is my deepest intellectual commitment – reading texts, spending a long time with just a single classic, and reflecting on what can be learned by contemporary readers from a powerful religious text and the cultivated habit of reading it. Professor Catherine Cornille's invitation to contribute to her new series, *Christian Commentaries on Non-Christian Texts*, gave me the opportunity to spend a great deal of time with the *Śrīmad Rahasyatrayasāra* (*Auspicious Essence of the Three Mysteries*), itself a prolonged reading of three holy Mantras, and to spell out in detail what I have learned from Śrī Vedānta Deśika's reading of the three holy Mantras of his tradition. Though aware of the great riches of other Śrīvaiṣṇava authors whose work must also be honored – Śrī Piḷḷai Lokācārya, for instance, stands at the fore – this was the opportunity to read Deśika at length and in detail; perhaps other occasions will allow me to explore the Śrīvaiṣṇava tradition still more broadly, and to try to write from my reading in a way that is helpful to other readers as well; in this case my audience is primarily Christian, though hopefully not exclusively so.

As is most often the case in writing, projects weave together and borrow from one another. I first presented materials on the *Essence* in seminars at Boston College (beginning in the late 1990s) and the Center for Hindu Studies at the University of Oxford (in 2002), and as recently as May 2007 returned to Oxford to present further reflections on the study of the three Mantras. The Bellarmine Lecture at St. Louis University in October 2006 afforded me the opportunity to discuss my approach to commentary on the text of another tradition. A recent essay for the *International Journal of Hindu Studies* was devoted entirely to Deśika's exegesis of the Dvaya Mantra, and some of the ideas, translations, and choices of texts that eventually found their place here in Chapter 3 were first articulated for that essay. I was also honored to give The Prof. K. R. Sundararajan Endowment Lectures (2006-2007) in the Department of Vaishnavism at the University of Madras on Deśika's reading of the Carama Śloka in light of the parallel reading by Piḷḷai Lokācārya and Manavāḷamāmuni, and am grateful to Dr. V. Raghavan and Dr. M. Venkatakrishnan for that opportunity. I am of course grateful to Professor Cornille for the opportunity to publish in this new series.

Most notable, in terms of time commitment, was the other book project that occupied me during my sabbatical year of 2006-2007: *Beyond Compare: St. Francis de Sales and Śrī Vedānta Deśika on Surrender to God*, an exercise in a double and increasingly intense reading of these powerful authors on the major theme of their works, surrender to God; much of my year was spent in reading and writing back and forth from one manuscript to the other. In an ideal world where readers have very great patience, *The Ṭruth, the Way, the Life* would begin a reading that would be completed in *Beyond Compare*, interreligious reading and learning oriented to and then fulfilled in the act of surrender as perfected by two great authors, Hindu and Christian, in their great texts. And if all these seminars, lectures, and publications overlap, it was inevitable that they should do so, since they all grew out of my need to put into words what Vedānta Deśika taught so powerfully. I am indebted to all those who provided these contexts in which my interconnected projects could thus grow, together, each with its own character yet echoing the other as well.

I am grateful to Harvard Divinity School for the 2006-2007 sabbatical and to my new colleagues there for their encouragement during the year. I am indebted to my Jesuit brothers at Boston College where I continued to live during the writing of what has turned out to be the last project completed during my 23 years at BC. I am grateful in particular to my most patient brothers in community, Nicholas Austin, Thomas

Regan and, most poignantly, my very good friend Ronald Anderson who died just as this book was nearing its conclusion.

Professors Mangalam R. Parameswaran, Retired Professor of the University of Manitoba, and Anuradha Sridharan, Associate Editor of *Nrsimacharya* in Mylapore, Chennai, were most generous in their willingness to read the manuscript and give me their detailed comments. With their help, I have avoided some of the smaller and larger mistakes I would otherwise have made; had I the opportunity to read for a long period of time with them and other teachers, many of the remaining imperfections too would have been eradicated.

I have done the best I could in the writing of the Mantras and Deśika's commentary and yet, of course, the more I have delved into the tradition, the more I have become aware of how much more there is to learn, and how little a beginning I have made in this learning. Vedānta Deśika himself prefaces the 32 chapters of his *Essence* with a preface entitled "The Essence of the Lineage of Teachers," in which he emphasizes that it is imperative to begin teaching – or writing – only after due acknowledgment of and reverence for one's teachers. For reasons of opportunity, time, and religious commitment I could not sit with a Śrīvaiṣṇava teacher for a thorough study of the *Essence*, but I did, at every turn consult the commentaries listed in my Bibliography, from the early *Sārāsvādinī* of Sri Vedanta Ramanuja and Sri Gopala Desika, to the *Sārabodhinī* of Sri Srirangasankopa Yatindramahadesika, and the classic of our era, the *Sāravistaram* of Sri Uttamur T. Viraraghavacharya. In the spirit of Deśika's admonition that we remember our teachers with gratitude when taking up something so precious as the Mantras, I, a latter day Ekalavya, dedicate this volume to the great teachers of our era, such as Sri Uttamur T. Viraraghavacharya, and to his predecessors, all the way back to Deśika and his teachers as well.

INTRODUCTION

THE THREE HOLY MANTRAS: COMMENTARY AND CHRISTIAN COMMENTARY

Aum, obeisance to Nārāyaṇa! (Tiru Mantra)

Having completely given up all dharmas,
to Me alone come for refuge... (Carama Śloka, 1st Line)

I approach for refuge the feet of Nārāyaṇa with Śrī.
Obeisance to Nārāyaṇa with Śrī! (Dvaya Mantra)

...from all sins I will make you free. Do not grieve. (Carama Śloka, 2nd Line)

In *The Truth, the Way, and the Life*, I offer a Christian commentary on three Hindu mantras, specific sacred words which, as meditated on and interiorized with a clear understanding of their meaning, are powerful in transforming the practitioner. More specifically, I am reading the three holy Mantras of the Śrīvaiṣṇava Hindu tradition, and exploring how they have been understood in that Śrīvaiṣṇava tradition. On that basis and by extension, I ask also what they can mean for readers today (presumably for the most part) from outside that tradition and, given the nature of the Series in which this book appears, for Christian readers in particular. This chapter serves as a brief introduction to the project of (Christian) commentary on the Mantras.

Given all the important and interesting things – mostly everything in life, I suppose – that occur outside texts, it may be that commentary as dedicated close reading goes against the grain, with its insistence that we go deeper into a text itself, finding ever deeper meanings within it. Although such a focus may seem rather narrow, or even impossible given sensitivities to context, history, and what texts do not tell us but rather hide, commentary is worthwhile, as the following pages will show. As the dedicated reading of texts, particularly in loyalty to a tradition of earlier interpretation, commentary is a most effective way to learn religiously; it generates specific concerns and insights that ultimately disclose a very wide view of reality. The value of close reading is evident even when the challenges are modest; while some texts are extraordinarily difficult and require commentary if we are to make sense of them at all, difficulty is not the main reason for commentary. Regarding more typical texts that are demanding without being particularly obscure, these are quite often rich enough in meaning and implications that they merit continued reading and exploration, over a longer period of time, because we keep learning from them. Although we can always wish for more historical and cultural context and desire the benefits of reading with a wise teacher, a steadfast commitment to reading offers a simple approach that works better than most alternatives, if we want to understand a text of our own or another tradition.

In the following pages I first reflect upon the process of commentary and Christian commentary in general, and then turn to the three Mantras of the Śrīvaiṣṇava tradition and the commentator with whom I will read them; I will close this chapter with a brief preview of my method in the chapters to follow.

I. Commentary, Religious Reading, and Christian Commentary

Commentary is first of all simply a responsible *academic* activity, sensibly requiring that one be able and willing actually to read; it is also a *spiritual* activity, by which one cultivates close reading as a necessary basis for further reflection and deeper insight. As patient learning, primary[1] commentary is necessarily a matter of language learning and cultural and historical study; it requires the acquisition of skills for linguistic, cultural, and historical study, and then the actual practice of these skills. We need to take seriously whole texts, not merely select ideas or the more interesting parts of texts; we need to notice the specific characteristics of the whole literary documents before us in any given instance; genre, manner of writing, and the intentions of author (and redactor) are intrinsic to a text's significance, in addition to any theses or concepts proposed inside the text. Strategies for the use of prose and poetry, scriptural citation, anecdotes, allusions to divine and human spiritual exemplars, rebukes to opponents and appeals to readers to take the teaching to heart in practical ways – these are all substantive dimensions of what we are

[1] I do not preclude the idea that some commentaries may be done, and very well done, using translations.

reading and what is to be understood, requiring of us some similarly complex response.

Adherence to the close reading that is appropriate to commentary, along with the humility and openness that such reading requires, enables an intellectual and spiritual approach to interreligious truths and values, including even realities not easily expressed in words. To reconsider reading and reflection as deliberate spiritual activities, I direct our attention to two pertinent books.[2] Pierre Hadot's *Philosophy as a Way of Life: Spiritual Exercises from Socrates to Foucault* stands forth as particularly sensitive to philosophy as a way of life and spiritual practice, exemplified in certain instances in ancient Greece and (ideally) in some contemporary contexts as well.[3] Hadot expresses well the demands of this kind of learning as an interpretive, even commentarial practice:

> It was believed that the truth had been "given" in the master's texts, and that all that had to be done was to bring it to light and explicate it. Plotinus, for example, writes: "These statements are not new; they do not belong to the present time, but were made long ago, although not explicitly, and what we have said in this discussion has been an interpretation of them, relying on Plato's own writings for evidence that these views are ancient."

The claims of the consequent "exegetical" philosophy are therefore formidable: "Each philosophical or religious school or group believed itself to be in possession of a traditional truth, communicated from the beginning by the divinity to a few wise men. Each therefore laid claim to being the legitimate depository of the truth."[4] This depository often takes a textual form, and the teacher (most often as commentator) is the agent of the transmission of the text and also of the proper way of reading it to the next generation. In oral discourse, and then in writing, the enduring truth of the tradition is made available for new students, new readers. I suggest that for an adequate reading of a religious text of another tradition, we do well to adapt ourselves to the older model to which

2 Works such as de Lubac, and Leclerq confirm the rich contextualization that is possible and beneficial for learning that is intentionally rooted in scripture, tradition, and religious practice.

3 See also McGhee and Stalnaker. Fowl offers a specifically Christian reflection on the interplay between reading – engaging – the Bible and the theological dispositions one generates from and bring to that reading. Highlighting virtues that we can recognize as applicable to Hindu traditions as well, Fowl explores the communal, educational (and catechetical) and liturgical context of becoming a properly engaged reader of the Bible. He adjudicates the tensions and divergences between a Christian theological reading and the professional analysis of Biblical texts in academic settings.

4 P. 74

Hadot points us, even if this older way of reading is less systematic, necessarily prolonged and resistant to closure, and requiring "new" skills of the reader. The older way of reading – such as Hadot envisions in the Greek context, but also as might be found in numerous premodern religious cultures – is more adequate to what the authors of the great texts of other traditions had in mind; the subject matter of those texts makes fuller sense to readers whose reasoning is disciplined by tradition, and thus become vulnerable to the imaginative and affective dimensions of the writing that so intensely and insistently engages us in such texts.[5]

This spiritual reflection can be further nuanced by attention to Paul Griffiths' *Religious Reading: The Place of Reading in the Practice of Religion.* Even while describing particular details of reading and book production in several religious traditions, Griffiths too draws our attention to the worldview and habitus of faith proper to religious reading. Over against a consumerist (and rather too often academic or theological, narrowly and primly conceived) mining of texts in service of a preconceived agenda neglectful of the texts' own purposes, religious reading has to do

> primarily with the establishment of certain relations between readers and the things they read, relations that are at once attitudinal, cognitive, and moral, and that therefore imply an ontology, an epistemology, and an ethic... [I]t will, in every case, imply a distinctive set of relations between religious readers and their works.

Griffiths' estimation of this religious reading aptly mirrors our expectations regarding what goes into commentary on a text of another tradition; for in all such cases, we must submit ourselves, at least for a time, in order to learn:

> The first and most basic element in these relations is that the work read is understood as a stable and vastly rich resource, one that yields meaning, suggestions (or imperatives) for action, matter for aesthetic wonder, and

[5] Hadot notes that in ancient Greece and in cultures in continuity with Greece, study itself was thus reconstituted as a philosophical and religious act, an exegetical reasoning divergent from the philosophical expectations regarding "system" that were to become common in early modernity: "It is not the case that every properly philosophical endeavor is 'systematic' in the Kantian or Hegelian sense. For two thousand years, philosophical thought utilized a methodology which condemned it to accept incoherences and far-fetched associations, precisely to the extent that it wanted to be systematic. But to study the actual progress of exegetical thought is to begin to realize that thought can function rationally in many different ways, which are not necessarily the same as those of mathematical logic or Hegelian dialectic." (p. 76) A real shift occurred, when philosophers in the 17th century and thereafter "refused the argument from authority and abandoned the exegetical mode of thinking." (p. 76)

> much else. It is a treasure-house, an ocean, a mine: the deeper religious readers dig, the more ardently they fish, the more single-mindedly they seek gold, the greater will be their reward. The basic metaphors here are those of discovery, uncovering, retrieval, opening up: religious readers read what is there to be read, and what is there to be read always precedes, exceeds, and in the end supersedes its readers.

Griffiths' sense of the obligations incumbent upon the reader draws on and ably parallels the expectations of religious authors, Christian and in other faith traditions, who see their work as imposing high expectations on readers willing to read and reflect with a full awareness of the implications of that practice:

> The second, and almost equally important, constituent of the relations between religious readers and what they read is that readers are seen as intrinsically capable of reading and as morally required to read. Their capacity for retrieving the riches of the work by an act of reading is something intrinsic to them: they are essentially and necessarily readers, to the point where *homo lector* can be substituted for *homo sapiens* without loss and with considerable gain.[6]

Learning to be and act as a *homo lector* – obviously an identity dependent on but also beyond *homo sapiens* – is not a neutral or cost-free activity. It requires self-effacement before the text, patience, perseverance, and imagination; it is a humble practice that discloses productive ways of thinking and changes the reader, as she or he is drawn into the world of the text, even the text of another religious tradition.[7] Such are the readers who become competent to read the religious texts of their own and other traditions, receiving wisdom in the process.

Ideally, the issues and questions of the original, commented-on text take precedence over the concerns of the commentators, even the very concerns that motivate the project of reading across the boundaries of time, culture, and religion, and even if such concerns never entirely let go of their influence on the commentator. This is therefore a kind of writing in which the person and personality of the writer, the commentator, do not take center stage; indeed, the very best commentators seem intent upon self-effacement, as it were erasing themselves from their own writing about the text/s on which they are commenting. In our autobiographical age, this pattern of choosing to read intensively, self-effacement

[6] Pp. 41-42

[7] Such is my own extension of Griffiths' position; he does not see his model of religious reading as necessarily adaptable as a practice of interreligious reading.

in the reading, personal writing and yet an erasure of personal creativity, is all the harder to achieve and yet, in this context, all the more refreshing if it actually happens.[8]

Commentary requires self-effacement before the text, patience, perseverance, imagination and humble practice. Disclosing productive ways of thinking, it changes the reader as she or he is inevitably drawn into the world of the text and faced with the implications of its truths. Commentary is thus an intellectual activity that becomes a spiritual activity, a patient and long-term practice that involves the reader in the inscribed project of the text that is commented on. In understanding, learning, appreciating, appropriating slowly and over a long period of time, we become what we read, and ambiguously or not become part of the tradition of the text, though never perfectly if we begin from outside the tradition. We learn to re-read the tradition to which we already belong, and thus at least have a chance to renew and reform the values we began with.

To write a Christian commentary on a text of another religious tradition is therefore a delicate operation, if it is more than comments from a distance. The demands of *commentary* make it likely that readers expecting the early, prominent, and frequent appearance of the *Christian* commentator will be disappointed; it will be only after immersion in the discipline of commentary that this Christian reader can find and write words appropriate to a Christian reception of the text of the other tradition.

Nevertheless, we can say a little more about the character of a *Christian* commentary on a non-Christian text. In such a project, if it is truly Christian, we are not starting from nowhere; even apart from the Christian learning and sensitivities of the commentator who is a Christian, commenting as a Christian implies openness to drawing up a Christian tradition that itself is rich in examples of commentary ripe for application in interreligious reading.[9] After all, the traditions of the West were for a long time also commentarial traditions, dedicated to literary, philosophical, and religious classics – such as David Tracy has characterized as possessed of abundant and inexhaustible meanings.[10] While we could

[8] It is not incidental that it is difficult to write about a commentator as person, or even about the ideas of commentators; except in controversial contexts, commentators rightly tend to submerge their identities and agenda into the text of their commentaries.

[9] On the commentarial tradition see for instance "Theology, Scripture, and the Fourfold Sense," the first chapter in Volume 1 in de Lubac. For a recent reflection on our appropriation of the Bible, see Fowl, and Clooney 2002.

[10] See Tracy, and also Stendahl, who most aptly distinguishes kinds of classics, and the need to found broader notions of the Bible as classic literature in claims about the

look to any number of disciplines in the humanities for examples of commentary – great works of literature, the writings of Aristotle and Plato, the plays of Shakespeare – most apt as guiding examples are the commentaries on Biblical books, for example, the *Song of Songs*, the *Psalms*, and the letters of St. Paul. We can also look to commentaries on specific prayers, including commentaries on the Our Father by Cyprian or Aquinas, Bonaventure's *Mirror of the Blessed Virgin Mary*, essentially a commentary on the Hail Mary, and the Orthodox tradition of reflection on the "Jesus Prayer." Even in today's interreligious context, as we learn better to read the great texts of other religious traditions, we can still draw on these older examples for guidance.

It is important to admit the importance of other Christian predispositions for how one learns and makes use of the texts of another tradition. As Cornille indicates in her introduction to *Song Divine*, the first volume in this series, it should not be taken merely for granted that a Christian can and should read the great texts of other traditions closely and for religious purposes. Even sincere efforts in commentary undertaken for the benefit of Christians may be perceived of as problematic: "post colonial theory and the critiques of Orientalism have made us more hesitant to assume the right to interpretation of the religious texts, practices, or doctrines of traditions other than our own."[11] And so, Cornille indicates, it is a wise corrective to interreligious arrogance to decide not only to read a particular text of another tradition, but also, as I have suggested, to learn from traditional commentaries on that text: hence the importance of rejecting any notion of a merely superior reading from outside the other tradition that is studied.[12] We must consider ourselves accountable to those in whose tradition we read, welcoming even their more critical rejoinders to what we write. It seems most sensible to expect that friends in that other religious tradition we study will to some extent respect our work and to some extent notice and indicate shortcomings – even if, in the end, seeing it as different in kind from works written in the tradition. Thus, while the "Christian commentary on the three

Bible as Scripture(s) and Revelation – lest the notion of "classic" be impoverished and eventually proven inadequate. By extension, every commentary works with an implicit understanding of its text as classic, literature, scripture, guide to religious practice, and even revelation.

11 *Song Divine*, p. 4.

12 This is so, I suggest, even if new and old readings, from outside and inside a tradition, can be mutually corrective; at certain times, and in some respects, a Christian might do Śrīvaiṣṇavas a great service by reading a familiar text in a new way, just as Śrīvaiṣṇava readings of Christian classics may be of great value to Christians.

Mantras" that comprises this book will, I hope, have value for both Christian and Śrīvaiṣṇava readers, there is no reason to expect that Śrīvaiṣṇava Hindus will accept it as "a commentary of the Śrīvaiṣṇava tradition". It is wiser to hope for modest success, and moderate openness to the new possibilities of interreligious commentary.

What then makes a commentary "Christian"? Cornille suggests the following:

> Broadly speaking, a Christian commentary on the sacred text of another religion may be seen to involve a deliberate assumption of the Christian worldview and faith tradition as the hermeneutical lens through which a particular text is understood and interpreted. It attempts to elucidate the meaning and importance of a particular sacred text for a Christian readership, and to point to the way in which the reading of the text may come to deepen Christian self-understanding.[13]

A Christian may then read from a more or less definite Christian confessional and denominational basis, with varying degrees of certainty regarding the (possible or likely) superiority of Christian texts and doctrines, and similarly varied levels of openness to deepening and possibly challenging Christian views and practices through this study of the other.

But we must not run too hastily to the interreligious and Christian values of such reading; a commentary must first of all be well done. The demands of modern academic scholarship have raised the standard regarding any kind of close reading today, as a measure for judging the quality of the interpretation of a text. We know that perfectly adequate commentaries are written on Biblical and later Christian texts by authors who have no religious commitments or, at least, who bracket personal beliefs for the sake of academic scholarship. It should not be very easy to distinguish a "commentary on the *Gospel according to John*" from a "*Christian* commentary on the *Gospel according to John*," if we mean more than the prospect of Christians adding pious and pastoral comments after the scholarly exegesis. Similarly, it should not be easy to explain "a *Christian* commentary on a Hindu or Buddhist text" as distinct from (simply) "a commentary on a Hindu or Buddhist text." While the issues at stake are complex, we can at least say that a commentator who is an informed and committed Christian is first of all committed to close reading, contextual reading, and reading with a respectful awareness of indigenous tradition. *Then*, we hope, such a reader, shown to be a professional in her or his commentarial work, will *also* be mindful of and attuned to

[13] *Song Divine*, p. 5.

Christian spiritual realities communicated in and through Biblical and later revered writings of the Christian tradition, such as will bear on the interpretation and reception of a text of another tradition.

Issues of method and attitude aside, however, the significance of this kind of project for Christians will necessarily remain complex and uncertain. Complicated loyalties are in play when a Christian comments on a religious text from another tradition. If there are sacred truths inscribed in the text commented on, these will have to be considered alongside the enduring truths of the Christian tradition; if the prayers in such texts are prayerful communications with the deities of another tradition, the Christian will have to think more deeply about her or his prayerful relationship to Jesus and the God of Jesus, and how to understand these other deities respectfully and yet with fidelity to Christian faith. So too, being a Christian commentator should most often involve continued loyalty to a Christian community, in my case the Society of Jesus within the Roman Catholic Church, even while cultivating empathy with the tradition of the text being commented on – in this current book, the south Indian Śrīvaiṣṇava Hindu community of south India. Writing as a professedly Christian commentator clearly rules out any pretense of writing neutrally, even if complex multiple loyalties create problems that would be obviated by professing no loyalties at all. If Christian commentary on the texts of other traditions is worthwhile, it will also be worthwhile to find our way through the uncharted waters of mutual respect, openness to the other even while maintaining faith and loyalty in the Christian context.

Some Christian readers may still press the question of whether writing a commentary on another tradition's text, even if possible, is a good thing for a Christian to do – or instead, a dangerous activity that ultimately unsettles or even threatens the Faith. A close Christian reading of another tradition's text can, if read by others or discussed by second-hand report, confuse at least some Christians, particularly those who hear about the reading without venturing to do it themselves. Cornille, in the same introduction noted above, suggests that the work of commentary entails the question of "the *religious status* of sacred texts of other religions,"[14] a question on which there is a variety of views, ranging from contentment with the view that the text we approach is revelatory, a true transformative sacred word, to the view that such texts may (at best) contain "seeds" and "rays of Truth" – but also, inevitably for some, the view that there is nothing much at all for a Christian to learn from such texts. Let

[14] *Song Divine*, p. 5

the reader decide: while my close reading of a Hindu text – to which we now turn – is very much a respectful and positive reading, written in the conviction that we have much more to learn from the other tradition than we could possibly anticipate, I have also tried to make the content and meaning of the text available in a clear enough way that readers may decide for themselves at what level to take it to heart and learn from it.

But it is only in commentary and the reading of commentary, and not in more abstract discussion of methods and presuppositions, that the significance of the text of another tradition for the Christian becomes evident. In all seriousness, I hope that it will be impossible for readers to assess the value of *The Truth, the Way, the Life*, unless they read it first. But now let us get into the substance of this study, by turning to the three Mantras and their tradition.

II. The Three Holy Mantras of the Śrīvaiṣṇavas

1. The Śrīvaiṣṇava Tradition

Śrīvaiṣṇavism is devoted to the worship of Nārāyaṇa as the sole God who is ever accompanied by his consort, Śrī. While the existence of other deities is admitted, they are firmly subordinated to Nārāyaṇa and Śrī. Theology and ancillary disciplines (cosmology, ethics, ritual, language) are enlisted to emphasize the centrality of Nārāyaṇa with Śrī, theologically, in practice, and in the rarer, experiential, advanced states of the mystical life.

Flourishing primarily in the areas of Southeast India known as Tamil Nadu and Andhra Pradesh, Śrīvaiṣṇavism is rooted in the great Sanskrit tradition of India, drawing on the Vedas and Vedic way of life, the Upaniṣads, *Bhagavad Gītā*, *Mahābhārata* and *Rāmāyaṇa*, various *Purāṇas*, and a host of other texts in the Pāñcarātra tradition. But, in its most distinctive feature, it is also rooted in the culture and literature of the Tamil language, most notably the devotional tradition of the ālvārs (7th-9th centuries), thus appropriating a rich affective tradition of religious commitment and desire for God founded in south Indian locale, culture, and temple cult. In the 9th century and thereafter, great teachers such as Nāthamuni, Āḷavantār, and Rāmānuja began weaving together more systematically the teachings of the Sanskrit and Tamil traditions, into what is often called the "Ubhaya Vedānta," that is, the "double" Vedānta possessed of Sanskrit and Tamil literary, theological, and spiritual values. This "weaving" was of course a complex process, and one not a matter of easy synthesis, given the variety of approaches, styles of writing, and particular issues operative in the textual traditions at issue in the syntheses of these early, influential theologians. While eventually the tradition divided into "northern" (*vaṭakalai*) and "southern" (*teṅkalai*) schools that might be understood as giving priority, respectively, to Sanskrit or Tamil dimensions of the joint heritage, the social and theological factors dividing schools was and remains insufficient to gainsay their larger and more important commonality as Śrīvaiṣṇava schools.[15] While in this commentary I rely on just one commentator of the *vaṭakalai* school, I readily admit that a rich and interesting interpretation could just as well be based on the commentaries of the *teṅkalai* tradition.

2. The Three Mantras[16]

The three holy Mantras are at the heart of the Śrīvaiṣṇava faith, taken to be expressive of the core truths, practices, and goals of the tradition. They encode in three ways *prapatti*,[17] which is the act of taking refuge with the divine couple Nārāyaṇa and Śrī – surrendering all responsibility and concern for one's well-being to them; and they show by implication all that is at stake in a life that leads up to, is built around, and consequent upon, that act of surrender.

Despite the voluminous commentaries they generate, the Mantras themselves are brief and seemingly rather clear:

> Tiru Mantra: Aum, obeisance to Nārāyaṇa.
> Carama Śloka, First Line: Having completely given up all *dharmas*, to Me alone come for refuge.
> Dvaya Mantra: I approach for refuge the feet of Nārāyaṇa with Śrī. Obeisance to Nārāyaṇa with Śrī.
> Carama Śloka, Second Line: From all sins I will make you free. Do not grieve.

[15] Both traditions are located primarily in what is today the Indian state of Tamil Nadu. While "northern" and "southern" may be taken to indicate the intellectual and spiritual centers located respectively in Kanchipuram and Srirangam, it may also indicate the greater Vaṭakalai use of the Sanskrit tradition, even if both Vạtakalai and Teṅkalai affirm and draw on both Sanskrit and Tamil sources.

[16] There is a significant body of literature on the meaning and use of mantras in Hindu and other Indian traditions. See for example, Coward and Goa; Alper; Padoux; and Patton. The best starting point is probably Gonda, "The Indian Mantra," an essay both detailed and comprehensive. On the specifically Śrīvaiṣṇava understanding of mantra, see Mumme, and Gupta.

[17] Other terms for this act of surrender are *śaraṇāgati*, taking refuge, and *bharanyāsa*, laying down with the Lord one's burden. The standard word for devotion, *bhakti*, might in some contexts be taken as having this same meaning but, as will become clear, in the Śrīvaiṣṇava context *bhakti* is a longer and more arduous path of practices that must be distinguished from *prapatti*.

The Mantras encode in three ways the ideal of complete dependence on God:[18] a confession of the dynamic of the human toward the divine person (in the Tiru Mantra), leaving behind all encumbrances and listening to God's invitation to have total faith in God (the first line of the Carama Śloka), the enunciation of the words recited while surrendering (in the Dvaya Mantra), and the divine response to those who have taken refuge (the second line of the Carama Śloka), a promise of freedom and the ending of grief.[19] Such words are rich in meaning, but they are also actual prayers appropriate for devout recitation and attentive listening, as regular moments in individuals' and communities' ongoing relation with the divine couple.[20]

For Śrīvaiṣṇavas and for ourselves as readers and commentators, discipline is required if we are to discover the full theology and practice of this tradition in three mantras that are so very brief. We have to learn to see how they stand in for a large body of revelation (*śruti*) and revered tradition (*smṛti*), offering a succinct distillation of whatever else can be said in the tradition, an implicit creedal formulation of Śrīvaiṣṇavism. Traditional teachers have for centuries found in the Mantras an effective catechesis of great subtlety that can be remembered easily and uttered by anyone who knows their several words. They are also more than ideas; they are descriptive and effective with respect to the psychology and enactment of radical devotion. A reflective appropriation of the Mantras opens the way for their enactment by a person who is transformed by them: to hear them well, is to begin to live them. They detail the grief and desire, the resolve and helplessness, the alienation and the loss of

[18] Occasionally in the pages to follow I will use the word "God" as a reliable shorthand for the technically more correct "Nārāyaṇa with Śrī." I do not use "God" to the exclusion of Śrī, and do not intend any uncritical assimilation of Nārāyaṇa and Śrī to the God of the Christian tradition.

[19] I must leave to others the important fieldwork required to understand the "on the ground" meaning of the mantras for Śrīvaiṣṇavas today and their actual use in devotional practice today. While my personal conversations with contemporary Śrīvaiṣṇavas make it clear that the Mantras are still held in the highest regard and are still taken as guides to life and in particular to taking refuge, I have not done any systematic inquiry into contemporary belief and practice.

[20] Each Mantra has its own history, most clearly the Carama Śloka, which is verse 18.66 of the *Bhagavad Gītā*, part of Kṛṣṇa's climactic final instruction. The Tiru Mantra (and similar mantras combining the divine name with *namaḥ*) can be found widely in Sanskrit and even in Tamil literature. The Dvaya Mantra, though also very old, is harder to trace. For at least 1000 years the Mantras have been read together, complementing and reinforcing one another. The textual evidence for this goes back at least to the time of Parāśara Bhaṭṭar, whose *Aṣṭaślokī* is the oldest commentary we have, the verses of which we will cite in the following chapters.

safety that characterize the true devotee, and also that person's determination to come home to self and God. These are all features characteristic of the ideal act of taking refuge, utter dependence on Nārāyaṇa and Śrī, who invite the devotee to liberation through surrender. The Mantras state enduring truths, but they are therefore also about change; a reflective appropriation of the Mantras changes the person who hears them, opening the way for that person actually to live a life of worship, radical trust, and freedom from fear and grief.

Fundamentally too, the Mantras are acts of prayerful communication with the divine persons, words addressed to them or received from them: praise, divine initiative, and human response, all compressed into these few words. Those who study the Mantras and begin to understand them are thereby also challenged to decide whether and when studying the Mantras becomes also praying with them.

3. Reading with Vedānta Deśika

If we are to be commentators, we must keep learning from earlier commentators. Key to comparative theological reading is simply to learn from one's theological colleagues, those who are thoughtful and learned practitioners in the other theological tradition. The Mantras yield little of their rich meaning if read alone without commentary – they are so short, and so densely packed with meanings – and it is necessary to be connected to the Śrīvaiṣṇava tradition, reading with it, if we are to learn anything worthwhile. We must therefore resist the tendency to seek only original meanings by examining primary texts separately from the traditions wherein they originated and have been preserved. Reading by ourselves, we are more likely to fall into the bad habit of reading independently, out of context, missing more than we discover.[21]

But reading with the commentators is a formidable task, and a desire to be thorough in consulting all available commentaries could end only in a very long and very large project. In lieu of attempting to synthesize the interpretations found in all the commentaries, I have chosen to read with just one leading commentator: Vedānta Deśika (Veṅkaṭanāta;[22]

[21] There is a rich commentarial tradition on the three Mantras, beginning with the *Aṣṭaślokī* of Parāśara Bhaṭṭar (1078-1165), the *Nigamanappaṭi* and *Parantappaṭi* attributed to Periyavāccāṉ Piḷḷai (1167-1262), and then the *Mumukṣuppaṭi* of Piḷḷai Lokācārya (1205-1311), particularly with the commentary of Maṇavāḷamāmuni (1370-1443). See Mumme 1987.

[22] Veṅkaṭanāta is his name, and "Vedānta Deśika" – the Teacher of Vedānta – an honorific title. But since he is most often called by the title "Vedānta Deśika," I use that term in referring to him and, henceforth, simply "Deśika."

1268-1369), an honored Śrīvaiṣṇava teacher (of the incipient *vaṭakalai* community) and one of the most versatile and important theologians in the Indian tradition. Deśika composed a number of brief commentaries on the Mantras, most of which are included in the *Cillarai Rahasyaṅkaḷ*, "Assorted Works on the Mantras/Sacred Realities."[23] In addition to these smaller works, we have what may be Deśika's greatest work, and what is said also to be nearly his last: the *Śrīmad Rahasyatrayasāra* itself (*Auspicious Essence of the Three Mysteries*; henceforth, the *Essence*), a detailed exposition of the exegesis, philosophy, theology, practice and religious sociology of Śrīvaiṣṇavism. This is the most complete available to us, and itself the source of a number of important sub-commentaries over the centuries. Deśika writes with an awareness of interpretations of the Mantras preceding his, and he is determined to correct the record while being as generously inclusive as possible.[24]

Thorough exegesis of the Tiru Mantra, Dvaya Mantra, and Carama Śloka occurs respectively in Chapters 27, 28, and 29, which comprise nearly 40% of the whole. This exegesis is complemented by the expositions found in Chapters 3-19. Thus, Chapters 3-6 offer philosophical and theological underpinnings for the entire project – the Truth – while Chapters 7-12 offer the logic and psychology of taking refuge – the Way – and Chapters 13-19 spell out the manner and motive of a life lived in accord with the Mantras – the Life; other chapters raise questions about the transmission of the teaching of the Mantras, and the implied cosmology, epistemology, etc. Here is an overview of the *Essence* as a whole:

[23] In the *Cillarai Rahasyaṅkaḷ* we find paired works that most often focus on the Mantras (*rahasya*) and works that focus on the "realities" (*tattva*) correlative to what is invoked spiritually in the Mantras. These works, mostly very short, give us a profile of the *rahasya* commentary and its relation to doctrinal (*tattva*) expressions of the tradition. Thus, for instance, the *Tattva Padavī* indicates that for the sake of liberation one must humbly seek a teacher who will explain reality, and that consequently one must take refuge with the Lord who is both the means and the result of taking refuge; the *Rahasya Padavī* speaks more specifically of the three truths to be known, regarding what is real (*tattva*), what is beneficial to do (*hita*), and what is the goal of human life (*puruṣārtha*), and explains how these are encoded respectively in the Tiru Mantra, Dvaya Mantra, and Carama Śloka. In addition, still other works by Deśika – *Sāradīpa*, *Sārasāram*, *Abhaya Pradāna Sāram*, *Sāra Saṃgraha* – reflect on "the essence" (*sāra*), presumably "the essence of the Mantras." On all these texts, see Deśika 1993.

[24] So too, one may notice the clarifications that occur in the subsequent *Virodha Parihāra*, also collected in the *Cillarai Rahasyaṅkaḷ*, in which Deśika makes further clarifications and meets objections.

	mantra	*exegetical chapters*	*the teaching*	*further exposition*	*additional points*
Truth	Tiru Mantra	c. 27	*tattva* (truth, reality of total dependence on God)	cc. 3-6	the lineage of teachers; introductory perspectives; the journey after death; the clarification of disputed issues; the transmission of the tradition[25]
Way	Dvaya Mantra	c. 28	*hita* (the beneficial: Nārāyaṇa and Śrī as means to salvation)	cc. 7-12	
Life	Carama Śloka	c. 29	*puruṣārtha* (the goal, living in service, for the Divine Couple and the community)	cc. 13-19[26]	

In this way Deśika offers us an exhaustive exegesis of the Mantras; a narrative about the truth and psychology of the path; a moral guide to a life consequent upon taking refuge.[27]

Deśika constantly reminds his readers that attention to even the details of the Mantras must be placed in the context of a full appreciation of the overall Śrīvaiṣṇava faith perspective. He insists that the three Mantras cooperate in shaping a Śrīvaiṣṇava worldview, and thus need to be understood together; in a number of texts, he introduces and praises them together. Thus, in Chapter 2:

> Among the three mysteries (*rahasya*) the Tiru Mantra, when it makes known its own meaning, makes all meanings known; as it says,
>
> The three Vedas, their six subsidiary disciplines,
> the hymns, the varied musical notes,
> all this and everything else too that is made of word
> subsists in these eight-syllables.[28]

[25] These points are developed respectively in the Preface (*Guruparaṃparāsāra, Lineage of the Teachers*); Chapters 1-2; Chapters 20-23; Chapter 23-26; Chapters 30-31. Chapter 32 is a concluding summation of the whole.

[26] I have omitted from the Table the prefatory reflection on the teaching tradition (*Guruparaṃparāsāra*), and these later chapters: cc. 20-22: Eschatology; cc. 23-26: Further consideration of disputed topics; cc. 30-31: The duties of the teacher (*ācārya*) and the student (*śiṣya*), on the importance of tradition; c. 32: Summary.

[27] See also Srinivasaraghavan, p. 69, for a similar division of the *Essence*.

[28] *Aṣṭākṣara Brahmavidyā* 1.9; or, Ramadesikacarya notes, *Haritasmṛti* 3.65. Here and throughout, I occasionally add, from the cited passage in its context, a few words to fill out Deśika's very laconic citations. Here, for example, he cites only the last words, "everything else too that is made of word subsists in these eight-syllables."

> Yet too, when the Carama Śloka says, *Having completely given up all dharmas*, it establishes the single means, and how by it the results of all means are achieved.
> Likewise, the Dvaya Mantra... makes the person who utters it even once into a person of great power, who has done all that needs be done in any way at all. Thus, the three mysteries are to be respected by all who desire liberation.[29]

And, in the Sanskrit verse concluding Chapter 2, all three are again given their due:

> First he gains his self by the Tiru Mantra[30] that stands above all the disciplines of learning and practice;[31]
> then he passes his every moment with the Dvaya Mantra which, recited just once, makes for true existence;
> when his confidence is deepened by the compassionate summation [that is the Carama Śloka],
> offered by the One who is the supreme adornment of the Veda,
> the Charioteer at play,
> then a person knows all that's essential;
> whoever is such a person is the leader of our community in this world.[32]

The distinctive doctrine of the Śrīvaiṣṇava tradition is explained in Chapter 3, as the dependence of the self on God in a body-soul relationship. In concluding the chapter, Deśika indicates how this truth is articulated in the Dvaya Mantra in relation to the other two Mantras:

> The *Dvaya Mantra*'s first line illumines the fact there is no other refuge; the second, that there is no other goal; both clauses, that there is no other foundation. The same points are made in the Carama Śloka too, explicitly and implicitly, and in it we find specified the means that is to be accomplished[33] if one is to win over the Lord. By the *Dvaya Mantra*, we learn what needs to be meditated on during the time of performance. The *Tiru Mantra*, like a small mirror illumining large objects, succinctly illumines all the prerequisite truths.[34]

[29] 43/19. Here and throughout the chapters to follow, the first number indicates pages in Ramadesikacarya's standard edition of the *Śrīmadrahasyatrayasāra*, and the second number indicates pages in Rajagopala Ayyangar's 1956 English translation – for while I offer my own translations, I am indebted to Ayyangar, and wish to enable the reader to profit from consulting his translations.

[30] "Fundamental Mantra"

[31] I have added "of learning and practice."

[32] 46-47/21

[33] That is, the act of taking-refuge

[34] 54/27

In Chapter 6, Deśika shows how the three Mantras are in their detail the vehicle of correct doctrine and confession:

> One should meditate on the highest reality of this supreme God in the first letter of the Tiru Mantra [the *a* in *aum*] and in the word *Nārāyaṇa,* in *Nārāyaṇa* with its specifications [*with-Śrī* and *feet*] in the Dvaya Mantra, and also in the words *I* and *Me* in the Carama Śloka.

Deśika goes on to emphasize the proper theology communicated in the Tiru Mantra:[35]

> ...Having seen the highest reality of this supreme God in the Tiru Mantra, he becomes firm in his abandonment of other deities and their people, and then too in belonging to the Lord and also to His people.

Deśika then cites Tirumaṅkai Āḻvār on the religious transformation ignited by the Tiru Mantra, the "eight-syllabled Mantra:"

> After I learned Your eight syllables
> – regardless of what else might be said –
> I have no bond with those who say there is some other deity;
> my only bond is to serve Your devotees,
> O Lord of Kaṇṇapuram.[36]

The Tiru Mantra's exclusive focus on Nārāyaṇa enables the āḻvār to break free of other gods, their cult, and to distance himself from the communities worshipping such deities.

In Chapter 14, Deśika suggests that the three Mantras together highlight total orientation to and dependence on God, as best fragile words can point to ultimate truths:

> By the dative ending of *to Nārāyaṇa* in the Tiru Mantra and *to Nārāyaṇa with Śrī* in the Dvaya Mantra, and by *obeisance* in both mantras, and by *from all sins I will make you free* in the Carama Śloka, it is pointed out to us that we are to be established in the highest, unlimited human goal – just as when an ocean is pointed out by an outstretched hand.[37]

35 "There is no protection other than that of Kaṇṇaṉ," (*Tiruvāymoḻi* 2.2.1), "Whether you weed out my suffering, or not, I have no other refuge," (*Tiruvāymoḻi* 5.8.8), "Except for you, I know of no support for my soul," (*Tiruvāymoḻi* 10.10.3) and the whole song beginning, "If you do not withhold the suffering [my karma] gives..." (*Perumāl Tirumoḻi* 5.1.1) On the multiple meanings of *kaṇ* – refuge, eye – in the first quotation, see Parameswaran, p. 56.

36 *Periya Tirumoḻi* 8.10.3; only the first two lines are actually quoted. The entire citation is from 153-155/84-85. On Tirumaṉkai Āḻvār and the Tiru Mantra, see the beginning of Chapter 2.

37 262/145

Chapter 27, which begins by an overall prelude[38] to the complete exegesis of all three Mantras in Chapters 27-29, presents the relationship among them as comprehensive of a whole way of life:

> The *Tiru Mantra*, first among them, makes clear our proper form, as having its sole enjoyment in being entirely dependent on the highest [Person]; it then increases our eagerness and taste for attaining that highest Person, after ending all obstacles. It thus makes us fully competent for that means. By *I come for refuge...*, the *Dvaya Mantra* clearly illumines this competent person's manner of performing the specific means, after experiencing a desire for its result. By *to Me alone come for refuge*, the *Carama Śloka* commands this specific means.[39]

The key rule generously allows for multiple interpretations:

> Although we can see, explicitly or by implication, all the truths in each of the Mantras by itself, nevertheless in each one we see one truth in particular.[40]

The Mantras thereby both imply and reinforce one another:

> That the object of refuge is the highest reality is stated concisely in the first letter of the first word [the *a* of *aum*] of the Tiru Mantra; likewise, in the middle and third words [*obeisance* and *to Nārāyaṇa*] the means and the goal are respectively taught. The Dvaya Mantra reveals all this clearly. In turn, the Carama Śloka clearly identifies the specific competent person indicated by the first person ending of the verb *I approach for refuge* in the Dvaya Mantra. It also suggests a lack of need for any other means, and the ending of obstacles that is stated concisely in the [Dvaya's] *obeisance*.[41]

The Mantras are thus an integral whole, encompassing the Faith of the Śrīvaiṣṇava tradition. They are the primary context for one another; even as Deśika analyzes the details, he also keeps reminding his readers that none of the Mantras is to be dissected by itself. In the following chapters, as we treat topics specific to each Mantra, we find ourselves continually in a situation where there will be too much to say – even as all that can be said is in fact said in each Mantra and yet most fully in all three. This is why commentaries are to be read as wholes, not selectively; one cannot skip to the last chapter of a commentary to get its meaning.

Reading the Mantras with Deśika is also an exercise in reading with the whole Śrīvaiṣṇava tradition. Inclusive in tone and manner, Deśika seems determined to fashion a consensus for all Śrīvaiṣṇavas as to the meaning of

[38] 615-617/346-348

[39] The means that is total surrender to God, who alone is the means; 615-616/346

[40] 616/346-347

[41] 616/347. The Carama Śloka identifies the person ready to take refuge by its first words, *having completely given up all dharmas*, which identify the person to whom the subsequent injunction is addressed, *to Me alone come for refuge*.

the Mantras. He seeks to enhance the inner cogency of the tradition by a complete and clear presentation of it, and he has no time for heated polemics. He continually maps common ground, appeals to widely accepted sources, and respects alternative interpretations of the Mantras; he does not attack possible rivals by name. He seems rather to want to present his ideas as logical developments that pass beyond, without contradicting, what had been said previously. Deśika regularly quotes other teachers, including Āḷavantar, Rāmānuja, Parāśara Bhaṭṭar, and his own uncle and teacher, Appuḷḷār, along with other lesser-known figures. Although he never mentions by name Piḷḷai Lokācārya, the premier *teṅkalai* teacher, at least on occasion he seems to take the implications of Lokācārya's interpretations into account. Deśika is always locating himself within the tradition of such teachers, since continuity with Tradition is to him more important than individuality.

Good theology and continuity of tradition are also at the service of spiritual progress. The focus of the *Essence* is of course exegesis of the three Mantras, but this exegesis is located within a complete religious world in which those Mantras can be fully appreciated as meaningful and powerful. Throughout the *Essence*, exegesis, argument, rhetorical appeal, and conscious reflection on the nature of teaching and learning religiously combine in educating the reader, expanding her or his understanding and affective reach, and thereby making an extraordinary demand on this person: total surrender to God, in a moment of realization and choice, becomes a real possibility, daunting yet simple. To create this prospect, thorough interpretation is paired with a vivid attention to the imaginative and affective implications of the Mantras, as meaning comes to life in guiding religious and moral practice.

On multiple levels, the *Essence* is a very good place to learn how to read the three Mantras, and consequently to reflect on that learning process and its implication for Christian readers. My project is thus a micro-project – the explication of just three small mantras – and a complex macro-project as well – engaging the long commentarial tradition generated by the Mantras, as this tradition is accessible in the *Essence*, an inquiry into commentary, and a comparative project. And all of this is written with an eye toward the Christian tradition of faith and worship, theology and prayer – in what ultimately is entirely a Christian commentary.

4. Who Can Understand Sacred (Rahasya) Mantras?

Thus far I have rather optimistically argued for commentary as an act of religious reading that opens up deep interreligious understanding. And yet, by common usage and in accord with the title of Deśika's work, the

Mantras are *rahasya*,[42] sacred truths, mysteries. To say that they are *rahasya* is a meaningful and important assertion, but not primarily due to secrecy in the material sense of excluding listeners and keeping knowledge private; in fact, the Śrīvaiṣṇava community is dedicated to the publication of its texts, and welcomes readers willing to learn from the tradition. Rather, *rahasya* indicates a body of meaning/s that become available – to those who take to heart and receive humbly wisdom that has been transmitted from generation to generation by teachers and that has been encoded in the Mantra as properly read in accord with tradition. *Rahasya* seems first of all to refer to this extraordinary demand placed on a person who ventures to know what the Mantras mean and what is to happen in accord with their meaning and recitation. As *rahasya*, the Mantras expose the reader to truths not immediately accessible to uncommitted observers, and demand a surrender to God that would seem out of place and beyond bounds, according to the ordinary expectations even of religious people. But since there is an extraordinary demand placed on whoever would venture to teach or learn the Mantras, and since, for that reason, they are not accessible to most people, therefore they are *rahasya*, sacred, precious.

In the following somewhat autobiographical passage from Chapter 32, Deśika notes a fidelity so severe that it seems to overshadow values of individuality and creativity:

> All the prior and following verses[43] about the three mysteries are the words of Maṭaippaḷḷi, by tradition called "Vedānta Udayana" from whom, in turn, Kiṭāmpi Appuḷḷār heard them. And then, in accord with the mercy in his heart, he made this servant learn them too, as a parrot learns. He made me speak them without error exactly as the Lord had first made them clear; he shed light on them, ensuring that they not be forgotten, and made me speak them without error.[44]

Deśika's writing is introspective, yet also in submission to what has been given to him by another, the divine teacher:

> We are at the feet of the White Horse, our teacher,
> who wrote inside us, His servants,
> and that we have etched on palm leaf...[45]

[42] *Rahasya* can indicate actual secrecy, or a sacred truth or value that demands reverential treatment by those who are competent to teach and receive it properly. See my comments on *rahasya* in Clooney 2007b.

[43] Since this passage occurs in Chapter 32, he is indicating the entirety of the *Essence*.

[44] 965-66/572

[45] 1008/591. The White Horse is Lord Hayagrīva, an *avatāra* of Nārāyaṇa as teacher, honored in Deśika's home village.

The given truths are sacred; the understanding and writing of them are precious acts not to be taken for granted. Learning these things is a gift normally available only in the oral communication of the teacher. Nevertheless, by the Śrīvaiṣṇava tradition's own standards, it seems that it is the intention of the divine teacher, and of the teachers submissive to the divine teacher's plan, to further propound the three Mantras and their meanings for the benefit of the community – in writing "etched on palm leaf." As I have mentioned, there are few religious traditions more literate and book-oriented that Deśika's Śrīvaiṣṇava community.

A long passage from Chapter 31, on the duties of the student, makes perfectly clear the kind of learning that is at stake:

> A person who speaks without tradition about the *rahasyas* related to the self is merely teaching what he has read on a palm leaf or heard by climbing a wall.[46] Like someone who wears a stolen jewel, he will be afraid of all those who see him; and he comes to a bad end, as it says in texts such as this:
>
> When by chance a mantra is heard, by a person in hiding,
> or by deception, or from what is seen on a palm leaf, it has no value;
> rather, it causes misfortune.[47]

Deśika cites two texts that by contrast indicate the proper approach to learning:

> Know this by prostration, by posing careful questions, and by service;
> Those who have knowledge and have seen the truth
> will impart knowledge to you,[48]

and, remembering traditional practice,

> Maitreya prostrated himself before Parāśara
> who had completed the rites prescribed for the early part of the day;
> he reverenced him,
> and then he carefully posed his questions to him.[49]

Proper teaching requires the same remembrance and gratitude:

> One is to teach after listening in the proper way; but even so, if one speaks without first glorifying the teacher, then all his ideas are rootless, like a

46 That is, as if eavesdropping on a conversation she or he is not intended to hear.

47 *Padma Saṃhita* 23.81

48 *Gītā* 4.34

49 *Viṣṇu Purāṇa* 1.1.1

> parasitic, rootless plant. Such teaching is content given without respect, and this causes nothing but great anxiety in the student.[50]

The logical conclusion might be that neither the Mantras nor Deśika's own teaching about them will do any good for the reader who has not learned from a teacher in the proper way; on the contrary, great disrespect is shown, and harm done.

And yet we can read, and by reading we learn; and this learning cannot be called merely "intellectual," as if studying the Mantras through the *Essence* could be a simply intellectual endeavor. Even if we readily grant the Śrīvaiṣṇava view that the full meaning of the Mantra lies within that community, we can still insist that the words can be considered to have their own efficacy, even as understood through the study of books, guided by teachers who wrote works as instructive and persuasive as the *Essence*.

The Truth, the Way, the Life is therefore best understood as written at the periphery, between the Śrīvaiṣṇava tradition and a wider world, thriving, insofar as it does, as a commentary founded in reading what the Śrīvaiṣṇavas have so prolifically made available in writing – and as a commentary nourished by the wisdom and expectations of traditional Christian commentary and learning. Even if my work cannot claim to be a Śrīvaiṣṇava commentary, my dependence on Vedānta Deśika suggests that *The Truth, the Way, the Life* can, as rooted in two traditions, be seen as a *Christian* commentary deeply indebted to *Śrīvaiṣṇava* tradition. All of it is, of course, infused with a Christian hope that meaningful and efficacious learning across religious boundaries is possible in the 21st century.

III. The Order of the Chapters to Follow

I comment on the Mantra in this order:

a. human recognition of the human-divine relation as one of utter dependence (Tiru Mantra; Chapter 1): *Aum, obeisance to Nārāyaṇa.*
b. the divine invitation to enact this relation by surrender to the Lord and trust in him (Carama Śloka, first line; Chapter 2); *Having completely given up all dharmas, to Me alone come for refuge.*

[50] 978-979/577-578

c. the human response in affirmation of the invitation, by an utterance of complete surrender (Dvaya Mantra; Chapter 3); *I approach for refuge the feet of Nārāyaṇa with Śrī; obeisance to Nārāyaṇa with Śrī.*
d. the divine response, a promise of liberation and grieflessness (Carama Śloka, second line; Chapter 4); *From all sins I will make you free. Do not grieve.*[51]

Thus we have:

My Chapter	*Mantra*	*Speaker*	*Message*
1	Aum, obeisance to Nārāyaṇa	The person, in God's presence	Truth: this person's primal recognition of dependence on God.
2	Having completely given up all *dharmas*, to Me alone come for refuge.	The Lord's response as an invitation.	The Way: the divine invitation to take refuge without hesitation or compromise.
3	I approach for refuge the feet of Nārāyaṇa with Śrī; obeisance to Nārāyaṇa with Śrī	The person's response to the divine invitation.	The Way: in response, the act of refuge.
4	From all sins I will make you free. Do not grieve.	The divine response to the person taking refuge.	The Life: God's promised liberative act, and a new life without grief or fear.

[51] A word of explanation on this division – my major innovation – of the Carama Śloka into two parts. I read its first line immediately after the Tiru Mantra, since the Carama Śloka can thus be taken as the divine word in response to the devout person who has uttered the Tiru Mantra, now giving a specific and special invitation to the listener to respond – as the devout listener does respond, with the Dvaya Mantra. In turn, the second line of the Carama Śloka is a consequent divine promise to the person who has taken refuge by the Dvaya Mantra. This order then reflects the dynamic of the divine-human interaction envisioned in the three Mantras. While my division of the Carama Śloka has no precedent in the tradition, we can note that there was early on some debate among Śrīvaiṣṇavas on whether to discuss the Carama Śloka before or after the Dvaya Mantra. In his commentary on Piḷḷai Lokācārya's *Mumukṣuppaṭi*, Maṇavāḷamāmuni notes that different teachers ordered the Mantras differently, depending on the points they wished to stress. He concluded: "there is nothing wrong with doing it either way." (Mumme 1987, 108). While my approach is different yet again, I hope that Śrīvaiṣṇava readers will recognize the good faith and honest intention of my ordering of the Mantras.

All of this makes sense to me, and I am hopeful that it will be vindicated as a fruitful way of reading the Mantras, even if I thus diverge from the standard Śrīvaiṣṇava order of reading, Tiru Mantra, Dvaya Mantra, and Carama Śloka.

In each chapter, I offer a simple statement of the meaning of each Mantra – its individual words and then its meaning as a whole. This is a rather straightforward procedure, necessary before the insights of the *Essence* are taken into account. I then recount what Parāśara Bhaṭṭar[52] has to say on the mantra under discussion in his *Aṣṭaślokī*, the oldest available commentary. Thereafter, at length, and for the bulk of each chapter, I follow what Vedānta Deśika has to say in the *Essence* regarding the Mantra in question. In a sense, much of my commentary is simply reading along with his commentary, and it may be that 70% of my "Christian commentary" is simply a reading in accord with Deśika's commentary. But originality is not a major feature of commentary, and even *Christian* commentary has to be dedicated to illumining the Mantras in accord with their tradition. And yet throughout, I read as a Christian; the questions I raise and passages I highlight are those that make sense and are most interesting to a Christian reader. Even in reading the *Essence*, I read as a Christian; the foundation of "Christian commentary" lies not in the quantity of recognizably Christian words, but in the continuing presence of a Christian reader. Occasionally in each chapter, though, I add an explicitly Christian comment, indenting them and introducing them with *reflection*.

In the final section of each chapter, I deal more explicitly with the Christian context of this commentary. I advert to questions generated from the Christian theological tradition, questions not directly rooted in the Śrīvaiṣṇava tradition, yet which arise in light of the meaning of the Mantras and Deśika's reading of them. To widen the base for the practice of reading within traditions and yet across religious boundaries, I suggest Biblical texts that can be read fruitfully along with the three Mantras. While I do not suggest that we Christians have a mantra tradition,[53] I do

[52] Parāśara Bhaṭṭar, an important teacher in the generations after Rāmānuja, was a disciple of Vatsaṅka Miśra (Kūrattāḻvaṉ), Rāmānuja's disciple; in addition to his commentary on the Mantras, Bhaṭṭar's works include the *Śrī Guṇa Ratna Kośa*, 62 verses in praise of the Goddess Śrī. See Clooney 2005b.

[53] The closest in Christianity outside of India may be the tradition of the Jesus Prayer: *Lord Jesus Christ, Son of the Living God, have mercy on me a sinner*. On this tradition, see Billy. I also do not take into consideration Christian prayers in India that are consciously modeled on mantras, terms found in litany form, such as *Jesuve namaḥ, Christave namaḥ*.

wish to draw parallels with specific, narrowly chosen Biblical texts, in order to highlight the possibility of re-imagining Biblical prayer in light of the mantra tradition of the Śrīvaiṣṇavas. Such double readings can be significant, influential interpretive tools, yet without laying claim to any specific theological positions; for there is no reason for the commentator who is a conscientious reader to be conservative or liberal.

At the very end of each chapter I pose a probably still more difficult question: Can a Christian reader pray with this Mantra? Since the Mantras are prayers, this is a kind of limit question that assesses the implications of the Christian reading, which must remain somewhere between detached assessment and an entirely engaged "insider" reading but yet which, as understanding opens into spiritual appreciation, cannot be entirely located on the side of "not praying." But we shall see more of this as we go along.

CHAPTER 1

TO KNOW THE TRUTH: THE TIRU MANTRA[1]

Abba, Father

Aum, obeisance to Nārāyaṇa

Reflection: As Christians, we are called to recognize that God is the creator of all, and possessed of innumerable beneficent qualities; all beings depend on God entirely and forever. Such is the truth of human existence and indeed the existence of all else. Recognizing this fundamental orientation and dependence is innate to human nature, and also a consciously appropriated primary duty of the religious person; out of this reality also grows our commitment to one another. The Tiru Mantra enables us to explore these truths more deeply, from the fresh perspective of another tradition.

I. INTRODUCTION

Auṃ namo Nārāyaṇāya

Aum – Aum;[2] *namo* – praise (reverence, obeisance);[3] *Nārāyaṇa* – Nārāyaṇa; *Nārāyaṇāya* – for Nārāyaṇa

Aum, obeisance to Nārāyaṇa

As the familiar story goes, Tirumaṅkai Āḻvār was taught the Tiru Mantra by the Lord himself, who sought out the saint (*āḻvār*) when, having lost his fortune, he was living as a highway robber. Lord Nārāyaṇa came in the guise of a traveler who, when accosted by the robber, was willing to give him everything. When Tirumaṅkai Āḻvār found curiously that he

[1] Occasionally, in chapters 2-5, I insert more explicity "Christian comments," as secondary reflections on my more detailed interpretations.

[2] *Om* is the more familiar English spelling of what is, in Sanskrit, three letters, a-u-m.

[3] Although "obeisance" is not in common usage today, it seems to capture well the mental and physical dimensions of a complete orientation to the Lord: "Obeisance… a movement of the body (as a bending or prostration) or other gesture made in token of respect or submission; an attitude of respect, deference." (*Webster's Third New Dictionary*, 1993)

could not lift the bundle, his victim offered him the Tiru Mantra itself. Tirumaṅkai āḻvār boldly accepted the Mantra, but he had not anticipated its power. Upon receiving it from the Lord and then receiving his further instruction on the meaning and power of the Mantra, he was enlightened; seeing himself in a new light, he began to rethink his priorities; no longer could he be an autonomous agent, but instead he became entirely dependent on the Lord who had thus surprised him. His robber career was finished, and he became an āḻvār, a great poet saint; his major work, the *Periya Tirumoḻi*, is inspired by his learning of the Tiru Mantra.[4]

Given this ancient account, it is not surprising then that Tirumaṅkai Āḻvār – as we know him from his verses – seems particularly devoted to the Tiru Mantra. One well-known verse refers to the saint's new and exclusive commitment to the Mantra's eight syllables (*aum* + *na* + *mo* + *na* + *ra* + *ya* + *na* + *ya*), and to the implied service for Nārāyaṇa, Lord of the Tiru Kaṇṇapuram temple:

> After I learned Your eight syllables
> – regardless of what else might be said –
> I have no bond with those who say there is some other deity;
> my only bond is to serve Your devotees,
> O Lord of Kaṇṇapuram.[5]

He also composed an entire song (6.10), each of its ten verses ending with *obeisance to Nārāyaṇa* (*namo Nārāyaṇa*):

> Our Lord dwelling in Kuṭantai as a boar lifted our world,[6]
> our Lord who by fire destroyed the hostile fortress of Laṅkā,[7]
> our Lord who crossed Laṅkā and the world itself in two steps –
> if you would speak His name, let it be *obeisance to Nārāyaṇa*!
>
> The Earth Goddess garlanded with the churning oceans,
> The great Lady in the lotus,
> Brahmā, Śiva, Indra, the gods –
> He is their leader,
> our revered Lord, leader of the immortals – to destroy our deeds,[8]
> let us speak His name, *obeisance to Nārāyaṇa*![9]

[4] See Govindacarya, 162-165

[5] *Periya Tirumoḻi* 8.10.3

[6] Rescuing the world, when it had sunk into the ocean. Tiru Kuṭantai is a famous temple town.

[7] Belonging to the demon king, Rāvana.

[8] "Deeds" surely means "sins," of course, but the neutral terms also suggest the eradication of "self-righteous good deeds."

[9] *Periya Tirumoḻi* 6.10.1, 9. See also 1.8.9. Earlier āḻvārs (poet saints) such as Poykai Āḻvār, Tirumaḻicai Āḻvār, and Periyāḻvār, had already alluded to and praised the power of

The Mantra brings together elements that are considered forceful in themselves. Elsewhere in the songs of the āḻvārs and in later literature as well, there are numerous references to the potency of the name *Nārāyaṇa* by itself; so too, as we shall see in a moment, the initial syllable in the Mantra, *aum*, has its own history and efficacy, even apart from the Mantra. In this chapter, however, we focus on the dynamics of the divine name and *aum* as located within the Tiru Mantra itself, which by its structure of deep reverence (*aum*) and obeisance (*namo*) makes evident the speaker's most essential and intimate relationship to Nārāyaṇa.[10]

Deśika begins his own Chapter 27, the chapter devoted to exegeting the Tiru Mantra, with his own praise of the Mantra, highlighting key points. It is rooted in tradition:

> First is Tāra [*Aum*],[11] followed by the Heart [*namaḥ*][12] and then *Nārāyaṇāya*:
> this we know as stated in Tradition,
> given with its meaning by the teacher.[13]

Still near the beginning of the chapter, after general comments on all three Mantras,[14] Deśika presents the Tiru Mantra as authorized in scripture and tradition:

> This Tiru Mantra's glory is well known in the *Atharvana*, *Kaṭha* and other *Upaniṣads*, in other texts such as *Manu*, in the variety of ritual handbooks such as the *Nārāyaṇātmaka Hiraṇyagarbha*, *Nāradīya*, and *Bodhāyana*.[15]

namo Nārāyaṇa. Periyāḻvār, for example, gives us a sense of this early devotion; *Nārāyaṇa* has great power, and so too praise of it is beneficial: "I know nothing of good and bad, nothing but to cry *Nārāyaṇa*! See, I do not praise You with flattering selfish words, Tirumāl! I do not know at all how to comprehend You, but I chant *obeisance to Nārāyaṇa* without stop, such is my strength, being a Vaiṣṇava living in Your temple: what strength!" In another of Periyāḻvār's verses, the tradition of Vedic theology and worship is juxtaposed with the chanting of the Mantra: "O Kṛṣṇa, creator of the Four-faced god, Primal cause, Dark One, I Your servant have never hungered even a day due to not eating; but a day when I am not chanting without ceasing *obeisance to Nārāyaṇa*, a day when I am not approaching Your feet with flowers and with the Ṛg, Yajur, Sāma Vedas, that day I starve." (*Periyāḻvār Tirumoḻi* 5.1.3, 6.)

[10] It is possible then that the issue is not the removal of *aum*, but rather its addition as an assertion of orthodoxy even in obeisance to Nārāyaṇa.

[11] As interpreted by the commentators, *Tāra* is a common name of this mantra in the tantric texts: it is the mantra that enables one to cross over (*tārayati*).

[12] Commentators suggest that in the offering of one's limbs (*aṅga-nyāsa*), *namaḥ* is uttered at the heart; by thus indicating *Tāra*, heart, and *Nārāyaṇāya*, the Mantra is indicated without being expressly given.

[13] 614/345

[14] See Chapter 1.

[15] 617/348

Along with the Dvaya Mantra and Carama Śloka which too are "encompassing",[16] the Tiru Mantra is deserving of the highest praise:

> Just as the Lord's Mantras are greater than other mantras, and just as the three encompassing Mantras [Tiru, Dvaya, Carama Śloka] are great compared with the innumerable other mantras, so –
>
> Among mantras this [Tiru Mantra] is supreme;
> secret among those which are secret, the highest,
> purifying those which purify –
> this Tiru Mantra,[17] everlasting.[18]
>
> And so, this [Tiru Mantra] is greater than the other encompassing Mantras; it is the essence of all the Vedas, capable of ending all that is undesirable; it aids all other means; in accord with the respective competences of the various religious classes and in both its orthodox and common forms, it is sustenance;[19] it states all things directly, both that which encompasses and that which is encompassed;[20] it is effective without needing any other mantra; it is common to all the forms of the Lord. For these reasons, all teachers enjoy it.[21]

After citing āl̲vār verses and the words of ancient seers,[22] Deśika affirms that the Lord is the teacher of the Tiru Mantra and initiator of the lineage of teaching, when he prompts the sage Nārada to teach Puṇḍārika this Mantra and thus enable him to reach liberation:

> The Lord of all had the revered Lord Nārada teach the Tiru Mantra to Śrī Puṇḍārika; he listened to it as his highest benefit, and became established in this Mantra, and so was liberated: as it says,
>
> Puṇḍārika, the soul of dharma, accepted Nārāyaṇa as his highest abode,
> and softly recited the eight-syllable Mantra, namo Nārāyaṇa[23]

Deśika too recollects that this is the Mantra "the Lord himself" taught to Tirumaṅkai Āl̲vār.[24] Traced back to Nārāyaṇa's own divine word, the Mantra has the highest revelatory status.

[16] "Pervasive" (*vyāpaka*) is taken to mean mantras praising the Lord who is the all-pervasive one.

[17] "Fundamental" Mantra

[18] *Nāradīya* 1.11

[19] Vedic or Tantric: respectively, with *aum* and assigned to upper caste males, or without *aum* and for everyone.

[20] Respectively, the Lord, and all else.

[21] 617-618/348-349

[22] 618-619/349-350

[23] *Itihāsa Samuccaya* 31.124; 620/349

[24] 620/350

For Deśika, the tradition of teaching and learning the Mantra remains potent. He promises that by the grace of a teacher, the student will have access to the deeper meanings of the Mantra that most people miss, even when they have its words before their eyes:

> Even here anyone can experience with nothing left out
> the meaning concealed in this Tiru Mantra[25]
> like a treasure placed under a crystal surface –
> with the eye given by his teacher.[26]

What it says is not obscure, however: it stresses dependence, divine action, and human service:

> May God accept the burden of protecting our selves –
> though we are so weak in mind –
> and quickly cast aside all obstacles to the power that lies in service.[27]

Though concise, nothing is missing from the Tiru Mantra, which is above all other mantras.[28] As such, it is the object of great praise:

> Praise to this great Mantra,
> first among the encompassing Mantras –
> within it is contained, nothing omitted,
> all that is made of word,
> including the Veda itself and all that is Vedic.[29]

Deśika thus advises us right from the chapter's beginning to treat the Mantra not simply as an interesting historical artifact or admirable prayer – as if to say only, "I praise God." Rather, it is an act of potent, transformative praise: to study it is already a grace, and the student is to look for its deeper truth, admitting that it is potent and able to illumine the true meaning of human life – and on that basis help us change how we live.

1. The Tiru Mantra in the *Aṣṭaślokī* of Parāśara Bhaṭṭar

But before turning to Deśika's detailed exegesis of the Mantra, by a practice I shall follow in each chapter, I begin by noting the exposition of the Mantra by Parāśara Bhaṭṭar, whose *Aṣṭaślokī* (*Eight Verses*) is the earliest

[25] Literally, the "Fundamental (*Mūla*) Mantra"

[26] 615/346

[27] 614/345

[28] It is customary for Deśika to describe each of these three Mantras as best and most important – but without, in fact, relegating the other two to lesser places.

[29] 615/345

extant commentary on the three Mantras.[30] In Verse 1, Parāśara Bhaṭṭar parses the meaning/s of the letters of the sacred syllable *Aum*:[31]

> The meaning of the letter *a* is Viṣṇu who causes the creation, protection, and dissolution of the world...[32]

Right here, we are already in a religious and theological context where there are no multiple deities, nor a subordination of named deities to a transcendent and unnamed divine reality beyond the different gods. Rather, in the beginning is the God whose name is Viṣṇu or Nārāyaṇa,[33] Lord of the universe, its beginning and end, protection and foundation while it exists: Bhaṭṭar rejects the popular notion of the "Three forms" (*trimūrti*), in accord with which creating is attributed to Brahmā, preservation to Viṣṇu, and destruction to Śiva; all power is reserved to Nārāyaṇa.[34] Bhaṭṭar's opening words also offer an analogy between the world and language, as the first letter and the first being of the world stand parallel to one another, verbalized alongside each other. As the famous opening verse of *Tirukkuṟaḷ* indicates, "As *a* is the first of all letters, of this world the eternal God is first."[35]

Bhaṭṭar then stipulates the *m* in *Aum* to be indicative of all dependent, living and conscious beings,

> The meaning of *m* is the living being who is Viṣṇu's instrument.

The intervening *u* in *aum* marks their relationship:

> *u* specifies their relationship [of Lord and soul, *a* and *m*], belonging to no one else.[36]

[30] The *Aṣṭaślokī* succinctly captures crucial points regarding each; four of its eight verses refer to the Tiru Mantra, and two each to the Dvaya Mantra and Carama Śloka.

[31] *Aum* – OM – is of course familiar in popular discourse on religion, both in India and in the West. It is important to read OM as *aum*, so that it can be parsed with an eye to meanings specific to each letter, *a*, *u*, and *m*. On the meanings of *a-u-m*, see also *Praśna Upaniṣad* 5.3-5 and *Maitrī Upaniṣad* 6.3. The *Māṇḍukya Upaniṣad* 8-12 also points to a fourth meaning, beyond *a-u-m*. For a translation of all these Upaniṣads, see Hume.

[32] I am indebted to Mumme whose translations I have used, although I have made some revisions based on my reading of the text and attention to the commentaries.

[33] Several other names are often found: "Viṣṇu," for instance, and "Rāma" and "Kṛṣṇa" with reference to divine appearances in this world.

[34] See Clooney 2001, c. 3. In the *Essence*, see particularly Chapter 6.

[35] *Tirukkuṟaḷ* 1.1

[36] There are places in the *Essence* itself and in its commentaries, where *u* marks the presence of Śrī as the mediator (*puruṣakāra*) and intermediary between the Lord [*a*] and individual selves [*m*]. Parāśara Bhaṭṭar, however, does not suggest this.

In summary:

> *Aum*, made of the three letters (a + u + m), the essence of the three Vedas,[37] teaches this truth.[38]

Verse 2 explicates *namaḥ* in two ways: as indicating not only *obeisance* (*namaḥ*), but also the denial of ego (as *na mama*, "not mine"):

> *Namaḥ*, the middle word in this potent mantra,[39] teaches the person's true nature, its way, and its goal.

The self is fundamentally oriented to the Lord:

> By looking at what is placed before and after *namaḥ*,[40] it can be clearly discerned that independence and self-protection, and the behavior consonant with these, are appropriate to Hari and no one else; therefore, we do not exist for ourselves.

In Verse 3, he links his previous exegesis of the *a* to *Nārāyaṇāya*, *Nāra-ayana-āya*. We exist for God, depending on him; to live entirely in service for him:

> I myself exist for the one [*Nārāyaṇa*] denoted by the *a*. So I am "not for myself." The word *Nārāyaṇa* means the abode [*ayana*] of the host[41] of eternal beings [*naras*]. The dative case-ending [Nārāyaṇa-*āya*] indicates that my innate acts of service should occur at all times, in all places and conditions.

Bhaṭṭar's fourth verse summarizes the Mantra's meaning, and is more usefully considered at the end of this chapter.[42] But for now, it suffices to see that even before Deśika's time, the meaning of the Tiru Mantra was both highly prized and carefully articulated in great detail. Deśika is creative and insightful – within a well-established tradition.

II. Exegeting the Mantra

Now let us turn to Deśika's analysis of the words and component parts of the Mantra, as he reads it in Chapter 27. He follows the general purport

[37] The *Rg*, *Yajur*, and *Sāma* Vedas.

[38] The truth about Nārāyaṇa as the supreme deity.

[39] Literally, *mantrabrahman*, *brahman* – most potent speech – among mantras.

[40] That is, the *aum* and the *Nārāyaṇa*.

[41] *nivahāḥ* (group, multitude), the word ending the first line, is not easily interpreted in context; Mumme notes (211) that commentators suggest it be taken as a genitive.

[42] See pages 57-58.

of Bhaṭṭar's interpretation,[43] even while adding numerous details and insights. While never losing sight of the Mantra's simple devotional intensity, Deśika is determined to disclose as much as possible the subtleties of the meaning inscribed in its simple words.

Aum

Deśika first asserts the potency of *Aum* even apart from the rest of the Mantra. That he does so is appropriate, given the fame and sanctity of this sacred syllable in the widest reach of the Hindu traditions and given its independent symbolic value even before it serves here to inaugurate the Tiru Mantra and encapsulate its full meaning. It has an efficacy of its own, as sacred syllable and as utterance of surrender:[44]

> In the meditation on surrender, *aum* by itself appears as a complete mantra that refers to the surrender of self. As it is said,
>
> Taking up the oblation in the form of self
> and using the mantra "You are wealth, You are pervasive..."[45]
> let him offer his self into the everlasting fire called Unfailing,
> with the mantra that is *aum*.
>
> In the same way, here too [in the Tiru Mantra], people construe *aum* as indicative of surrender. *Aum* is principally about knowledge of the proper form of self, and so it can be taken as nothing but a meditation on total dependence on the Lord.[46]

In part, this praise of *Aum* in itself recognizes that *Aum* and *namo Nārāyaṇāya* (or even, as in the āḻvārs, *namo Nārāyaṇa*) have distinct and often separable histories, and yet are parallel in meaning. *Aum*, perhaps the most famous syllable in the Hindu traditions, is usually taken as complete in itself. As we have seen, *namo Nārāyaṇāya* (or *namo Nārāyaṇa*, without the dative ending) is popular in the Tamil tradition of the āḻvārs; taken together, *Aum* and *namo Nārāyaṇāya* are read as stating in two ways total dependence on the Lord: what is already the case (as is stated in *Aum*) is freely reaffirmed (in *namo Nārāyaṇāya*).

After praising *Aum* in general terms, Deśika begins to explain its three letters in the same way as Bhaṭṭar: *a* indicates the Lord, *m*, all beings as

[43] Presumably he is also knowledgeable of other prior interpretations, such as those of Periyavāccāṉ Piḷḷai and Piḷḷai Lokācārya.

[44] 624/352

[45] That is, with the mantra beginning with the words, "You are wealth, You are pervasive..." (*Mahā Nārāyaṇa Upaniṣad* 79.17); see Vimalananda, 349.

[46] 624/352. I have added "on the Lord."

dependent on the Lord, and the intervening *u*, the dependent relationship connecting the one to the other.

a

Citing the *Aṣṭaślokī*'s first verse, Deśika affirms that the *a* in *Aum* indicates that the Lord is the beginning of all that is:[47] just as *a* is the first letter, the Lord is first and foremost of all realities. Since *a* comes first, before the *m* that refers to the human self, any idea of being "for oneself" rather than "for God" is ruled out from the start.[48] God is first; from this truth, all else follows. Similarly,[49] the conjunction of the *a* and the *m* [indicative of the human] in the same syllable [*aum*] yet as different letters rules out the opinion that the self and God are unrelated or simply identical.[50]

m

After first asserting that the *m* in *Aum* simply indicates all beings that are not God – *m* includes all inanimate things, as well as every living being[51] – Deśika adds two stipulations. First, *m* indicates the self in its true and ideal state as innately oriented to God, and not in its worldly, fallen (*saṃsāric*) state, as is known from ordinary human experience. It also indicates an entire class of such selves, not just a single self. Deśika thus finds in *m* the orthodox Viśiṣṭādvaita Vedānta doctrine articulated most famously by his predecessor Rāmānuja, that there are multiple selves that are not God, but in an eternal and dependent relationship with God.[52]

[47] 625/353

[48] 631/358

[49] 630/357

[50] It is striking, but consistent with Deśika's overall theology, that he finds Śrī implicit in the Tiru Mantra. (628-629/355-356) Śrī is Nārāyaṇa's most distinctive attribute and the source of his fundamental excellence, so one must presume her presence even when she is not explicitly mentioned.

[51] 633/360

[52] 635-636/362. At the opening of Chapter 12, *aum* is again identified as indicative of the self's total orientation to God: "For the person who is competent because desirous of liberation, the proper form of the means to liberation is as follows: just as one best returns a jewel, to wear and protect, to the person to whom it belongs, the surrender of self is similarly specified. That is, by the nominal root [*a*] and its case-ending [the implied dative form of *a*] in the first letter of *aum*, the Lord of all appears as the protector of all and the one to whom all belongs. [That is, the verbal root *ava*, here taken to be implied by *a*, means "protect."] The work of protecting the self and what belongs to the self as well as the result of that protection have no connection to oneself in terms of dependence on oneself or one's own purpose. This is the defining feature of the meditation on belonging-to that is specified by the utter dependence primary to surrendering the burden." (232/127)

Second, *m* also suggests *man*, a Sanskrit verbal root indicative of the verb "to think" or "to know," and yet too as possibly correlated with bliss:

> In accord with grammatical usage, we know that *m* indicates the root *man* and thus too "knowledge." Explicated in this way, it indicates the atom-sized self[53] which by its proper nature is knowledge, and which is qualified by knowledge.[54] This is in accord with *Uttara Mīmāṃsā Sūtras* 2.3.19.[55] Even if the self thus has knowledge as its proper nature, it is keeping with this fact and also with textual authority to add that the self is also specified as of the form of bliss.[56]

In this way, the basic attributes defining self – knowledge and bliss – are found to be stated in the Mantra.

u

The *u* is treated briefly as the mediating term, the link between God and selves; or, when taken to mean "only," it also marks the exclusive relationship of living beings to the Lord, the impossibility of conceiving of such beings apart from that relationship, and the consequent ruling out of relationship with other deities.

It is important finally to notice that in Deśika's initial reference to *aum*,[57] he reaffirms the view that it is a sacred syllable reserved to initiated upper caste males.[58] For women and the lower castes, he recommends the utterance of the Mantra without *aum*, and even without proper Sanskrit declension, that is, simply *namo Nārāyaṇa*, a form found in the a̲lvār songs. As such, it could then be read as a Tamil mantra, stripped of its Sanskritic orthodox boundaries. Yet, he still insists, in this non-orthodox form – *Namo Nārāyaṇa* rather than *Auṃ namo Nārāyaṇāya* – the Mantra has the same salutary effect.[59] Since the Mantra is conceived of as an

[53] As "atomic," the self has a material location, but only as a point and with no extension in space.

[54] The self is essentially comprised of knowledge – consciousness – and yet too is qualified by a series of acts of knowledge that are necessarily object-dependent and transient.

[55] This sūtra, which Rāmānuja explicates in the *Śrī Bhāṣya*, argues that the self, in itself, is essentially a knower.

[56] 635/361

[57] 621-623/350-351

[58] We can also note that not all Śrīvaiṣṇavas were or are concerned to restrict access to the Tiru Mantra; it may even be that the majority, then and now, permit all to utter *auṃ namo Nārāyaṇāya*.

[59] With some agility eight syllables can be identified.

intentional, highly condensed distillation of the tradition, his juggling of two readings of the Mantra also reflects his view of the Śrīvaiṣṇava community itself as orthodox and inclusive. It is a compromise – orthodoxy balanced with accessibility – that illustrates the supple balance between form and content in the potency of the properly uttered Mantra, and exemplifies how Deśika wants to adhere to orthodox brahminical strictures, while yet too safeguarding the inclusivity of the community, as open to all. The implied tension also reminds us that commentators do not work in a vacuum, but with social and even cultural concerns affecting how they interpret the text before them.

> *Reflection*: Nothing in Deśika's exegesis of *aum* appears obviously contrary to the Christian view of God or of the human condition. On the contrary, Christians can benefit from so succinct a reminder of the deep orientation of all beings to God, and God's determination, by grace alone, to make the human journey toward God successful. Even the notion of the mediation (*u*) is recognizably a shared one, even if the Christian and the Śrīvaiṣṇava may be inclined to identify different divine persons – Jesus, or the Spirit, or the Goddess Śrī – as fulfilling this role. Accordingly, *aum* has a viable and specific theological meaning that can be appropriated by the Christian, in remembering her or his fundamental orientation to God – and hopefully, possibly guided by the *Essence*, in also affirming that orientation joyfully. Even if we give due respect to the orthodox view that the recitation of *aum* is for upper caste males only, it seems possible for us to recite aum with the Śrīvaiṣṇava community, affirming a shared understanding of God, self, and mediation. But I will say more on this later, after we have considered the meanings Deśika attributes to *namo* and *Nārāyaṇāya*. The sheer compactness of meanings found in *aum* should also impel us to think more deeply about the key, most intense sites in which Christian scripture speaks the truth of the divine-human relationship: what word or words does a Christian say, in order to say all that we believe? I return to this point at the chapter's end. As for the social concerns evident in Deśika's cautions about the recitation of *aum* by women and men from outside the upper three religious classes, we will inevitably be ambivalent about this kind of social restriction, even if, as Deśika assures us, nothing is lost by recitation of the truncated Mantra. And yet too, if we are honest, we may recognize ways in which Christians too have read scripture to accommodate social expectations.

Obeisance: *namo*

Deśika adheres to a traditional exegesis of *namaḥ*; this word – obeisance, praise – indicates an orientation to God, but at the same time also forcefully negates self-centeredness. In addition to meaning some act of reverence, the *namaḥ* can be parsed differently: the second syllable

– *maḥ*[60] – is taken as a shorthand for *mama*, the possessive "of me" or "my," while the first – *na* – denies the self-centeredness of "I" and "mine:" *aham – na mama*, "I – am not mine."[61] *Aum* already indicates that one belongs to the Lord and not to oneself. Even if this God-oriented person seems an agent and a possessor, agency and possession are really the Lord's, not her or his own. *Namaḥ* thus reinforces the notion of total dependence on the Lord as a way of acting that can also be implemented, lived. We may therefore read *namaḥ* as reinforcing and stating more expansively the negation of self-centeredness already indicated by *aum*.[62]

Deśika also discusses at greater length why total dependence on the Lord can be seen as a positive value, once incorrect notions of dependence and sovereignty are removed.[63] This expression of *obeisance* announces our desire to affirm our dependence, and to take refuge with the Lord.[64] To elaborate this point, he quotes thirty-two verses from the *Ahirbudhnya Saṃhitā*[65] – strikingly, the longest quotation in the entire *Essence* – for the sake of a fuller elaboration of *obeisance* as external or material/physical (*sthūla*), subtle/psychological (*sūkṣma*), and supreme/spiritual act (*parama*). According to these verses, *namaḥ* is to be read on three levels in illumining submission to the Lord:[66]

> The external meaning [*sthūla-artha*] is the *external* gesture and word of reverence and worship.
> The subtle meaning [*sūkṣma-artha*] is the cognitive denial of the egocentric life – *na mama*, not mine; it indicates the interior realization of what visibly enacted on the exterior level; the repeated utterance of *namaḥ* helps break down and pierce stubborn patterns of self-assertion and falsely imagined independence.

60 The word translated here as obeisance is most spelled *namas*; in various settings one may also find *namaḥ* or (as in the Mantra) *namo*.

61 637-638/365

62 639/366

63 Extraordinarily, he adds that the Lord is dependent on selves just as selves are dependent on the Lord; the difference is that dependence is a necessary condition for those selves, while the Lord freely chooses to be at the service of humans, for their sake and his own pleasure. (642/368)

64 The resultant union becomes evident only in the Dvaya Mantra (which itself includes *namaḥ* in its second line); there, *namaḥ* is seen more fully as also a statement of fact, an affirmation of one's dependent relationship on Nārāyaṇa with Śrī, and of union with them as the goal of life.

65 52.2-33

66 Vss 1-22 (645-649/370-372), *sthūlārtha*; vss. 23-29 (649-650/372-373) *sūkṣmartha*; vss. 30-32 (651/373-375) *paramārtha*.

> The supreme meaning [*parama-artha*] pertains to the supreme meaning, supreme goal [*parama-artha*], primarily the fact and identity of existing entirely for God; for this, a still more esoteric reading of the word is required: *namaḥ* as *na* (= means) + *ma* (= most important) + *ḥ* (= Lord).[67] The Lord is the means to liberation; it follows that nothing the devotee does counts as a means to liberation.[68]

The move from the ontological state inscribed in *aum* to the dynamic, responsive utterance of *obeisance* is a move from a recognition of the way things are to an affirmation of that state, increasingly interiorized as a matter of insight, a personal and deepening realization that God and not self is the means and the goal of human existence. *Aum* and *obeisance* together mark religious practice as an intelligent human activity, as the interiorization of that practice, and as a conclusive shift from discourse about oneself to discourse about God. Liberation is what happens when one stops thinking of oneself first, and thinks of self – and all things – only in God; and the double declaration *aum, obeisance* is potent in bringing about this new state. But to whom exactly is it addressed? That is our next topic, the meaning of the third word, *to Nārāyaṇa* (*Nārāyaṇāya*).

> *Reflection*: Here too, there seems to be nothing of great difficulty for the Christian. In *obeisance* and in the still deeper renunciation of ego that also underlies *namaḥ*, God is praised, and the conventional understanding of the autonomous self overturned in favor of a recognition of dependence on God, and life for God. The stylized analysis of *namaḥ* – which, like the analysis of *aum*, is hard to replicate in English – helps us to sort out material, psychological, and spiritual dimensions of praising God, with the realization that we belong to God and not to ourselves. As Christians, we can easily say, *aum*, *obeisance*, and respect the powerful reorientation underlying this prayer.

67 651/373

68 652/374. After a comment on the technical derivation of the three meanings, Deśika adds: "[*Namaḥ* in the Tiru Mantra] first explains [as the external meaning] a person's behavior in accord with his own, entirely dependent self. This is the core of the means to be accomplished; it takes the form of renunciation with all its requisite helps. But then too [as the subtle meaning] there is a purification of the self's proper form, such as is prepared for by terminating autonomous freedom and the like. All this is required if someone is to be competent (for taking refuge,) the means to liberation. As for the last [and supreme meaning], *obeisance* points to the objective means [Nārāyaṇa with Śrī], who can be won over by the particular means [taking refuge] that is to be accomplished." (652/374) While this kind of interpretation is exceedingly technical and difficult for us to grasp, we do well at least to acknowledge the rarified analysis of spiritual advancement and practice to which it points.

For Nārāyaṇa: *Nārāyaṇāya*

But the preceding insights still require specification: who is this divine person to whom all beings are radically oriented? Deśika's exposition of *Nārāyaṇa-āya* unfolds in three stages. First, he analyzes the word *Nārāyaṇa* into its component parts, "beings" (*nara*) and "abode" or "foundation" (*ayana*). Second, he reflects on the dative ending, *-āya* ("for the sake of" or "to" [*Nārāyaṇa, Nārāyaṇa-āya*]) which is explained rather simply as emphasizing again the orientation of everything to the Lord, Nārāyaṇa.[69] Third, Deśika offers a lengthy list of meanings related to *Nārāyaṇa* and the qualities and deeds of God; he also lists, again at length, related meanings pertaining to the individual self, and errors that threaten to problematize the divine-human relationship. Let us consider each in turn.

Nara-ayana

Nārāyaṇa is rich in theological meanings that can be discovered first in exegeting it as *Nara-ayana-āya*, and then again as a single word rich in theological meanings. At the beginning of his exegesis of the name, Deśika states succinctly:

> *Nārāyaṇa* is the person who is to be propitiated by the means that has to be accomplished, taking refuge, the act signified explicitly and implicitly by *obeisance*. He is the referent of the service signified by the dative, and the protector of all. He is the one to whom all belongs. He is the object of refuge that wants nothing and that corresponds to the first letter [*a*, in *aum*]. All this is evident.[70]

In accord with tradition, the meanings implicit in *a* is elaborated in *Nārāyaṇa*; as *a* is to *m* in *aum*, so the Lord is the foundation (*ayana*) to all beings (*nara*).

Like earlier commentators, Deśika elaborates the relationship between "beings" (*naras*) and their "foundation" (*ayana*). *Nāra* indicates the class of entities that do not (*na*) perish (*ṛṇ*),[71] "the eternally existent [*naras*]."[72] As Deśika explains at some length, the broad category of *nara* includes persons of various kinds, but also substantive divine qualities, and even eternal material realities such as time and Heaven. Deśika notes also that *nāras* exist only in their relationship of dependence, affirmed in taking refuge with the supreme person, Nārāyaṇa. *Ayana* can be construed as

69 669-670/387-388
70 653/375
71 660/379
72 664/380

"the way," the "goal toward which one goes," and "the abode on which something rests." Lord *Nārāyaṇa* is the way, goal, and abode for living beings.[73] Deśika spells out these basic points in detail, again relating the meanings thus uncovered back to the *a* and *m* in *aum*.[74]

Nārāyaṇa-*āya*[75]

Deśika then briefly takes up the meaning of the dative ending of *Nārāyaṇāya*. Since in Sanskrit, even a grammatical case tells us something about reality, the dative ending of "Nara-ayana-*āya*" is significant, reinforcing the dynamic human dependence on the divine person. In this Deśika follows without significant change Parāśara Bhaṭṭar's view; Nārāyaṇa is the one *to whom* one directs oneself, *for whom* one exists.

This analysis of *Nārāyaṇāya* in a sense completes Deśika's exegesis of the Tiru Mantra; other commentators, such as Piḷḷai Lokācārya and Periyavāccāṉ Piḷḷai, satisfactorily completed their explanation of *Nārāyaṇa* at this point. But for Deśika, theological commentary can still be more amply developed.

On the Multiple Meanings of *Nārāyaṇa*

He consequently elaborates the meaning of *Nārāyaṇa* by listing 108 qualities that are implied by the name and that are to be meditated on with respect to it – and thereafter he adds, as also implicit in *Nārāyaṇa*, a second list of 68 qualities of the self, and third list of 57 errors that threaten true devotion but that are eradicated by meditation on this name. In his transition to these lists, Deśika compares the Tiru Mantra to a mirror:

> The mirror that is the Tiru Mantra shines after flaws arising from the views of outsiders are removed by careful reflection on its words, accomplished in accord with grammar, etymology, etc. This makes entirely clear the proper nature and other features of the highest Reality, and the various states of the self's own proper nature that are (otherwise) hard to discern.[76]

[73] See 661-662/380-381. Deśika also notes [668/386] that all beings are in relationship with one another by their relationship to the Lord.

[74] It is striking that he does not mention Śrī in this context, even if we should presume his inclusion of her presence even in *Nārāyaṇa*.

[75] 669/387-389

[76] 672/389; for a similar image, see also the passage already cited in Chapter 1: "The Tiru Mantra succinctly illumines all the things that are required, just as a small mirror illumines great things." [54/27] So too, at the beginning of Chapter 3, the Tiru Mantra and other Mantrae are again compared to a mirror: "All this world, what is and endures, its activity and results, is the first maker's body, in accord with rules regarding what it is to be depended upon, and the rest: when one sees all this, the Lord is seen in the mirror of the encompassing Mantras, and one plumbs the workings of the intent of the deep, uncreated peaks [of the Vedas]." (49/22)

To anticipate where Deśika is leading us with his list of Nārāyaṇa's qualities, it is helpful to look first at the verse with which he concludes:

He is with Śrī;
He is the protector;
to Him all belongs;
there is no one equal to Him or higher than Him;
He is our refuge;
He has all as His body,
He is the one to be reached,
to be honored,
to be meditated on by good people.[77]

While space does not permit detailed consideration of the 108 qualities listed by Deśika, the list is worthy of our reflection; I give them here simply in the order followed by Deśika, though with my sub-headings:[78]

Protector

1. He is the protector, and
2. this protection is accomplished (innately) in accord with His proper way of being;
3. it pertains to all things, and
4. it occurs in various modes, in accord with the specific nature of what is to be protected;
5. He protects at all times,
6. everywhere,
7. in every manner, and
8. for His own sake;[79]

Possessed of the qualities of a protector

9. As the protector of all must be, He is omniscient,
10. omnipotent,
11. deterred by nothing except His own will,
12. unsurpassable in His ardor to protect,
13. supremely compassionate,
14. looking for opportunities (to save),
15. requiring only some pretext (for His saving act), and
16. accessible to those taking refuge;

[77] 674/392
[78] The list covers pages 672-674/389-392.
[79] That is, not as compelled by someone else.

17. He is worthy of trust,
18. and distinguished by His qualities of healing sinners, etc.;

For whom all exists

19. He is the one to whom all belongs, and this is
20. without conditioning factors, eternally, and with respect to all;
21. He belongs to no other, and is
22. the one to whom all belongs in accord with His good qualities;
23. along with His spouse,
24. He is devoid of equal and superior, and is
25. designated the fitting recipient of the oblation of self;
26. He is entirely different from non-conscious, bound, liberated, eternally free beings;[80]

He is the cause why beings are those to whom others belong;

27. Agent and prompter of all action
28. He acts on His own accord,
29. He bestows power and
30. instigates (others), but is
31. instigated by no one else;
32. He permits and
33. witnesses karma and
34. cooperates with it,
35. bringing about what is pleasing and
36. bringing about what is beneficial;

Possessed of Paradoxical Qualities

37. He is to be honored unconditionally
38. but is able to be won over (by devotion);
39. He is the objective means (to liberation) and
40. the cause for the means that has to be accomplished;
41. He gives commands in the form of revelation and tradition;
42. He carries the club (of justice) and
43. is impartial toward all, yet also
44. partial toward those taking refuge;
45. He is the cause for ignorance, etc.,[81] but He Himself

[80] These are the four states in which selves may be found.

[81] He veils the minds of those who need to suffer through the effects of their deeds. "Etc." refers to other flaws and limitations that accompany ignorance.

46. is untouched by ignorance, etc.,
47. He ends the ignorance of those who take refuge;
48. He is devoid of change in His proper form, and
49. devoid of change in His proper nature;
50. He is leader of all, and
51. all that happens in the world is His play;

The primary topic of the scriptures, and of religious practice

52. He is expounded as primary in all the Vedānta texts,
53. He is the material cause of all and
54. the efficient cause of all;
55. All His wishes come true;
56. everything is His body;
57. He is what is expressed in every word,
58. He is propitiated by all rites and
59. He gives all their results;
60. He is in every kind of relation (with humans),
61. He pervades all;
62. He is unsurpassably subtle,[82]
63. the foundation of all,
64. firmly established in Himself,
65. He is truth,
66. knowledge,
67. the infinite,
68. bliss,
69. the pure;
70. He is possessed of infinite qualities, even those unmentioned, that specify His proper form that has been described;
71. He is possessed of an eternal, divine, auspicious form, and
72. transcendent and emanatory states, and other forms;
73. His descents (*avatāra*) are real but
74. His proper way of being never fails (even during those descents),
75. His (bodies during those) descents are not comprised of material nature,
76. nor compelled by karma,
77. nor limited by time;
78. They are a flood of good qualities for those taking refuge,
79. the auspicious foundation for all states, and

[82] The smallest of the small, beyond ordinary perception.

80. in all those states Lakṣmī cooperates with Him, and
81. He has divine ornaments, weapons, queens, places, servants, paraphernalia, gate-keepers, attendants, etc.;

God and the destiny of the self

82. He separates (the self) from its gross body,
83. He is a place of rest,
84. He offers special graces,
85. He illumines the doorway to the path of the brahma-nerve[83] and what follows,
86. He makes people enter there,
87. causing them to rise up through the *brahmarandhra*,[84]
88. preparing for them subtle bodies for the *arcira* path,[85]
89. leading them by the door of the sun,
90. enabling them to go beyond the natural cosmos and the obscuring cosmic egg,
91. making them reach the bank of the celestial Virajā River and
92. leave the subtle body,[86]
93. giving them a body not made of natural matter,[87]
94. causing them to be welcomed by divine nymphs etc.,
95. making them enter upon the scent of Brahman, etc.,
96. arranging for them a special welcome by eternal and liberated beings,
97. receiving respect even up to the time of their ascending the couch,[88] and
98. causing perfection in their experience;
99. He Himself is the primary object of attainment,
100. connecting them to all kinds of service done with-body, without-body, and in many bodies;

The ultimate divine bliss

101. all of their desires are satisfied, and there is
102. unsurpassable bliss,

83 The pathway up through the body that leads to the final ascent at death.
84 An opening in the top of the skull.
85 The path of light traveled after death by those who are liberated.
86 The "remnant" of the earthly body by which the self had traveled after death.
87 But rather comprised of the extraordinary (*aprākṛta*) matter of the divine body, Heaven, etc.
88 That is, the couch of their celestial repose.

103. unsurpassable enjoyment and
104. enjoyment in every mode,
105. by His proper nature He is benevolent at all times;
106. He gives perfectly equal enjoyment,
107. He is unable to endure separation from those who take refuge, and
108. He is the cause for their not returning (to this world).

All these divine perfections are latent in the name *Nārāyaṇa*; they have mostly to do with the divine relationship to the world and living beings, particularly those seeking refuge. Or, to use a familiar Christian terminology, it is the "economic," engaged reality of God that is stressed in the context of the Tiru Mantra, not "God in Himself."

It is notable too that almost every quality mentioned could apply universally to "God" understood in relationship to the human race, the naming of specific deeds left to particular believers. This generality need not preclude attention also to Nārāyaṇa as a specific deity who is the object of popular cult and devotion, engaged in specific divine descents, doer of deeds celebrated in the epics and mythic narratives – that is, much of what would be popularly known about the divine Person with the proper name Nārāyaṇa. But none of these more specific, "local" attributes is mentioned here, and Deśika's careful choice of these 108 attributes opens a way for us to reflect upon and learn from this understanding of *Nārāyaṇa*.

Reflection: While it may have seemed nearly impossible for a Christian, as a Christian, to meditate religiously on the Nārāyaṇa worshipped in the Tiru Mantra, we can see now that we need not exclude a significant even if not complete meditation. *Nārāyaṇa* is and can be honored as a proper name particular to Vaiṣṇava traditions; and yet even when it is thus honored by Deśika and his community, it is clearly also a name possessed of a rich array of universal meanings, rooted in both the exegesis of *Nara-ayana*, and in the 108 divine attributes listed by Deśika. There is almost nothing in the exegesis just rehearsed – *nara* + *ayana* + *āya* = *Nārāyaṇāya* – that could not be accepted by the Christian. The entire chapter, though devotional and theological, does not make much of claims specific to Vaiṣṇavism, the narratives of Rāma and Kṛṣṇa, or even the songs of the āḻvārs taken as intensely Vaiṣṇava devotions. While Deśika would not separate out the proper name from the name as a more universal indicator of qualities, we can, in our understanding of the Mantra, find our own way – and limits – in learning from *Nārāyaṇa*, for our theology and prayer. So too, the subsequent meditations on the self and the obstacles blocking the way to God – to which we now turn – can only be helpful in enabling us to be simpler and more transparent in our personal acts of obeisance. It seems then that the Tiru Mantra, *Auṃ namo Nārāyaṇāya,* is able to be affirmed and uttered by the Christian, even if we cannot ignore complications that also arise when a Christian ventures to utter *Nārāyaṇa* prayerfully.

On the Qualities of the Self

Implied by the listed divine qualities are the 68 qualities of the self who, in keeping with its true nature, chooses to take refuge with the Lord.[89] Here is the list, again in Deśika's sequence and with my subdivisions:[90]

In relation to protector[91]

1. Being protected by the one who is with Śrī and
2. protected by no one else;
3. having a protector who protects everywhere, all the time, in every way,
4. having a protector who is most well disposed;
5. having a mediator,
6. being endowed with great faith,

On being a servant[92]

7. being a servant of the one who is with Lakṣmī,[93]
8. being always a servant,
9. unconditionally and
10. meant to serve no one else;

Basic qualities[94]

11. being comprised of knowledge and
12. bliss,
13. self-illuminating and
14. luminous to oneself;

[89] Commentators on the *Essence* have made point by point connections between parts of the life and parts of the Mantra, but Deśika himself does not make any such explicit connections; he simply lists all the relevant qualities of the self.

[90] Covering pages 674-675/392-394

[91] I have followed the *Sārāsvādinī* commentary in making these divisions, and noted the correlations made in that commentary; but there is no indication that Deśika has in mind any such particular correlation to the Matra's parts.

[92] *Sārāsvādinī*: the elided *a* in *Nārāyaṇāya*; That is, when *Nārāyaṇa* is given in the dative as *Nārāyaṇa+āya*, the 4th and 5th *a*'s are merged, the (human) *a* "lost" in the divine *a*.

[93] Śrī.

[94] *Sārāsvādinī*: with respect to the *m*.

15. the referent of the word "I,"
16. atomic in size,
17. subtle,
18. unable to be cut, etc.;
19. entirely different from the twenty-four elements,
20. pure,
21. different from the Lord, and
22. (essentially) a knower;

Capacities of the self[95]

23. connected to what is suitable,[96]
24. desiring the highest human goal,
25. fit to be commanded,
26. fit for service,
27. fit for direct manifestation of everything,
28. fit for unsurpassable bliss;
29. an agent in need of another,
30. a ruler, but only in a conditioned manner,
31. dependent on those belonging to the Lord
32. and at their service;

The plight of the self

33. this self has no other means;
34. it suffers ignorance, etc.;
35. the expansion of its knowledge depends on the senses, etc.;
36. it is beset with fear of this world,
37. needs to end ignorance yet
38. has no resources to do so;
39. but it does have the good-heartedness of the Lord, and
40. is able to attain a good teacher;

Help for the self[97]

41. this self is suited for the performance of (taking refuge as) the means that is to be accomplished, and
42. is firmly established in this means,
43. has great power,

[95] *Sārāsvādinī*: obeisance.
[96] Suitable to pleasing the Lord, and thus conducive to liberation.
[97] *Sārāsvādinī*: Nārāyaṇa.

44. is subject to creation and destruction because of its current garb[98] yet
45. is imperishable;
46. selves are in essence plural and even
47. countless in number;

By the Lord's choice,

48. the self is pervaded by the Lord,[99]
49. controlled by the Lord, and
50. supported by the Lord, and on that basis
51. the self is the Lord's body,
52. the cause of His enjoyment in His divine play,
53. a fit instrument of His enjoyment;
54. the self's movement is dependent on the Lord, and
55. its gaining of its goal likewise depends on Him;
56. it has no need for lordship or total isolation,[100] and instead
57. desires to gain the Lord;

The final state of the self[101]

58. The self becomes free from all ignorance,
59. and its proper form is made manifest;
60. it sees all,
61. has enjoyment only in experiencing the Lord in every way,
62. has unsurpassable bliss,
63. enjoys the objects of the Lord's enjoyment,
64. takes on forms, etc., such as it wishes,
65. has no obstacles to its wishes,
66. attained supreme sameness (with the Lord) excepting features unique to the Lord,[102]
67. takes pleasure solely in total service, and
68. never returns here.[103]

[98] That is, the self is born and dies because it currently has this particular, finite body.

[99] Wherever the self is, the Lord also pervades that space.

[100] These are two highly desired human goals: total power, total separation from all that is contingent.

[101] *Sārāsvādinī*: the dative.

[102] The divine role as creator, as the one to whom all belongs, etc.

[103] After reaching the liberated state with Nārāyaṇa and Śrī in Heaven.

After the list of qualities of the individual self, Deśika adds another passage in praise of the Tiru Mantra and its inclusive truth:

> As it says,
>
> The three Vedas, their six subsidiary disciplines,
> the hymns, the various musical notes,
> all this and everything else too that is made of word
> subsists in these eight-syllables,[104]
>
> and accordingly we find everything inside the Tiru Mantra: the forms of conscious beings, non-conscious beings, and the Lord; the differences among living beings; the unconditional differences between selves and the Lord, in terms of their existence as dependent and depended-upon, and so forth; the specification, etc., of distinctive features of the highest deity who is the efficient and material cause for the universe.[105]

Or, more simply, Deśika affirms strongly a realist philosophical and theological position as most appropriate to the Tiru Mantra and its profession of innate orientation and chosen surrender to the Lord.

Erroneous Views about God and Self

But it also follows, Deśika adds, that people who know these things about the Lord and self due to the Mantra ought not be disturbed by errors that distract the meditating person and thwart refuge with the Lord. Conversely, people who do not understand the Tiru Mantra are prey to many errors, of which 57 are listed here. As expected, these are mainly errors about the Lord or self, and follow fairly directly from the key characteristics of Nārāyaṇa and the individual self.[106]

To anticipate Deśika's summation, we can note that the concluding verse for this third list gives us the real point behind the list by pointing to the serene state of the person who, settled in the orthodox views of the community, remains untouched by these errors:

> The person who knows the essence of the twice-four Mantra[107] will be like a deep Gaṅgā pool, undisturbed by ideas contrary to this settled state, by views contradicted by his own positions, or by any other errors.[108]

[104] *Aṣṭākṣara Brahmavidyā* 1.9; see Chapter 1.

[105] 675/394. Here too Deśika gives a concluding verse, although this one seems to summarize what needs to be known about the self in light of the entire Tiru Mantra, and not just the word *Nārāyaṇa*: "In the three words, concisely: being entirely dependent – on no one else; having no other means; having no other human goal for ourselves." (675/394)

[106] The *Sārabodhinī* meticulously identifies the heterodox traditions holding these wrong views, particularly 1-37.

[107] That is, the eight-syllable mantra, the Tiru Mantra.

[108] 677/396

The 57 errors too can be subdivided thematically:[109]

Errors regarding the Lord[110]

1. There is no Lord;
2. the Lord is devoid of distinguishing features;
3. He is nothing but witness;[111]
4. His lordship is but a mirage;[112]
5. it is accomplished due to His specific karmas, and
6. He is sometimes overcome by karma;
7. the "three divine forms"[113] are equal, or
8. they are one, or
9. there is a highest reality beyond all three divine forms;
10. the Lord is just one among Brahmā and other deities;
11. He suffers evolution in his proper form;
12. instrumental and material causes can never be one;[114]

Errors regarding differences between the Lord and human selves

13. living selves and the Lord share a single self;
14. their differences are due only to conditioning factors, or
15. they are eternally different and non-different;[115]
16. dependence (on the Lord) is merely a matter of karma;
17. dependence is not absolutely necessary;[116]

Erroneous views of the qualities of self

18. the self is insentient, or
19. its proper form is nothing but knowledge;
20. it is eternally free;
21. its enjoyment is merely a superimposition (but not real);

[109] Covering pages 675-677/394-396

[110] 675-677/394-396

[111] And not active, not an agent.

[112] A reflection apparent in this world, but not real, since he has no relation to contingent realities.

[113] The *Trimūrti* popularly conceived as three deities, Brahmā, Viṣṇu, Śiva.

[114] The argument of the Vedānta traditions is that God is both the efficient (or instrumental) and material cause of the world.

[115] The so-called *bheda-abheda* position, by which God (or Brahman) and other beings are from different perspectives alike, and one, but also different and not one.

[116] That is, the utter dependence of self on God is due to karma, or temporary.

22. it is not an agent, or
23. it is an agent independent of the Lord;
24. it survives only up to the cosmic dissolution;
25. it survives only up to liberation;
26. it is self-established;
27. it is an effect even in its own proper form, or
28. it never experiences being an effect;
29. the means (of liberation) is nothing but action;
30. in the state of liberation, it is like a stone;
31. it rejoices only in the bliss of its own self,
32. it is entirely free,
33. it becomes entirely one with the Lord;
34. it is entirely devoid of activity,
35. it has the power to be separate from the Lord or not,
36. (in liberation) it experiences degrees of bliss;
37. it experiences fixed differences with respect to the states of "sharing the same place (as the Lord),"[117] etc.;

Erroneous views regarding Nārāyaṇa and Śrī[118]

38. weakness of faith regarding the spouse of Śrī;
39. seeking other protectors;
40. arguing with the Lord, "You are mine," "No, I belong to myself..."[119]
41. mistakenly imagining unconditional dependence on someone other (than the Lord);
42. inclination toward other deities, and
43. relationships with their devotees;
44. taking pleasure in serving people not worthy of service;

Erroneous views about the self and body, and life in the world

45. errors regarding the body and self, etc.;
46. errors regarding the self as independent, etc.;
47. grasping things for one's own sake;

[117] *Sālokya* ("sharing a place") is one of the higher (but not ultimate) states of union with God.

[118] The following errors occur within the Śrīvaiṣṇava fold.

[119] In reference to the *Tirumañjana Hymn* of Parāśara Bhaṭṭar, in which he portrays himself as engaged in argument with the Lord about dependence and independence, during the time of a festival ritual bath of the temple image.

48. offending people belonging to the Lord;
49. forgetting that we have nothing;
50. taking pleasure in remaining in this world;
51. fearing the destruction of the self, etc.;
52. taking pleasure in bad behavior;
53. distinguishing enemies and friends, etc.;[120]
54. grasping at relationships (other than with God),
55. taking pleasure in purposes other (than the Lord and the Lord's people),
56. lacking interest in the highest goal;
57. and many other such obstacles to one's proper establishment[121]

Finally, it is important to remember that all these qualities of the divine person, the human person, and the errors to be avoided are evoked simultaneously as one says, *Aum, obeisance to Nārāyaṇa.* Remembering them in detail or not, we express them in reciting the Mantra. While all of this knowledge can be concisely tabulated, it is ultimately practical, to be recollected and uttered in recognition of the nature of reality and for the sake of worship. The Tiru Mantra offers a therapeutic knowledge by which relationships are healed, our self-image corrected, and errors cured.

Parāśara Bhaṭṭar's Fourth Verse on the Tiru Mantra:
After his long reflection on the meanings of *Nārāyaṇa,* Deśika moves into the summary portion of the chapter, tabulating the meaning of the Tiru Mantra in several ways.

But first we can finally introduce the fourth verse of Bhaṭṭar's *Aṣṭaślokī,* a straightforward summation of the meaning of the Tiru Mantra in correspondence with the mind and attitudes of the person who has taken refuge:

> If he thinks the self is attached to the body – let him remember well the third syllable [*m*];
> if he is blindly independent – the first syllable [*a*];
> if he has a mind for dependence on someone else[122] – the second [*u*];
> if looking to protect himself – *namaḥ*;
> if hankering after seeming relatives – *Nārāyaṇa*;

[120] Rather than relating to all with equanimity.
[121] The *Sārabodhinī* identifies heterodox views connected with each of these erroneous positions.
[122] Anyone other than the Lord.

if his mind moves toward things – the dative [*-āya*]:
thus the person who takes refuge.

Thus read, the Mantra is both demonstrative of the truth and therapeutic, purifying the individual who utters the Mantra and meditates on its meanings. For those who understand it and utter it with understanding, transformation follows.

Summarizing the Tiru Mantra in Chapter 27

As should be no surprise, Deśika's summary statements are considerably more complex than Bhaṭṭar's. As if to take into account all prior interpretations, and possible ones as well, Deśika recognizes and affirms ten different ways of construing the Mantra, as encoding one, two, or three statements. First, the Mantra can be read as *one sentence*:[123]

	Aum, obeisance to Nārāyaṇa
1	The One to whom I am exclusively oriented: Nārāyaṇa, indicated by *aum*, the cause, protector, the One to whom all belongs, is the One to whom I have given all.
2	The behavior of the entirely dependent person: I worship the Lord, reverence Him, and for Him perform all service.

Second, it can be read as *two sentences*:[124]

3	The Lord is the protector and support of all.	I am neither suitable for nor dependent on any other means.
4	I have offered myself to the Lord.	The burden of protecting my self is no longer mine.
5	I perform service for the Lord.	I no longer act on my own behalf, independently and to achieve my own results.

[123] 677-678/397

[124] 678-681/397-401. While it is not hard to read the Tiru Mantra as one statement or three (one for each word), the division into two requires exegetical agility – the complexity of which need not be demonstrated here. It would seem easiest, however to see my first column as explicatory of *aum* and *Nārāyaṇāya*, and the second of *namo* taken to mean "not mine."

Third, it can be read as *three sentences*:[125]

	Aum	obeisance	to Nārāyaṇa
6	The self is oriented to and entirely dependent on the Lord.	I am not oriented to or reliant on myself.	Experiencing the Lord and Śrī fully, I serve in all times and places.
7	The self is oriented to and entirely dependent on the Lord.	I have rejected all opposing and harmful views, such as the idea of existing for myself.	I serve Nārāyaṇa and Śrī in all times and places.
8	I am oriented to and entirely dependent on the Lord.	You alone must be the means for me who am not capable of any other means.	I pray that You give me all the desired forms of service.
9	I have offered myself to the Lord.	I have managed to end all things that are undesirable.	I perform service for the Lord.
10	I am oriented to, entirely dependent on the Lord.	I have taken refuge with Him.	I perform perfect service for Him.

Is there a point to listing all ten interpretations,[126] beyond the value of a comprehensive summation of respectable views? It is surely an intellectual tour de force, an enjoyment of the sheer possibilities of interpretation, and with the further goal of showing that all such meanings converge. Deśika indicates that he respects all ten possibilities:

> The Tiru Mantra is the womb of endless meanings pertaining to the truth, the means, the human goal, and the prayer for these… But in the ways [recounted above, scholars] have interpreted ten meanings of the Mantra in accord with tradition. Even if one meditates on just a few of these as primary, the rest are still implied.[127]

All ten are possible, since none is excluded by other possible meanings. If the list is taken as full and balanced, it also stands as a comprehensive bulwark against wrong interpretations:

> Therefore, by the meanings of these words and sentences shown by gurus
> who know the truth,

[125] 681-691/401-412
[126] My interpretation follows Ramanujadesikacaryar's gloss, 711-712.
[127] 692/412

> other construals expressed by various wrong-seeing people are destroyed.[128]

A person with knowledge of the right meanings will never be shaken by alien and misdirected views:

> Having ascended the tower of wisdom,
> this ungrieving man of knowledge observes those who grieve in ignorance;
> like one standing on a peak who observes people on the ground below.[129]

On a sophisticated intellectual level, the Tiru Mantra becomes, like other mantras, a charm that wards off evil – in this case, the evil of wrong views and harmful patterns of thought.

In each chapter of the *Essence* Deśika offers concluding Tamil and Sanskrit verses. As is also his custom,[130] the final Tamil verse usually praises the teachers who pass down the Mantra, as is the case here:

> Refusing allegiance to anyone but their exalted Protector
> these living beings ended their confusion;
> having no other recourse they reached the feet of Nārāyaṇa
> who has made everything and is our refuge:
> these ancient devotees lovingly recited this Mantra that teaches service.[131]

And likewise too, the final Sanskrit verse usually offers a kind of summation for key points learned in the chapter, in this case stressing the superior value of such knowledge as "the end" or high point of what can be known, decisive in transforming the world of the three constituents – the world in fluctuation – as we commonly experience it:

> Thus composed of three words –
> one plus two plus five syllables,[132]
> with three meanings, the truth, the way, and the goal,
> all three spiritual in their essence –
> the Mantra is primal, in its three letters[133] it generates the Veda,
> it never loses its three levels of meaning, the material and the other two,[134]

[128] 692-693/413

[129] *Mahābhārata, Śānti Parva* 150.11. (693/413)

[130] See Clooney forthcoming a., Chapter 3.

[131] 700/418; Here and in the Sanskrit verse, "Mantra" is *Manu.* It is striking that the value of service appears so prominently in the interpretaion of the Tiru Mantra.

[132] Respectively, *aum, na-mah,* Na-ra-ya-na-ya.

[133] *a-u-m*

[134] That is, the material, subtle, and supreme meanings, as noted earlier in this chapter, pp. 42-43.

and for good people it extinguishes the three constituents,[135]
it is the essence of the apex of the Three Vedas.[136]

III. Insights Elsewhere in the *Essence*

In each of this book's chapters, we focus on one of the Mantras as exegeted by Deśika in a single chapter of the *Essence*. But it is also important to follow up on a point stressed in the Introduction to this book: the *Essence* is an integral whole, so that what Deśika explains explicitly and in detail in any given chapter on a particular Mantra is reinforced and explained from other angles elsewhere in the text. Here I mention some particularly interesting references.

The verse opening Chapter 2, already cited in my Introduction, shows us the purpose of the Tiru Mantra with respect to the Dvaya Mantra and Carama Śloka: "Having gained his self by the Tiru Mantra[137] set above all the branches [of learning and practice]..." The Tiru Mantra distills the truth of the tradition as the truth of the self; as such, it is also the basis on which one can then profit from the Dvaya Mantra and the Carama Śloka. The opening verse in Chapter 4 succinctly calculates the value and meaning of the Tiru Mantra:

The goal, highest and flawless – in the first letter [*a*],[138]
the form of the one who attains – in the *m* and what follows,
the desired means – in the (*Nara-*)*ayana* and *namaḥ,*
the most desired goal – in the dative [*-āya*],
the obstacle – in the word expressing "mine" [*namaḥ*]:
the [Tiru] Mantra explains all this, and the Dvaya[139] says the same:
knowing this, one knows all and becomes agreeable to all.[140]

In Chapter 14,[141] Deśika lists the signs indicative of the fact that one is firmly established with respect to the truth of reality (*tattva*), the means

135 That is, the constituents of all material reality known as *sattva* (the true and light), *rajas* (the passionate) and *tamas* (the dark, lethargic);

136 "The Three:" the *Rg, Yajur,* and *Sāma* Vedas; the apex of the three Vedas is the Upaniṣads. Ramadesikacaryar suggests that by "the essence of the apex of the three Vedas" is meant Nārāyaṇa. (701/418-419)

137 The "Fundamental Mantra"

138 The *a* which also stands for *Nārāyaṇa.*

139 It is tempting to interpret "dvaya" here as "the two," referring to both the Dvaya Mantra and Carama Śloka.

140 61/32

141 "Recognizing One's Own Firm Establishment [after Taking Refuge]"

(*upaya*), and in one's focus on the final goal (*puruṣārtha*), respectively geared to the Tiru Mantra, Dvaya Mantra, Carama Śloka. Here is the first installment:[142]

Chapter 27
tattva (truth)
knowing the self, detached serenity with respect to bodily flaws and criticisms by others
compassion toward those who criticize
remembrance of the help being given even by those who criticize
seeing that criticisms are really from the Lord who controls all
rejoicing that by these criticisms, karma is being expended

The Tamil verse at the end of Chapter 14[143] highlights the power of the Tiru Mantra's instruction:

People established in the three truths[144]
shown in this primary Mantra,
never desire what is improper,
nor anything but what is proper;[145]
reflecting deeply, they realize, "Proper deeds are for us;"[146]
by this measure, they are heaven-dwellers on earth.[147]

And finally,[148] at the beginning of Chapter 32 Deśika asserts the importance of the Tiru Mantra as the basis for right teaching and right living:

By the glance of the teacher
a person finds all this[149] as obvious as a jujube berry in one's hand,
all illusion is dispelled, and thus too

[142] We complete this chart in Chapters 3 and 5.

[143] "The Characteristics of the Person Firmly Established in Refuge with the Lord."

[144] That is, the truth about total dependence on the Lord, expressed in the Tiru Mantra; the efficacious way to liberation, Nārāyaṇa and Śrī as Way or the Means, enunciated and enacted in the Dvaya Mantra; the highest and final human goal, union with the Lord, expressed in the Carama Śloka.

[145] That is, neither what is contrary nor what is merely neutral.

[146] That is, they recognize proper deeds as their duty, the correct behavior described in the chapter, and not the ordinary way ordinary people do things.

[147] 263/146

[148] In Chapter 25 (553/310), the recitation of the Tiru Mantra is cited as a means of purification and as a model (554/311) for the way to cherish spiritually important words.

[149] "All this" – all the world, all experience – or perhaps the entirety of the truth, the way, and the goal, taught here (see above).

he enjoys this Tiru Mantra[150] and the others too;
if (a student who is) an abode of good qualities is identified,[151]
one can teach him the tradition,
harvest good deeds, and by all this
become worthy of the heaven-dwellers' praise.[152]

There is, in the end, a harmony of Mantra, person, teacher, and tradition; studying the Mantra is thus a multi-dimensional cognitive, social, and religious event.

> *Reflection*: It is clear then that in Deśika's mind there is almost no limit to the praise due to the Tiru Mantra; while it is the gift of God and not a replacement for God, it is a most potent Mantra that changes recitants and their world. It may then be difficult for a Christian reader, accustomed to reserving such praise for Christ and for some of the many benefits and resources of the Christian tradition, to respond positively to such praise for the Mantra. Yet even if such praise is not to our taste, noticing it should help us to see differently, from another's perspective, the praise we do bestow on our own tradition, often without any sense that things might look very different from the outside. The Tiru Mantra is in this sense too a mirror in which we see ourselves.

IV. Reading the Tiru Mantra from a Christian Perspective

As I admitted in my Introduction, even the preceding description of the Tiru Mantra and Deśika's reading of it, though primarily textual and attentive to Deśika's Śrīvaiṣṇava environment, must be counted as Christian commentary. I have, consciously and surely at times unconsciously, selected insights more and not less consonant with Western or Christian interests. I have also offered a number of Christian reflections along the way. But even if all of this has been Christian commentary in a broad tense, our task at the end of each chapter is to reflect more explicitly on what we learn theologically, in a comparative textual practice, and with respect to actual prayer.

1. Theological Insights and Concerns, for a Christian Reader

It is clear that the Tiru Mantra, even as an utterance of praise, is also a highly condensed doctrinal exposition. Deśika wants to instruct, and in

150 "Fundamental Mantra"

151 That is, a good student who apt to become a receptacle of the teachings of the tradition.

152 990/581

that way also to persuade the listener/reader to take its truths to heart, and to affirm them by uttering the Mantra in an informed fashion. He is repeatedly putting his reflections on the Tiru Mantra into context by way of citations from scripture and tradition, and these are all the more potent precisely because they speak to – win over, persuade – insiders. At first, readers from outside that tradition may not be moved by the insights of Rāmānuja and other teachers, or by parallels drawn with the persons and events of the *Rāmāyaṇa*, or by the more rarified analyses of *a*, *u*, and *m*, etc. But the more we read, the more we learn and understand; we remember, and gradually begin to think with these texts and their images, etc., echoing in our memories and conscious awareness: *Aum, obeisance to Nārāyaṇa* becomes operative within Christian patterns of thought, imagination, and affective appropriation.

The Tiru Mantra indicates that all beings are fundamentally oriented to the divine person Nārāyaṇa, and exist only in relationship to that person. In turn, Nārāyaṇa is naturally and by choice ever welcoming the beings that seek him; he is for all eternity disposed to protect and care for such beings. Most of this basic truth, and all the truths subordinate to it, can quite easily be accepted by a Christian even if, as we shall admit again in a moment, the identity of Nārāyaṇa and the meaning of pressing his name remains an issue.

The Tiru Mantra should chasten us, reminding us to take more seriously the fundamental orientation to God that is surely at the heart of the Christian piety and theology as well. Because we now in some sense know the Mantra, we become able to act with greater reverence; we should understand more clearly and pointedly the theological proposition that everything belongs to the Lord; and we should become more vulnerable to the still more radical and spiritual denial of self, existentially, in our encounter with the Lord. By multi-leveled comparisons, we clarify not only our thinking regarding the Śrīvaiṣṇava tradition of Vedānta Deśika and the common ground we share, but we should also gain new insights into the fundamental and transformative truths of our own Christian tradition.

We can be more specific. The *a* and the *m* of *aum* provide for us rich theological and anthropological bases for reconsidering the human condition before God: who among us will say that we do not exist entirely for God? The *u* – as point of connection – prompts questions about the relationship of God and human persons. How are the divine and human connected, how does the orientation to God get satisfied in a humanly possible and comprehensible fashion? At least we can agree with Śrīvaiṣṇavas that we are not God, and yet destined to an intensely and intimately complete union.

Namaḥ seems unproblematic. As *obeisance* – worship, praise – it indicates the attitude of worship that one cultivates in the presence of God; again we exist for God, not for ourselves, and in prayer, we affirm this necessary truth. And if *namaḥ* is parsed as *na mama*, "not mine," the challenge is more stringent, but the point is same: whatever is mine is God's first and last, I am no longer my own, but God's.

Nārāyaṇa is a rich word, and tells us much about God, humans, and the better and worse aspects of the human condition. In accord with the richness of meaning inscribed in *Nara-ayana* as the foundation and abode of all beings, and also in the 108 attributes listed by Deśika, plus the 68 qualities of the self and the 57 errors to be avoided, the divine name indicates vast areas of potential agreement between the Śrīvaiṣṇava worshipper and the Christian. The reader is invited to maximize the widest extent of knowledge about Nārāyaṇa, living persons and the experience of life in this world, and the way to union and liberation, as truths to be couched in the nearly universal terms. But all of this learning is condensed into the words of the Tiru Mantra as a prayer of praise of Nārāyaṇa, a deity with a known history and specific presence in specific temples, etc. – a deity who is neither generic nor specifiable as the God of the Bible. Not only is the Mantra not merely knowledge-about; it is knowledge of and for a particular Deity, who persists in particularity even when Deśika goes so far in making him universal. We must therefore ask not whether to respect and take the Mantra seriously – that seems almost a necessity, once we understand it – but rather when we must stop affirming and uttering it as our own truth, a truth in harmony with Christian truth. However we read *Nārāyaṇa* and however we appropriate the Tiru Mantra, we have clearer, better theological choices on hand because we now do understand something of this highly concise, dense theological mantra.

Or, just one other example: one of Deśika's most notable borrowings in Chapter 27 is the long passage from the *Ahirbudhnya Saṃhitā* which indicates three levels of meaning, the material and physical, the psychological, and a supreme, spiritual meaning. All were taken as interpretive of *namaḥ*, respectively indicating the visible act of obeisance, the confession of dependence on God, and the more radical spiritual realization, *na mama*, "nothing is mine." This threefold distinction can harmonize well with analogous schemes in Christian practice, theological and spiritual insight, and models of practice and interior transformation. If we are well-disposed readers, we become gradually implicated in the larger world of the Mantra, the fuller world of ideas and images a learned Śrīvaiṣṇava would bring to bear on the texts, as truths about what we might for the moment call the "material, psychological, and supreme spiritual meanings" of the Christian faith. With full attention or more implicitly, we slowly grow more sophisticated, on multiple levels, in encountering the world in which the Tiru Mantra was cherished and passed down, and we are persuaded to take it seriously to heart, however unfamiliar the ground and necessarily incomplete our assent. Each of these, then, requires specific and multi-leveled reflection as a specific site for reflection.

From a stance of centuries later and from outside the Hindu tradition, it would be very surprising were we to understand and entirely agree with these ancient Mantras and their medieval interpretations. Just as contemporary Christians often seek some distance from the classic anthropologies and cosmologies of earlier ages, it is easy enough to imagine alternatives to the "medieval" worldview implied in the Tiru Mantra, perhaps even resisting the powerful *a – m* tension inscribed in *aum* and in the grammatical dynamism of the "*–āya*," preferring instead some newer view of a more autonomous human self. Yet we would surely be foolish were we to move too quickly away from the traditional reading, before becoming certain that we have understood it, with respect.[153]

2. Resonances in the Christian Prayer and Worship

At this point, I introduce a second dynamic to recur at the end of each chapter. No reader is a *tabula rasa*; we read as we have read before and not in a vacuum, but with often sharper memories of and sensitivities to

[153] And to touch again on the distinct point of orthodox expectations about *aum*, there is the issue of caste restrictions. As we saw, Deśika admits that women and low caste men might be barred from the recitation of the Aum, and even from the actual Sanskrit form *Nārāyaṇāya*, instead using *Nārāyaṇa*. The Tiru Mantra might then be or become a tool in defending a more conservative social order. *Aum*, which can have many meanings, may thus be narrowed by its usage in the Śrīvaiṣṇava tradition, to have not only a universal thesis about orientation to God, but also a socially constructed specificity limiting a full realization of the possibilities to upper caste males. Alternatively, however, we may well be inclined to be less severe, since it is possible, as the testimony of Tirumaṅkai Āḻvār and others suggests, to imagine two strands of the Tiru Mantra tradition, both of which are to be taken seriously: a Sanskrit and highly orthodox *auṃ namo Nārāyaṇāya*, and a Tamil version of fuller accessibility, *namo Nārāyaṇa*. Both versions of the Mantra seem to have the same range of meanings, even if in the latter case, *namaḥ* is required to bear the full burden in highlighting the radical orientation to the Lord. And if we as Christian readers begin to make sense of the Tiru Mantra in English – *Aum, obeisance to Nārāyaṇa* – it may be that the Mantra has yet another life in another language and cultural, religious context where different restrictions apply.

analogies arising in our own tradition. When we begin to read an unfamiliar tradition we bring to bear the resources of our own religious and cultural background. Much depends on what we bring to our work of reading and reflection. So we will do well to make explicit what we already know when we ponder the Tiru Mantra, or read a text like the *Essence*. We learn to read and hear the Mantra with a sense of continuities and differences between our own personal starting points and those of Deśika's expected audience. Even if our consideration of the Tiru Mantra might suggest a very wide range of possible parallels with prayers from the Christian tradition, for the illustrative purposes of this study, it seems economical to narrow our focus and look simply for parallels with Biblical texts that might be invested with greater expectations regarding their revelatory and transformative power.

It is not easy to find a Christian parallel to the Tiru Mantra, or even simply some "Christian mantra." As I readily conceded in my Introduction, we do not have a mantra tradition, there is not a similar ritual background; although there are many very important short prayers in the Christian tradition and in the Bible, we do not invest a special set of short prayers – and certainly not just favored three brief prayers – with quite the same theological and practical importance. But we can at least engage in experiments in reading the Tiru Mantra along with other texts more familiar to us, chosen in terms of theme and other correlations; rather than reconceptualizing the thought of another religion in Christian terms, as we often do, here we have the opportunity to reconfigure Christian piety and prayer in Śrīvaiṣṇava terms. It is therefore well to bring some examples of this experiment – it is only that – to the fore, as I will do now and in each chapter to follow. I invite the reader to think of other appropriate analogous prayers, Christian mantras.

Insofar as we wish to see in the Mantra an expression of praise, a confession of utter dependence – its simple evident meaning and enactment – we might think of any number of Biblical passages[154] in which praise comes to the fore, as a person acknowledges her or his complete indebtedness to God – for instance, Thomas' prayer and climactic words in *John* 20:

> Then he said to Thomas, "Put your finger here and see my hands. Reach out your hand and put it in my side. Do not doubt but believe." Thomas answered him, "*My Lord and my God*!"[155]

154 Or, more specifically, New Testament texts, to which I restrict myself.

155 *John* 20: 27-28. Throughout, for New Testament quotations, I use the New Revised Standard Version translation, with slight adaptations.

Insofar as we think of total dependence on God as the more pointed claim, the words of Mary become an apt companion to the Tiru Mantra:

> Then Mary said, "Here am I, the servant of the Lord; *let it be with me according to your word.*"[156]

Or we might reflect on this powerful yet most intimate prayer:

> Then Jesus withdrew from them about a stone's throw, knelt down, and prayed, "Father, if you are willing, remove this cup from me; *yet, not my will but yours be done.*"[157]

Many such parallels and echoes are worthy of consideration; several will recur in subsequent chapters, and in any case there is no need to narrow the possibilities to a single, best parallel. But I wish to examine at greater length just one particularly apt parallel that touches on the various possible levels of meaning, and in a mantra-like fashion. In *Romans* 8 Paul describes for us the deepest human orientation to God, and (building upon earlier chapters) the possibility of the marring of that relationship in sin:

> For those who live according to the flesh set their minds on the things of the flesh, but those who live according to the Spirit set their minds on the things of the Spirit.[158]

While sin does indeed turn people away from God, those reborn in the Spirit are dramatically changed, awakened to their true identity:

> ...you are not in the flesh; you are in the Spirit, since the Spirit of God dwells in you. Anyone who does not have the Spirit of Christ does not belong to him. But if Christ is in you, though the body is dead because of sin, the Spirit is life because of righteousness. If the Spirit of him who raised Jesus from the dead dwells in you, he who raised Christ from the dead will give life to your mortal bodies also through his Spirit that dwells in you.[159]

We are radically dependent on God, and yet have a choice to make that potentially changes the direction of our life:

> So then, brothers and sisters, we are debtors, not to the flesh, to live according to the flesh – for if you live according to the flesh, you will die; but if by the Spirit you put to death the deeds of the body, you will live. For all

156 *Luke* 1:38
157 *Luke* 22:41-42
158 *Romans* 8:5
159 *Romans* 8:9-11

> who are led by the Spirit of God are children of God. For you did not receive a spirit of slavery to fall back into fear, but you have received a spirit of adoption.[160]

In this situation of radical orientation to God, in realizing our true identity, we are given new words that speak both to our dependence and our freedom in choosing to affirm that dependence:

> When we cry, *Abba, Father*, it is that very Spirit bearing witness with our spirit that we are children of God, and if children, then heirs, heirs of God and joint heirs with Christ–if, in fact, we suffer with him so that we may also be glorified with him.[161]

Abba, Father, I suggest, stands forth as a kind of mantra, a most simple utterance that is most rich in theological, anthropological, and spiritual meanings. It is intimate, sacred, and likewise evocative of a fundamental orientation to God and yet too intimacy with that God. It is powerful as prayer, as an utterance in the Spirit. It shows Paul's fundamental insight into human and Christian identity, and is in some ways analogous to the Tiru Mantra in its succinctness and theological gravity and as a potent counterpart to it:

Aum, obeisance to Nārāyaṇa.	Abba, Father.

Henri Le Saux, O.S.B., on Aum and Abba, Father

An aside is necessary here, since my suggestion that *Abba, Father* is a kind of mantra is not a novel insight, nor even the proximity I am constructing between *Aum* and *Abba*. Henri Le Saux (1910-1973), better known as Swami Abhishiktananda, pioneered this path decades ago. He was a French Benedictine who, with Fr. Jules Monchanin, founded a Catholic ashram in south India in 1950. Le Saux studied the Upaniṣadic tradition carefully for a long time, personally appropriating the spiritual significance of that tradition, and he sought to find deeper and richer meeting points between the Christian and Hindu traditions. In his small

160 *Romans* 8:12-15

161 *Romans* 8:15-17. The older reference is in *Galatians* 4:4-7: "But when the fullness of time had come, God sent forth his Son, born of woman, born under the law, to redeem those who were under the law, so that we might receive adoption as sons. And because you are sons, God has sent the Spirit of his Son into our hearts, crying, *Abba, Father!* So you are no longer a slave, but a son, and if a son, then an heir through God." On "Abba, Father," see Grassi and bibliography; for a critique of the related patriarchal language, see d'Angelo.

spiritual classic entitled simply *Prayer*, Le Saux devotes the first part of the final chapter to meditation on *Aum* (though not on the Tiru Mantra) as the more precious and powerful of Indian mantras:

> As experience deepens, OM[162] appears as the reflection in man's mind of the universal theophany or revelation of *Being* in the world of *becoming*, the echo in his own heart of the heart-beats of the universe which count the time. OM is the awakening of every man in the secret place of his heart, the *guha*,[163] to the mystery that is hidden in each movement of the creation, revealing at any point of space or time its divine origin and final goal. OM is the sound which, at the ultimate boundary of meaning, gives everything its truth. OM, for anyone who has awakened to God, expresses the fullness of his communion with the whole universe, and also his communion with every other man who thinks, desires, and loves.[164]

After cautioning Christian readers therefore not to take up lightly the recitation of *Aum*, Le Saux seeks a parallel highest Christian mantra, and for this purpose turns to *Abba, Father*. Such is "the ceaseless prayer of Jesus,"[165] the expression and mode of his union with his Father. Does not the example Jesus thereby become, Le Saux asks,

> an invitation to Christian believers to make the invocation *Abba, Father* the centre of their spiritual lives – to make it their most cherished mantra ceaselessly on their lips, in their minds, in their hearts?[166]

In reciting it with Jesus, the Christian enters with him into the mystery of God. It is

> the sacred *mantra* which opens the doors of eternity, the doors of the inner sanctuary, the doors of the cave of the heart, and makes the soul share in the most intimate life of God in himself – a secret hidden from all generations of man, till the Son of God in person appeared as a man amongst men.[167]

In a true precedent to my own project of reading the Tiru Mantra with *Abba, Father*, Le Saux concludes his reflection by bringing *Aum* and *Abba, Father* together:

> Could we not say that OM introduces man into the mystery of the Holy Spirit, the Unspoken and Unbegotten Person, who will reveal to the elect the mystery of the Son, and whispers in the sanctuary of the heart the

162 Le Saux regularly uses OM, not Aum.
163 "Cave"
164 P. 61
165 P. 62
166 Pp. 62-63
167 P. 63

> eternal ABBA? ABBA then is the last word uttered by the creature, for it leads directly to the unfathomable mystery of the Father. ABBA is the mystery of the Son, OM the mystery of the Spirit...[168]

I am happy then to admit that Le Saux's *Prayer* has had a kind of subliminal influence on my own project. My own focus however is on the Śrīvaiṣṇava tradition, to which Le Saux makes no connection, the Tiru Mantra, which he does not mention, and a commentarial tradition, such as did not enter his reflection; and so my work constitutes an interesting variation on his project. It might then be fruitful to reflect on the difference between Le Saux's appropriation of OM as an independent mantra – quite in keeping with much of the Hindu tradition – and my interest in the Śrīvaiṣṇava incorporation of Aum into the Tiru Mantra, in close connection with *Namo Nārāyaṇa.*

Paul's intuition that in the *Abba, Father* we find expression of our deep orientation to God and our death and life in Christ can be given a still richer imaginative and intense power when, in a third New Testament usage, *Abba, Father* is remembered as the word spoken by Jesus on the night before he died:

> And they went to a place called Gethsemane. And he said to his disciples, "Sit here while I pray." And he took with him Peter and James and John, and began to be greatly distressed and troubled. And he said to them, "My soul is very sorrowful, even to death. Remain here and watch." And going a little farther, he fell on the ground and prayed that, if it were possible, the hour might pass from him. And he said, "*Abba, Father*, all things are possible for you. Remove this cup from me. Yet not what I will, but what you will."[169]

Spoken most profoundly by Jesus, *Abba, Father* is given a vivid existential enactment, a living out of what Paul meant in imagining new lives entirely and only for God. We pray *Abba, Father*, in imitation of Christ, who teaches us how to live, how to pray, and how to die. At stake are the illumination of the proper relationship of God, the flaws and enslavement of those who misunderstand and act without due cognizance of this relationship, and connaturality, intimacy, and a radically transformed way of life – truths and values deeply inscribed in the Tiru Mantra.[170]

168 P. 63

169 *Mark* 14: 32-36

170 Indeed, the insight of the *Abba, Father* also touches on the meanings of the Carama Śloka and the Dvaya Mantras, to which we shall soon turn; after all, as Deśika insists, each Mantra includes the meaning and significance of the others as well.

Similarly, the many contexts in which *Abba, Father* has been written, pondered, prayed, come to bear in nearly endless permutations alongside the Tiru Mantra: a vast space is opened for interreligious reflection.

At this point, we can simply allow *Abba, Father* to bring our knowledge of the Christian tradition to bear on the Tiru Mantra, and then too allow the Mantra to intensify how we hear "Abba, Father," thus deepening what we expect from either set of words, as we allow each to enhance and intensify our appreciation of the other:

Abba, Father	Aum, obeisance to Nārāyaṇa

This proximity allows us to return again and again to these mantras next to one another, as simple and deep utterances of worship and knowledge of God – and as inclusive of broad and rich theological worldviews. By remembering the complex ideas of the two traditions, we see the almost unlimited world of possibilities before us; by returning to these most simple words, theology is no longer confined to its worries and complications, but is rather returned to its roots in prayer, that prayerful instinct of obeisance deep in both traditions.

3. Praying with the Tiru Mantra?

We can pray with *Abba, Father*, of course, just as Śrīvaiṣṇavas can and do pray with *Aum, obeisance to Nārāyaṇa*. But now we can also profitably pray *Abba, Father* mindful of the Tiru Mantra, remembering and uttering highly revered words of our tradition mindful of these sacred religious words drawn from another tradition, and thus praying with Paul and with Jesus differently and more deeply. It would seem clearly worthwhile and fruitful for a Śrīvaiṣṇava and a Christian to sit together, the one praying *Aum, obeisance to Nārāyaṇa*, and the other, *Abba, Father*.[171]

But we can go further. Of course we can utter the Tiru Mantra with great respect and understanding, and even with some of the force of its speech resolutely directed to the Lord – even as understood to possess the attributes afforded to *Nārāyaṇa* by Deśika in Chapter 27. But can a Christian pray with the Tiru Mantra? In light of the preceding reflections,

[171] Here and in subsequent chapters, I move directly to the difficult issue of whether a Christian can pray using these Mantras; I do not dwell on the related, intervening issue, whether (as is likely) Christians can pray with Śrīvaiṣṇavas, perhaps using the pairs of texts I will be proposing. It seems better to preserve this important question for a context in which Śrīvaiṣṇavas are full participants.

we can see that the meaning and significance of "praying with the Mantra" is not so simple a matter as allows for a simple "yes" or "no" answer. We are fortunate now to know enough to rule out easy answers.

If we focus on the universal meanings detected by Deśika, we can pray with the Mantra; if we focus on the specific density of the Mantra as praise of Nārāyaṇa as a specific divine person who is exclusive of other deities and incompatible with God as understood in the Jewish and Christian traditions, then praying with the Mantra becomes nearly impossible. More likely, though, we will find ourselves on a difficult middle ground: it is an inclusive Mantra, yet by its power and tradition, it is exclusive too; and for us, finding where to stand is the key factor. But we will have made great progress if we at least understand better what the tradition of the Mantra tells us, and what it does mean to pray with a Tiru Mantra that is now on our minds and in our hearts too. And so we will be in the position where we can ask ourselves what kind of a spiritual act is taking place when we utter this Mantra we have been studying.

V. Looking Ahead

The Śrīvaiṣṇava tradition finds complete meaning in the Tiru Mantra and indeed in each of the three Mantras, yet by tradition too the community insists that the fullness of meaning is gained only when the three Mantras are understood together. By my reading, the Tiru Mantra establishes the parameters within which further considerations can be explored through study of the other mantras – the nature of reality is such that all exists for God, and God is perfect, just, and compassionate, and so ready to invite humans to turn toward the divine person/s. The next word spoken, then, is a divine word to the human who recites the Tiru Mantra – the first line of the Carama Śloka, an invitation actually to place full trust in God, surrendering to God.

CHAPTER 2

A DIVINE INVITATION: THE CARAMA ŚLOKA'S FIRST LINE

If you would be perfect, go,
sell your possessions and give the proceeds to the poor…

Having completely given up all *dharma*s,
to Me alone come for refuge…

Reflection: Our inescapable orientation to and dependence on God does not obviate freedom, the possibility and necessity of making our own personal choice for God. But before we make our choice and act, we need also to recognize that at our best, we are responding to a gracious invitation from God who is always before us, first. At the core of human identity is the fact that God addresses us in our freedom – and in our doubt, fear, alienation – and asks us to make a radical choice to risk everything, depending on nothing but God alone. Such is the invitation of Christ to those who would follow him in discipleship. The first line of the Carama Śloka too is such an invitation, expressed in simple, challenging terms. If understanding the Tiru Mantra was to risk putting new words in our mouths, with the Carama Śloka we take the risk of learning to listen anew.

I. INTRODUCTION

sarvadharmān parityajya mām ekaṃ śaraṇam vraja…
sarva – all; *dharmān* – *dharma*s; *parityajya* – having completely given up; *mām* – Me; *ekam* – alone; *śaraṇam* – refuge; *vraja* – come…

Having completely given up all *dharma*s, to Me alone come for refuge…

1. The Carama Śloka's First Line as Verse 18.66a of the *Bhagavad Gītā*

Having completely given up all dharmas, to Me alone come for refuge… Since the Carama Śloka has its own "pre-history," we must begin by recollecting the meaning of these words as from a verse of the *Bhagavad Gītā*. Over the eighteen chapters of the *Gītā* Kṛṣṇa had been teaching Arjuna the meaning of self and body, duty and detachment, service for the sake of the world, and through it all, Arjuna's love for Kṛṣṇa himself became increasingly evident. Near the conclusion of the *Gītā* and as the fruition of Kṛṣṇa's teaching in Arjuna's heart and mind, verse 18.66 appears a decisive, concluding word of challenge and comfort that Kṛṣṇa addresses to Arjuna the warrior, who now finally stands ready for battle. Kṛṣṇa tells Arjuna to trust him completely and, in that complete trust, to find a joyfulness that overcomes all grief, even on the battlefield:

> Reflecting thoroughly on this knowledge of yours,
> more hidden than the hidden yet expounded by Me,
> as you wish, so act.
> Listen again to this word of Mine, highest and most hidden of all;
> for you are surely my chosen, and so I will speak what is for your benefit.
> Be one whose mind is set on Me, be devoted to Me, sacrifice in Me, reverence Me;
> To Me alone will you come, I promise you truly, you are dear to Me.

And then the key verse itself:

> Having completely given up all *dharmas*, to Me alone come for refuge;
> from all sins I will make you free. Do not grieve.[1]

Encouraged by these words, Arjuna takes heart, stands up, and inaugurates the great war that will comprise the remainder of the *Mahābhārata*.[2]

Briefly, the meaning of the *Gītā* verse can be explicated as follows, in keeping with Deśika's tradition:[3]

> *Dharmas*[4] refers to the status and personal righteousness of the person performing them, the solid foundation and steadiness of this person's life. The *Gītā* seems to recognize all these *dharmas* as positive and valuable. Yet 18.66 is addressed to the person who has completely given up all such *dharmas*.

[1] 18.63-66

[2] For a detailed consideration of the words of *Gītā* 18.66 in the *Gītā*, see Clooney in *Song Divine* (Cornille), the first volume of the series in which *The Truth, the Way, the Life* appears. Here, I focus more exclusively on the Carama Śloka as Mantra, and on Deśika's reading of it.

[3] See also my essay in Cornille.

[4] "Dharma" is rich in meanings having to do with duty, righteousness, social and religious identity and location; in the plural, it also indicates more specifically the location of each individual within the larger schema of interlocking rights and duties. As such, *dharma* becomes famously hard to translate; while I have attempted in these pages to translate nearly every Sanskrit word, it seems wise to leave *dharma*, as a word in the Carama Śloka, in the original, as *dharma* and *dharma*-s.

Since *dharma* is given here in the plural (*dharmān*), we are steered away from a merely ontological or cosmic view of *dharma*, toward an array of particular duties and relationships, all of which are now at stake. *All* (*sarva*) emphasizes and reinforces the plural; all *dharmas* are to be given up, and a key challenge is to discern the extent and force of this *all*.

Having completely given up (*parityajya*) *all dharmas* indicates that the religious obligations constituting the right order of things and the righteous identity of the observant person should be let go of, as a prelude to taking refuge with Kṛṣṇa. As the past participle – *having given up* – indicates, the person addressed by Kṛṣṇa is a person who has *already* broken with life- and religion-as-usual. But as we shall see with respect to these words as words of the Carama Śloka, the Śrīvaiṣṇava tradition was hesitant to take the words literally. Even in the *Mahābhārata* – where the battle is about to begin, inaugurated by Arjuna – it is clear that the warrior ideal remains operative and honored, even after the *Gītā*: *completely giving up* is a radical act that requires careful interpretation for us to get a sense of what actually is at stake.

To Me alone (*mām ekam*) stands in contrast with the giving up of *dharmas*, the singular in tension with the plural. It highlights the *why* and *wherewithal* of giving up: you can and should give up all those *dharmas*, since *I* am here.

Refuge (*śaraṇam*) highlights the security and protection Kṛṣṇa is offering. He had obliquely made the same invitation in 18.62, with reference to the Lord of all: "Go to Him alone for refuge."[5] Immediately after this the second line of 18.66 refers to sins (*pāpa*), so a logical referent here is that refuge is "safety from sins," but the force of this first line indicates that one is discarding *dharmas* and not just sins – or *dharmas* as sins – in new dependence on the Lord; *then* one finds the refuge and safety.

Come (*vraja*) expresses movement – come, go; this word seems not to have any technical meaning in the *Gītā*, but does indicate the invitation, challenge, Kṛṣṇa poses to Arjuna and the wider audience.

This first line of 18.66 is rather clear, even if not entirely so: the person who has given up his or her *dharmas* – one's place in the larger order,

[5] "Refuge" (*śaraṇam*) was used earlier several times; for instance, *Gītā* 2.49 indicated that one must take refuge (*śaraṇam*) from the task of constructing a self in work; *Gītā* 9.18 indicates that Kṛṣṇa is the way, the support, the witness, and the refuge (*śaraṇam*).

a life oriented to what is dharmic because it is dharmic – and who instead takes refuge in the Lord alone and nowhere else, is the person who is freed from all sins, and freed too from grief (about one's life, duties, future). Taking refuge with Kṛṣṇa alone is possible, efficacious and, for those who know, an imperative.

2. The Carama Śloka's First Line in the *Aṣṭaślokī* of Parāśara Bhaṭṭar

In the tradition, *Gītā* 18.66 is singled out for special notice as a mantra that has a self-standing meaning of much broader application, beyond the *Mahābhārata* and Arjuna's plight.[6] For this we will look to its interpretation as the Carama Śloka by Deśika in Chapter 29 of the *Essence.*

> *Reflection*: In our Christian context, but also in the study of other traditions, we need to be cautious about venturing simply to pick up a scripture text and interpret it out of the context of tradition. A study of the original passage in its original contexts is necessary, but it is only a start. The double identity of the Carama Śloka as Mantra and as *Gītā* verse reminds us of the wisdom of learning from tradition.

But before turning to Deśika's exegesis, we must first note Parāśara Bhaṭṭar's comment in the *Aṣṭaślokī.* In his first verse on the Carama Śloka – the seventh of the *Aṣṭaślokī* – we find Kṛṣṇa's word to the anguished Arjuna who seeks Kṛṣṇa but cannot reach him on his own. *Dharma* – the array of means for reaching Kṛṣṇa, workable but in fact too hard for almost anyone to implement – is now an obstacle to union:

> You have completely given up all that *dharma*
> which had been expounded by Me for the sake of reaching Me;

The deeper roots of anguish must be confronted, because trust in anyone but God is inadequate:

> anguished, now make the determination
> that I alone am your refuge, your way to attaining Me;

Kṛṣṇa himself is perfectly capable of all that is required, and so the grounds for grief disappear:

> for I, full of all knowledge and all else too,
> will make you, thus determined,
> free of all obstacles to attaining Me.
> So be without grief.

[6] Just as the *Gītā* itself has a history apart from the plot of the *Mahābhārata.*

This is essentially a paraphrase, and a beautiful one, of the Carama Śloka itself.

The eighth verse offers a response to Kṛṣṇa's words, and as such it echoes the surrender enunciated in the Dvaya Mantra (which we shall see in the Chapter 3). We will return to Bhaṭṭar's verses on the Carama Śloka, particularly the second, in Chapter 4.[7]

II. Exegeting the First Line of the Carama Śloka

Now let us turn to Deśika's own exegesis. He opens Chapter 29, the long chapter devoted to the Carama Śloka, with two Sanskrit verses highlighting the compassion and power of Kṛṣṇa as teacher and liberator, and the prospect of the life without grief that Kṛṣṇa offers those who come to him:

> He stands at the apex of the Upaniṣads
> and from this boundless ocean of mercy
> spontaneously was born this Verse that ends everyone's sorrow;
> by its injunction, we take as our refuge Kṛṣṇa, the eternal dharma;
> our sins are extinguished, doubt and fear abandoned,
> and we become joyful.[8]

The second verse highlights the contrast between life before and life after acceptance of the words of Kṛṣṇa, who becomes sustenance in the great journey:

> Things hard to understand, heavy with restrictions,
> our place of rest too far away,
> the means for getting there multiple and unsuitable for simple people –
> over all this we have grieved:
> but He is the easy path,
> He loves leading us directly to His own feet,
> by His own greatness

[7] Here is Verse 8: "I have realized my dependence on You; I have no ability to perform those means, rites, etc., nor to give them up, nor even to take refuge – so I am indeed afflicted with sorrow; but I have this knowledge – so now be the destroyer of all my sins;' speaking thus, I am steadfast, remembering Your last word, O Charioteer." Arjuna – or the ideal speaker of this verse – thus shows himself the good student, appropriating as his own, in his own words, the teaching given to him by the master; he adds nothing, but makes it deeply personal. See also pp. 149-150.

[8] 792/465

He has prescribed this food that is right for the journey,
our Charioteer, guide for all.[9]

Appropriately, Deśika emphasizes Kṛṣṇa's power and determination to liberate, ending the sorrow and removing the fear of those trusting him entirely. There is a strong intellectual tone to every chapter of the *Essence*, but here in particular Deśika's exegesis manifests a meticulous concern for rules and law, the harmony of theology and ethics, law and freedom. Yet, even in the articulation of legal details, he still sees in the Carama Śloka evidence of a Lord who lovingly gives himself in the teaching that is this Mantra.

An accompanying Tamil verse expresses gratitude for Kṛṣṇa's decisive teaching:

By His single-minded intent
and also too of Lakṣmī whose bracelets shine,
– that all might live and beautiful Dvarakā city prosper –
He became Vasudeva's son[10] and charioteer to the prince;
He Himself, basil leaves on His chest,
uttered this peerless dharma that explains Himself to us,
and so he ends the game of blind man's bluff
that hinders the way
to seeing Him always,
rejoicing,
bearing His feet on our heads.[11]

The words of the Carama Śloka are Kṛṣṇa's; the entire reconfiguration of the world that will make liberation possible is also entirely his intention, put into practice.

Deśika introduces the actual exegesis with a clear reminder of his intention to rule out wrong interpretations of the Carama Śloka, while bringing together right views – and yet all of this without the technical detail and apologetic force he expended in earlier writings:

> We have refuted at considerable length in the *Tātparyacandrikā* and *Nikṣeparakṣā*[12] the interpretations given to the Carama Śloka by perverse interpreters such as Śaṃkara.[13] Here we state the best, most appropriate meanings as established in the tradition of the wise.

[9] 792/465; "guide for all" (*sarvanetā*), or "ruler of all."

[10] Dvārakā is Kṛṣṇa's home town, and he is the son of Vasudeva.

[11] 793/465; "on our heads" is implicit.

[12] Respectively, Deśika's commentary on Rāmānuja's commentary on the *Gītā*, and Deśika's concise Sanskrit treatise explaining and defending the taking of refuge.

[13] Śaṃkara, the great nondualist theologian, often portrayed as the great adversary of the Viśiṣṭādvaita tradition of Vedānta, to which both Rāmānuja and Deśika belong.

He identifies the first line of the Carama Śloka as key, because it indicates the true path – the renunciation of all *dharma*s, the acceptance of Kṛṣṇa as one's sole refuge:

> The first line[14] enjoins the means; the second[15] is the subordinate part that indicates the end to be obtained by this means; of course, the primary purpose is to prescribe the means.[16]

After this introduction, the rest of Chapter 29 is devoted to a careful, exhaustive exegesis of the words of the Carama Śloka.[17]

First Line: ***Having completely given up all dharmas, to Me alone come for refuge.***

All ***dharmas*****:** ***sarvadharmān***

Deśika indicates simply that in this context *dharma* refers to the complex of activities leading to the desired goal:

> *Dharma* is the means to that human goal which is known from the instructive scriptures. The plural (*dharmān*) indicates the plurality of *dharmas* enjoined in the instructive scriptures for the desired means. *All* indicates that the required subsidiary helps are present.

In particular, For Deśika, *dharma* indicates the pious meditations – those long, loving contemplations of the object of one's love that, as we know from Rāmānuja,[18] characterize devotion (*bhakti*) as a religious practice:

> This is stated here in general terms, but by the force of context we see that the point is to include all the meditations of the various kinds, plus their subsidiary helps, such as are enjoined by the instructive scriptures for the sake of liberation.[19]

Such meditations and related subsidiary practices such as reflection on the mystery of Kṛṣṇa's descents into the world, dwelling in holy places,

[14] Having completely given up all *dharmas*, to Me alone come for refuge.

[15] From all sins I will make you free; do not grieve.

[16] 795-796/467-468

[17] It is interesting to notice how Deśika invests his energy in Chapter 29. By the simple count of pages in the English translation, and omitting introductory and concluding sections, here are the numbers of pages devoted to each topic: *sarvadharmān*, 3 pages; *parityajya*, 31 pages; *mām*, 5 pages; *ekam*, 12 pages; *śaraṇam*, 1 page; *vraja*, 10 pages; *aham*, 1 page; *tvā*, 1 page; *sarvapāpebhyo*, 6 pages; *mokṣayiṣyāmi*, 14 pages; *mā śucaḥ*, 13 pages.

[18] Rāmānuja, *Śrībhāṣya* I.1.1.

[19] 796/468-469

etc., are all worthwhile and efficacious in their own way. When continued over a long period of time and practiced perfectly, they are quite successful. But in light of Arjuna's frustration and perplexity in the *Gītā* narrative, the Carama Śloka (as *Gītā* 18.66) implies virtuous religious practices that are effective but wearisome – and to be given up if a person is to become ready for taking refuge.

Having completely given up: *parityajya*

What does it mean to *give up* or *give up completely*? Deśika is clearly very concerned about assigning just the right meaning to *having completely given up*, as in some way indicating the complete abandonment of *dharmas*. His interpretation of the words is lengthy, longer than any other exegetical unit in the *Essence*,[20] but also strikingly spare in the citation of sources. It can be read then as Deśika's own extended argument, out of his own concerns, in favor of the true meaning of the abandonment of all *dharmas*. While it is not possible here to do justice to his lengthy and complex exposition, I indicate some key features in the following paragraphs.

Deśika values attention to the "spirit" of the Carama Śloka – inner abandonment into the hands of God, an experience of total helplessness wherein no human effort is efficacious.[21] But he is also cognizant of the evident injunctive nature of the two clauses of the verse – *come for refuge* (*śaraṇam vraja*) and *do not grieve* (*mā śucaḥ*) – and sees that *having completely given up* too might be read as injunctive, indicative possibly of a simple and stark abandonment of all *dharmas* that has necessarily already taken place as a prelude – as if to say, "First, renounce all *dharmas*; then, to Me alone come for refuge."

By some readings, this renunciation might well include renunciation of the orthodox norms of caste and stage of life and even, conceivably, of respect for one's guru. This possibility worries Deśika, so he seeks an interpretation of the renunciation of *dharmas* that is both forceful yet respectful of established religious and social norms, obligations that in his view are not to be contravened by a seeming command to give up all *dharmas*.

He therefore reads *having completely given up all dharmas* as signaling the new, extreme state into which Kṛṣṇa's attentive listener enters: "You who have given up all *dharmas*" indicates the kind of person ready to take

[20] 797-832/469-500

[21] See 798/470-471.

refuge, and not primarily whether or not certain actions are to be performed. If *having completely given up* implies an injunction, the Carama Śloka can be taken to indicate that other means are not needed for taking refuge; the person who cannot endure the slower process of devotional meditation is to let go of such practice and turn immediately to the Lord in the act of surrender:

> Taking refuge occurs independently of the subsidiary helps such as the rites, etc., that occur in the context of meditation. The point of seeing here an injunction of renunciation has to do with asking whether any such mode of *dharma* can be a help subsidiary to taking refuge.[22]

That is, if *having completely given up all dharmas* marks off a group of people who have already renounced in this way, then Kṛṣṇa is simply indicating a particular, restricted audience, comprised only of those who have already rejected all other means of salvation. But it may also indicate those who, even if competent for such means, cannot tolerate the long delay implementation would require:

> In this interpretation of *having completely given up* as an injunction to renunciation, the point is to indicate that competence for taking refuge belongs to those without the ability for other means, and to those who are competent but unwilling to bear delay. This is competence for taking refuge.[23]

The renunciation therefore is not a general prohibition of dharmic actions. Rather, the point is that neither performing dharmic acts nor refraining from them is essential to taking refuge; *having completely given up all dharmas* indicates that such means are not instrumental to the Lord's saving action:

> Therefore, neither the performance of these *dharmas* nor their renunciation is essential to taking refuge. What does matter is a lack of further interest in things we cannot accomplish.[24] The continued performance of the regular and occasional obligatory acts of which we are capable is nothing but the performance of acts of service in observance of a divine command.[25]

[22] That is, and not with whether such rites and related practices are to be done at all.

[23] 803/476

[24] And, we could add: need not complete, since they are not instrumental to the desired liberation God will perform.

[25] 811/484. These are the rites that are performed either regularly (for example, a morning fire oblation) or on specific occasions (for example, the New and Full Moon sacrifices, a wedding, a birth, etc.)

Since we cannot perform (theoretically possible) devotional meditations so perfectly as to reach the Lord by them, those among us who are wise lose interest in working out our salvation in that way. Obligatory ritual actions should still be performed, but they are not efficacious toward liberation – for that is the Lord's own work; but they are still required as expressive of obedience and human cooperation with God,[26] performed without any expectation that they bring about liberation. They are simply acts of service (*kaiṃkarya*)[27] that please God when enacted in obedience. It is therefore not the case that orthodox obligations are evil or entirely mistaken; it is just that the person who has taken refuge does not assess her or his life according to such calculations. Other possible interpretations are therefore ruled out as wrong:

> Such acts cannot be included along with actions counted as means;[28] nor are they helps subsidiary to taking refuge, which does not require such helps; nor does the person perform them because the Lord might be offended at their non-performance; nor does he perform them with the desire that of themselves they will bring about results such as the extinction of his sins or the attainment of heaven, cattle, children, and the like; nor does he perform them merely because he enjoys doing them, like worldly men playing dice and the like; nor does he perform them even to please the Lord, even after gaining direct insight (such as liberated selves enjoy) into what He favors.[29]

Even if extrinsic to taking refuge, such actions maintain an ordinary efficacy and obligation with respect to life as properly lived. So such actions must be performed. Moreover, there is a real satisfaction in them for those who love the Lord, even if pleasing the Lord is not simply one among many ordinary motivations for action:

> He continues to perform such acts because it is evident from the instructive scriptures that these acts of service result in the Lord's pleasure, just as they might have other results too. Because he is a person in whose nature *sattva* predominates,[30] he acquires a taste [for pleasing the Lord] and

[26] That is, while intention (*saṃkalpa*) is contributory to the action, commanded actions are carried out as commanded, neither initiated nor terminated by intention (and choice). See 811/484.

[27] Literally, "an attitude of what-must-be-done."

[28] Whatever their efficacy, such obligatory acts of service are not to be counted among actions assessed in terms of their effectiveness toward some goal.

[29] 811-812/485

[30] That is, the person in whom the highest of the three constituents, pure-being (*sattva*) is dominant over the tendency to passion (*rajas*) and the tendency to lethargy (*tamas*). Although ordinarily none of the constituents can exist apart from the others, in special cases, *sattva* may exist by itself.

> proceeds accordingly, with scripture as his lamp, delighting the Lord who is in every kind of relation to him, just as he might show affection for his friends, children, and others.[31]

Acts of service performed selflessly after taking refuge will give no delight if they are not in keeping with the duties of class and stage of life. It is only service performed within the bounds of orthodoxy that truly pleases God.[32]

> *Reflection*: Deśika is, therefore, institutionally a conservative. This is worth mentioning only because it is often presumed, in Christian discussions of Asian religions, that exposure to Hinduism will somehow make us more liberal. That may well happen, but not because traditional Indian thinkers are themselves liberal. Learning even from their orthodox and conservative instincts is, however, one of the important values of this kind of interreligious commentarial learning.

Deśika marks the end of his lengthy exegesis of *having completely given up* with two verses. In Sanskrit, he tabulates the points he has made:

> The wise agree on the meaning of the words *having completely given up all dharmas*:
> competence belongs to those without power;
> having no resources is the main thing;
> dharmic actions are not aids subsidiary (to taking refuge);
> we should not begin acts impossible (to finish) and
> we should dampen our expectations regarding such things –
> these words remind us of the maxim of the brahma-missile.[33]

That is, the famed weapon known as the brahma-missile (*astra*) has its terrible potency only if one has total faith in it and holds no backup plan in reserve. Taking refuge works if one risks everything on it, having no recourse, should refuge fail.

The concluding Tamil verse furthers the case for confidence in surrender and not in one's deeds – on the simple grounds that this is what Kṛṣṇa teaches:

> "Even if you are engaged in what is difficult,
> you need not keep trying;
> your strength lies first of all in giving up desires;

31 812/485

32 824-827/487-497. Deśika notes also (823/493-494) that a continued performance of recitation of the Tiru and Dvaya Mantras, along with regular and occasional obligatory ritual actions, is expected as part of one's service to the Lord.

33 830/499

other than the way of refuge, no means is required, and
if you desire such means, then like the Brahma-missile, refuge grows weak;
the lengthy path of those with full knowledge is not for you:
if in your lonely state you take My feet as refuge,
I will bear[34] all your faults."
We praise with all praise the Worthy One[35] who spoke these words.[36]

This act of trust is exceedingly simple but hard to accomplish precisely because of that simplicity, given the human tendency to arrange for backup support.

Reflection: The simple truth of this message, heard by the person meditating just as Arjuna heard the word of Kṛṣṇa in the *Gītā*, is that God speaks to certain people who are willing and able to let go of their *dharmas* – their righteousness – and instead trust entirely in God. Most Christians will recognize that Deśika makes good sense in moderating the act of abandonment with recognition of ongoing religious and social responsibility.

That *Gītā* 18.66 is ostensibly more radical than Deśika's reading of it as the Carama Śloka is another factor we need to take into account. We may hope for a more radical implementation of *having completely given up all dharmas*, and find ourselves disappointed at his caution. Yet this is the challenge commentators face, for we are not at liberty, here, simply to read the verse as we prefer. Rather, Deśika guides us into a traditional reading, and such is what we must reflect upon here.[37] Most Christians, too, should not be entirely surprised by Deśika's reading: our traditions are conservative enough, tempering and moderating what often seem to be obvious Gospel calls to radical change.

Me Alone: *mām ekam*

Deśika does not dwell at length on the meaning of *Me* in *take refuge with Me* (nor the *I* beginning the second line, *I will make you free…*), but in a series of Sanskrit verses he does identify prominent characteristics of this Lord who is active and engaged in the world, and who is both the goal (salvation) and the objective means to that goal. His brief characterization echoes and enriches the expansive reflection on *Nārāyaṇa* which we reviewed in the previous chapter. First, Kṛṣṇa – the *Me* – is truly born

34 Or, "forebear," even "forgive."

35 *puṇṇiyaṉ* [Sanskrit *puṇya*] here indicates the "meritorious one," perhaps even "the holy one."

36 831-832/499-500

37 I mentioned in Chapter 1 that there are other commentaries on the Mantras, many of which would be less evidently concerned about the details of orthodoxy than Deśika, and of course commentators might prefer such texts for their reading.

into the world by an act of his sovereign freedom, so that those who come to know him might escape rebirth:[38]

> The divine births are real, but He never loses His own proper being,
> (His body) is made of pure being[39] and
> (His birth) is caused only by His own will;
> this occurs whenever dharma declines,
> His intention being protection of the good:
> all this is the mystery of His birth,
> and whoever knows it
> will not be born again.[40]

Of great practical importance is that the Lord is accessible, free, and sovereign, and thus possessed of the mix of attributes in accord with which taking refuge is a best choice:

> There is no taking refuge with a lord who is sovereign but hard to reach;
> no result is gained from one who is not sovereign,
> even if such a one is easily taken refuge with;
> if he is not sovereign, the service will not be true,
> since it would be optional;[41]
> if he is hard to attain, service might still be accomplished,
> but would not be heartfelt:
> all this we know from ordinary experience.[42]

By contrast, the Lord is accessible, and reaching him is worth the effort:

> He is not merely easy to reach like grass and the like, for He is worthy of praise; He is not hard to reach like Mt. Meru; rather, this object of our refuge is the highest, yet easy to reach; He should be taken refuge with, and He can be reached.[43]

Deśika then describes the Lord's qualities in a theological exposition that is also a confession of faith in the mystery of divine identity. Qualities

[38] The words "Me" and "I" are understood to look primarily to the Lord's accessibility and freedom, as is explained in the "the teaching on the mystery of *avatāra*" [*Gītā* 4], and in the chapter expounding the highest person [*Gītā* 15].

[39] Pure *sattva*. On Rāmānuja's and Deśika's understanding of the nature of the bodies assumed by Nārāyaṇa in his divine descents, see Clooney 2007a.

[40] 833/500

[41] That is, if optional, lacking the requisite obligation that underlies pure, selfless service.

[42] 834/501

[43] 834/501

implicit in *Me alone* (*mām ekam*) echo the list of 108 qualities we saw in Chapter 1, with respect to the name *Nārāyaṇa*:

> This Lord who is propitiated is the clear and direct means to liberation. Meditation [on the Lord Himself, by way of *mām ekam*] is distinguished by the fact that the divine form to be known is a means requiring nothing else. This meditation's pertinent forms are all expressed in the words *Me* and *alone*. *Me* indicates that He is the refuge whose mode of being is indicated where it says, "This is Nārāyaṇa with Śrī" (*Harivaṃśa* 2.55.59) and in similar texts. This *Me* is illumined also by the Tiru Mantra and the Dvaya Mantra: the Lord who is the protector of all, to whom all belongs, who is the Lord of Śrī,[44] who has the qualities of *Nārāyaṇa*. The qualities underlying His accessibility and transcendence are omniscience, omnipotence, tenderness, good disposition, being most merciful, and so forth. These form the auspicious foundation, and are referred to by the word in the dual [*feet, caraṇau*] in the Dvaya Mantra. All these are made manifest in order to show the distinctiveness of the divine, auspicious form of the Charioteer.[45]

After a series of scriptural warrants highlighting additional qualities – tenderness, lordship, generosity of disposition, accessibility – Deśika concludes with further emphasis on the Lord's compassion:

> Thus (our forebears) meditated on the quality of mercy (*kṛpā*) as their support...;[46] they subordinated their relationship to the Lord and other qualities to that compassion (*kāruṇya*), on which they were entirely focused. So too, although the Lord has other qualities, the Lady graciously said,
>
> > It was because of His mercy (*kṛpā*), that Rāma[47] gave refuge to Kāka who deserved death.[48]

The story of Kāka, told in the ancient *Rāmāyaṇa* and well known in popular awareness as well, is an example that highlights the efficacy of refuge even in the most improbable circumstances.[49] Kāka is a crow that decides to peck at the breast of Sītā even while her husband Rāma sleeps, resting his head in her lap. Not wishing to disturb Rāma's sleep, she remains motionless even while under attack. Rāma awakes when a drop of Sītā's blood falls upon him. Enraged, he vows to kill Kāka, and furi-

[44] Even in discussing *mām ekam*, Deśika is careful to identify this Lord as forever "with Śrī."

[45] 835/502

[46] Illustrated in Tamil and Sanskrit texts cited by Deśika.

[47] Literally, "Kākutstha," a name of Rāma.

[48] *Rāmāyaṇa, Sundara Kāṇḍa*, 38.33; the crow is not named in the verse. 838-839/000, I translated *kāruṇya* as "compassion" and *kṛpā* as "mercy," in order to highlight Deśika's use of both words.

[49] *Rāmāyaṇa, Sundara Kāṇḍa* 38

ously pursues him across the universe. Kāka knows that he is doomed; with nowhere to go and no options left, he takes refuge at the feet of Rāma, who spares him, punishing him only by the loss of an eye.[50] Kāka, bereft of options, preparation, perhaps even good intentions, is saved soley because surrender works unconditionally – especially for those who have nothing else left. Deśika continues:

> In his *Śaraṇāgati Gadya*,[51] Rāmānuja too elaborated this primacy of mercy when he said,
>
> > Since you have uttered the Dvaya Mantra,
> > whatever the manner of that utterance,
> > Solely by My compassion
> > you will have entirely eradicated all obstacles
> > to exclusive and single-minded superior devotion, superior knowledge, and supreme devotion for My lotus feet...[52]

This text shows the ease of access to this Lord, who is himself determined to clear away all obstacles for the person who recites the Dvaya Mantra.[53] Rāmānuja too thus witnesses to the fact that the Lord's compassion alone suffices in freeing the devout person – marked by recitation of the Dvaya Mantra even imperfectly. By extension, the *Me* of the Carama Śloka emphasizes the value of sheer dependence on Kṛṣṇa alone, who is always accessible, no matter how one approaches him.

In explaining *alone* (*ekam*),[54] Deśika admits that the word may appear redundant, since *Me* is already a noun in the singular. *Alone* serves to emphasize that Kṛṣṇa and no other person or place, nor any human activity, is the refuge. While this point might be argued simply for theological reasons – in a defense of monotheism, for instance – here Deśika is concerned with an intense focus on the act of surrender: God alone, to whom one surrenders, is the sole, sufficient means to liberation. Deśika offers six reasons for the emphatic *alone*:

1. The Lord alone is the means to liberation, and union with Him alone is the fruit of refuge;
2. the individual self is not primary, but only the Lord;

[50] Hence the belief that crows have only one eye.

[51] *Śaraṇāgati Gadya*.

[52] 838-839/504-505. *Śaraṇāgati Gadya*, n. 17; in Rāmānuja 2002, p. 41 (Skt.) My translation, but see also the translation at p. 19. Here, "mercy" and "compassion" are respectively *kṛpā* and *dayā*.

[53] See Chapter 3.

[54] 839-863/505-516

3. the act of taking refuge itself cannot be means in the same way the Lord is means;
4. all means other than taking refuge are ruled out;
5. subsidiary helps other than the five intrinsic to taking refuge itself are ruled out;[55]
6. the Lord by Himself is the means to every result of every action.[56]

Deśika thus reorders the entirety of the religious world to "the Lord alone;" nothing is entirely obliterated or omitted, but everything is recentered on the Lord *alone* – Kṛṣṇa, the *Me* – as the only goal and means.[57]

While Deśika insists that his view is reasonable and well attested in the most authoritative scriptures, he is of course also working with the vivid images and memories of his own Śrīvaiṣṇava tradition. Each of his points is illustrated with inspiring examples. For example, in the course of the fifth interpretation of *alone*, he lists fifteen examples of surrender, wherein those who took refuge were saved precisely because they had no other option:

1. Draupadī desperately called on Kṛṣṇa when, after she was wagered and lost in a game of dice, she was to be stripped of her sari;
2. Damayantī took refuge with the gods in order to discover which among them was really Nala, whom she loved;
3. the demonesses tormented Sītā in her captivity, but came to depend solely on her for their own survival at the end of the war;
4. Vibhīṣaṇa, exiled from Śrī Laṅkā because he could no longer support his brother's kidnapping of Sītā, surrendered before Rāma and depended on him alone for his survival;
5. Kṣatrabandhu intended to rob Nārada, but after Nārada instructed him, he ended up surrendering to him;
6. Mucukunda, the powerful sage, surrendered before Kṛṣṇa, in order to be able to kill Kālayavana;[58]

[55] The five subsidiary aids are: 1. a choosing what is suitable to pleasing the Lord, 2. rejecting what is not suitable to pleasing him, 3. a realization of one's pitifulness and need of help, 4. great faith (confidence in the power of taking refuge), and 5. choosing a protector who can make refuge possible.

[56] Respectively, 839/505, 840-841/505-506, 841-842/506-507, 844-845/510, 845-847/510-511, and 857-858/513-514.

[57] Later, Deśika again summarizes the meanings of *ekam* by introducing six meanings of *ekam* taught by the teachers: 1. The goal alone – the Lord – enables reaching the goal; 2. self-importance is denied; 3. taking refuge is nothing but a pretext for sovereign divine action; 4. there is no connection with any other means; 5. there is no connection with their subsidiaries either; 6. yet no goals are given up (since all results are achieved, in the Lord). (860/516)

[58] *Bhāgavata Purāṇa* 10.51

7. Gajendra the elephant cried out to Viṣṇu for help when an alligator was dragging him under the water;
8. the five Pāṇḍava brothers, taught by the sage Mārkaṇḍeya during their stay in the forest, took refuge with Kṛṣṇa
9. the gods took refuge with Viṣṇu, hoping to secure the defeat and death of Rāvaṇa;
10. Sumukha, a serpent, took refuge with Upendra (Viṣṇu), to avoid being killed by Viṣṇu's eagle, Garuḍa;
11. Triśaṅku, suspended between heaven and earth, was protected by the sage Viśvamitra, with whom he took refuge as he sought to reach heaven;
12. Śunaḥśepha was to be sacrificed by his father, but prayed to Viśvamitra for protection;
13. A hunter, desperate and starving, took refuge with a pair of pigeons, who saved him from hunger;
14. Kāka, the crow – as above;
15. Kapota, a dove threatened by a hawk, took refuge with king Śibi who instead offered the hawk his own flesh;
16. and many others as well.[59]

The list offers an edifying and inspiring host of witnesses who by their actions testify to the efficacy of pure surrender. In concluding his list, Deśika emphasizes the main point, that none of these exemplary figures who took refuge had any other support, but had only one choice – their *ekam*, as it were:

> We do not see any manner of proceeding in such cases, aside from choosing what is suitable (and the other helps subsidiary to the taking refuge). Yet we also see that what was desired was accomplished immediately by those who took refuge, solely by the taking of refuge, an act accomplished in a moment's time.[60]

The overall effect of this exegesis of *alone* – surrender to this One only – is, perhaps unexpectedly, a universalization of the Lord's role and not a narrowing. Everything is oriented to the person speaking – the "I," the "Me" – who is the primary agent of liberation, and the one in whom *everything* occurs. This Person is Kṛṣṇa, about whom surely much can be said, but neither the Carama Śloka nor the tradition belabors this point

[59] Deśika does not elaborate on these examples; I have drawn on the commentaries and other sources to summarize each briefly. Ramadesikacaryar (847-856) recounts their stories in a series of ample footnotes.

[60] 847, 857/512

nor feels it necessary to highlight epic and mythic characteristics of Kṛṣṇa. While Deśika most certainly does intend to subordinate other known deities, such as Śiva, in his exegesis of *Me alone* he says nothing about them. Theological debates are not his concern in his exegesis of the Carama Śloka, but only the single-mindedness of the act of refuge invited in the Śloka: *Take refuge with Me alone.*

> *Reflection*: This preference for the universal and inclusive is analogous to the universalization of *Nārāyaṇa* by 108 characteristics, such as we saw in Chapter 1: in this unique and particular Deity who addresses the listener, innumerable universally recognizable good qualities are found. It is obvious that Christians and Śrīvaiṣṇavas name God differently; but it is also obvious that much of the same intellectual and affective force applies in both cases.

In a move that previews a major issue regarding the Dvaya Mantra, Deśika adds four verses asserting that *alone* does not exclude the goddess Śrī as sharing fully the liberative role of Nārāyaṇa. Her presence is a distinguishing feature of the Lord – what makes him different from other supreme deities. Śrī collaborates with him in all his saving deeds:

> Some say that the point of the word *alone* here is to indicate the singleness of the object of refuge,
> but even so, Śrī specifies this Lord, as do His qualities and His body.
> She is remembered in tradition as the ruler of all beings, the beloved of the Lord;
> She cooperates in the works of dharma dedicated to protecting all who take refuge.

Even claims about the world-maker's divine unity do not preclude her presence:

> Even when it is known authoritatively that the cause of the world is one,
> still there is some connection with requisite specifications;[61]
> even when meditation on the One is enjoined
> still there is connection with His qualities, etc.
> So too here: when it is enjoined that our refuge is one alone,
> [Her presence] is still to be inferred.[62]

A single-minded meditation on the Lord, authorized by the *alone*, is usually a meditation on his qualities too; so there is no reason to exclude Śrī

[61] The cause of the world may be simple and one, but it can also be characterized, without detraction from its unity, as intelligent, capable of making a world, intending to make a world, etc.; so too, the single Lord of the universe can be also characterized as the "consort of Śrī."

[62] 861/516. In Chapter 23, Deśika develops at length his position that Nārāyaṇa's inseparability from Śrī in no way diminishes his perfection and sovereign independence. See forthcoming d.

from even the most single-minded meditation on the Lord. The Lord is one, but the Lord is with-Śrī.

> *Reflection*: It could well be that *Me alone* will be for many Christians an obstacle, a stopping point, beyond which it is very hard to go. Because we know all about exclusive claims for Christ – "The way, the truth, and the life," in whose name alone there is salvation – and recognize the power of this exclusive language, we may be put off by the possibility that the Carama Śloka is voicing a claim of just that sort. But this recognition, that Śrīvaiṣṇavas have long understood the logic and power of Me alone, should do us good, by liberating us of the idea that we alone have had such sentiments. Here too, by staying close to the text, we may find some room for moving forward: neither the Carama Śloka nor Deśika's exegesis of it makes the exclusive claim so local and specific, in religious and cultural narrative and sentiment, that *Me* is "only" the name of Kṛṣṇa. Indeed, Kṛṣṇa might well have said, "to Kṛṣṇa alone come for refuge," but he did not. Admitting our problem, but also understanding the subtler possibilities our reading puts before us, we do well to keep listening, lest we take for granted that we already know everything we need to know about "God alone."
>
> Deśika insists on finding Śrī present in the *Me alone,* even when she is not explicitly mentioned. This too makes a Christian reception of the Carama Śloka more difficult, even if analogies in the Christian tradition can be found: the Wisdom of God, the Holy Spirit, or even Mary, mother of all graces. Reflection on Deśika's insistence that *God alone* is always accompanied by Śrī is at least instructive in reminding us how we carry truths and pieties of our faith, known from one part of scripture or tradition or local devotion, into other texts and contexts, where an impartial observer – who does not share our history and our expectations – will be puzzled by the meanings we find.[63]

Take refuge: *śaraṇam vraja*

In Chapter 3 we shall see more of what Deśika has to say about the meaning of *refuge* (*śaraṇam*), which is prominent in the Dvaya Mantra.[64] In Chapter 29, which deals with that Mantra, the major point will be that the Lord alone is the refuge; for refuge is an established, objective reality, not primarily the result of human choice or action.[65] But here, in exegeting the Carama Śloka's first line, Deśika stresses the universality of the refuge that is offered:

> Choosing this refuge is taught specifically to Arjuna, but even so it is really directed to everyone. As it says,

63 See Clooney 2005a.

64 We must remember too that in the *Essence*, Deśika treats the entire Dvaya Mantra before he takes up any part of the Carama Śloka.

65 Deśika himself refers his reader to his explication of *śaraṇam* in his chapter on the Dvaya Mantra.

> You are the refuge of the world without exception,
> without consideration of any further restrictions.[66]
>
> This is well known also from the *Śvetāśvatara Upaniṣad*.[67] That this refuge is meant for everyone without any restriction is indicated in verses such as these:
>
> The divine seers say that You are the refuge and the way of refuge.[68]
> (You are) yoga, leader among those who know yoga,
> [the Lord of material reality and of the person,
> in the form of Narasiṃha, with-Śrī, Keśava, the highest of persons]...[69]
> Whoever sees Him as the undying one, the means and the goal,
> the one to be known, the highest self, Viṣṇu,
> and then meditates (on Him as such) –
> that person does not grow despondent.[70]

Accordingly, the criteria for this sure state of taking refuge are simple:

> To be suited to Him who is to be chosen as the refuge, one must simply be a person who has no refuge but Him.[71]

Such are the desperate people to whom Kṛṣṇa is really speaking.

Despite Deśika's insistence on the importance of divine initiative and divine accomplishment of liberation, he also defends the value of human action, in relation to taking refuge. *Take refuge* (*śaraṇam vraja*) is, after all, an injunction, and injunctions indicate that an intelligent free choice is involved, a freedom compatible with divine initiative and power. As imperative, *vraja* expects a response that is obedient but free;[72] the "completely dependent self" still has the ability and obligation to act, assenting to the divine command. Just as Deśika discerned a possibility and choice latent in *having completely given up*, and not merely sheer obligation, here he argues at length that a dependent being can still be a doer. He rejects four opinions that in his view caricature agency as a misunderstanding of self, and incompatible with true self:

> *The self is not a doer*:[73] Just as non-conscious things carry sound and other [sense data] that the Lord has created, in this case accepting and exercising freedom are in accord with a person's complete dependence on the Lord. To say that [this entirely dependent person] is not really a

66 *Śaraṇāgati Gadya* 5; Rāmānuja 2002, Sanskrit 39; tr. 15. My translation.

67 "The benevolent hearted, refuge of all...", *Śvetāśvatara Upaniṣad* 3.17.

68 *Rāmāyaṇa, Yuddha Kāṇḍa* 120.18

69 *Viṣṇu Sahasranāma* (a litany of Nārāyaṇa's thousand names), nn. 18-19.

70 *Viṣṇudharma* 72.4

71 863/517-518

72 864-865/519

73 Here and below the introductory phrases are mine.

doer is the same as saying that agency belongs only to nature, ignorance, etc.[74]

The self effects the desired refuge: Were one instead to say that agency depends on the self [alone], there would be no meaning to the statement that there is a controller of all selves – and this would be tantamount to saying that there is no Lord.

The self's contribution is nothing but knowledge: To say that to be an agent dependent on the Lord is to be nothing but a knower would unfortunately result in excluding even the desire to accomplish the human goal by undertaking the means to it.

The self's contribution is nothing but knowledge plus the desire to act: Were one then to say that there is knowledge and also a desire specific to that state [of helplessness before God], but no other activity, there would be no way to enact any means with seen or unseen results, nor to act in accord with one's own purposes.[75]

Deśika concludes that in surrendering entirely to God a person is necessarily still possessed of three essential attributes, "knowledge, a desire to act, and effort."[76]

Deśika explains at length[77] the nature of the agency of the embodied self addressed in the Carama Śloka. There are indeed less perfect forms of agency – driven by desire, by fear, by opinions about independence from God, etc. But this fact need not preclude the notion that even the purest self is still a doer. When properly understood, divine sovereignty and human agency are compatible. To bolster his case, Deśika draws attention to a seemingly contrary verse by Āḷavantar that apparently discounts human action:[78]

> On account of Nāthamuni, my teacher's teacher[79]
> whose self was full of innate and overflowing love for Your lotus feet,
> be gracious toward me –
> but think nothing of my behavior.[80]

In Deśika's view, "think nothing of my behavior" is not a denial of the value of action. Rather, Āḷavantar was simply emphasizing that love and

74 That is, freedom is not innate, but given to the self in a dependent fashion.
75 And so the rest of life, dependent on human action, would come to a halt.
76 865/519-520
77 864-868/520-523
78 865-869/524-525
79 Literally, "grandfather;" see Parameshwaran, 161-162.
80 *Stotraratna* 65; 869/524

family matter far more than his own deeds, which certainly do occur, but only in a very flawed fashion. Humility and priorities are the issue, not a categorical denial of human agency. Hence, even if taking refuge implies a denial of the possibility of saving oneself, the new freedom from ego that comes with taking refuge still allows for human responsibility and does not allow one to ignore moral strictures, as if to transgress moral bounds and perform forbidden acts: "These are views that others [wrongly] hold: the self is not an agent; [surrender] is a matter only of utter dependence or pure knowledge; even intentional sins will not in any way stick; repeating the act of taking refuge is never needed."[81]

Similarly, although taking refuge includes a key moment of insight and simple recognition, Deśika insists that *come for refuge* is more than an injunction to a special realization, as some claim:

> Some make it out that injunctions like *come for refuge* have a different intent – to indicate that there is no means to be performed by the person desirous of liberation, and that nothing matters but knowledge of the relationship [with the Lord] such as is known from scripture. Such people even appeal to scriptural texts – yet without reflecting on their meaning...[82] For their view contradicts the inner meaning of the injunctions to devotion and taking refuge. Indeed, [by their logic] it would not be necessary even to enjoin knowledge that comes from knowledge of scripture, since [the kind of realization they promote] could be accomplished by the hearing and thinking that occur simply in accord with one's own wishes.

Knowledge is crucial, and has crucial consequences, but the imperative to knowledge occurs within the realm of continuing respect for scriptural injunctions that cannot be reduced to insight or knowledge:

> Through scripture a person can gain knowledge of the relationship between the highest self and the individual self, [knowledge] such as is shared by all persons who are desirous of liberation and who are firmly dedicated to all the proper meditations. [Such knowledge] helps them gradually. In such people there is born a desire for the means, a desire to know the way to reach our Lord, the consort of Śrī who is the object of unsurpassable enjoyment.

The conclusion is important:

> Devotion and taking refuge are thus enjoined upon specific competent persons, like other acts of knowledge.[83]

[81] 873/526
[82] Deśika lists three texts here; 526-527/873
[83] 873-874/526-527

That knowledge can be meaningfully enjoined is a claim we find also in much older ritual texts as well; knowledge as it were floats in a vacuum – in theory potent, but only for some theoretical, ideal audience – until it is geared to a specific body of potential knowers. It is by the force of injunction that this connection is made. Accordingly, even "to Me alone come for refuge" is not for every person who hears or reads the words, but for those who are desperate, who have given up all their *dharmas*, and who realize that taking refuge is their last chance: these are the people whose hearts are touched by the command, *Take refuge with Me alone.*

Deśika concludes his exegesis of the first line of the Carama Śloka with a Tamil verse that captures the divine initiative and its comprehensiveness:

> "I am the means and the good fruit;
> the practitioner of this means should become Mine and take hold of Me;
> taking refuge is not a means for you, nor are other means the means to it;
> for refuge, all the various painful subsidiary helps are unnecessary,
> for I stand in the place of every other means:
> I am the messenger, I am the Lord, so take hold of Me, end your sorrow:"
> that's what He said, as He surrounded me.[84]

This completes our basic reading of the first line of the Carama Śloka as interpreted by Deśika.[85]

Near the end of Chapter 29, however,[86] Deśika offers two summaries. First, he reviews each component of the Carama Śloka, identifying explicit and implied meanings of the individual words; here is his summation of the first line, in my own paraphrase:

1. *Having completely given up all dharma*s (*sarvadharmān parityajya*) specifies who is competent for surrender. It makes clear that this person has nothing and has no need for any other and difficult aids [*dharma*s], that initiatives which cannot be completed are inappropriate, that desiring what is too difficult is pointless, and that a

[84] 874/528

[85] In Chapter 24, Deśika clarifies the meaning of taking refuge as a "means that is to be accomplished" (*sādhya upāya*). He answers objections and refuting opposing views. At issue, as regarding the first line of the Carama Śloka, is a balance between a firm confession that the Lord alone is the means as well as the destination of taking refuge, and a continuing insistence that human effort is expected, as the "occasion" (*vyāja*) for divine intervention. God will do everything, if the human person signals her or his expectation and readiness.

[86] After the exegesis of the second part of the Śloka, which we see only in Chapter 4; as explained, we read that second line as a response to the utterance of the Dvaya Mantra by the person who has heard the invitation of the Carama Śloka's first line.

[religious] person chafes uncomfortably even at the very idea of other, specific means;[87]

2. *Me* (*mām*) identifies the Lord as the true refuge for the person seeking liberation, as a refuge full of good qualities, accessible, well-disposed, etc.;[88]
3. *alone* (*ekam*) indicates that the One to be reached is also the One who makes reaching Him possible, that He accomplishes all things without obstacle and independently, that He is always on the lookout for an excuse to be of help, that He does not need any intermediate means, that He can be propitiated even without subsidiary helps, and that He is the refuge for the one who desires all results but who cannot endure even the idea of turning to some other refuge;
4. *refuge* (*śaraṇam*) indicates that [the Lord himself] takes the place of all other means and assumes the burden of those who surrender to Him;
5. *come* (*vraja*) specifies the means to be accomplished, that is, the laying down of the burden, plus the aids subsidiary to that; it indicates that all are eligible, that laying down the burden need be done only once and is easy to do, that it gives results without delay and ends even karma[89] already under way;
6. the injunctive force of *come* indicates that the eligible person is the one who is able to act, even while also dependent on the one approached for refuge; such a person is subject to those directives of Scripture which indicate the need to surrender all independence.[90]

Second, Deśika offers an even more succinct summation:

1. having completely given up all *dharmas*	Having little knowledge, little power, moving in a restricted time period, not enduring delay – and not going along with other, slow results;
2. to Me alone	for I am easily accessible to all, the refuge of all the worlds, distinguished by all the forms useful to being your refuge;
3. come for refuge.	having determined that I am this refuge, surrender the burden of the protection of your self, accompanied by all five subsidiary helps.

[87] That is, there is no radical dismissal of *dharmas*, and no radical denial that the human person can act; rather, a radical change in attitude and self-conception is required.

[88] Not only is the goal one, but also there is a single means, God, to the goal, God.

[89] Both action and result.

[90] Paraphrased from 913-914/562-563

We will see the completion of these summaries in our consideration of the second line of the Carama Śloka in Chapter 4.[91]

The Carama Śloka as we have thus far understood it constitutes an urgent invitation to exclusive refuge with the Lord who perfectly fulfills the needs of those desperate enough to hear this invitation and take it to heart. The divine promise is inseparable from the divine initiative to make refuge possible, and its accomplishment likewise is the divine person's action and presence.

> *Reflection*: As this first line of the Carama Śloka indicates in its closing injunction (*come*), the renunciation announced in its first words was neither an end in itself nor selfish: the great act of abandonment opens us to hear the further challenge to take refuge. We who are Christian can and should reflect on the summons of Christ who asks us to leave everything and come follow him, and for us that should suffice; but the Carama Śloka's first line, so radical and so clear, can well be a guide to how we must prepare ourselves and then actually hear a summons from the Lord that is meant only for people on the edge.

III. The First Line in the Rest of the *Essence*

The Sanskrit verse at the end of Chapter 2 praises the Tiru Mantra and Dvaya Mantra, but climaxes in praising Kṛṣṇa as the charioteer who offered the efficacious, salvific teaching that is the Carama Śloka:

> First he gains his self by the Tiru Mantra that stands above all the disciplines of learning and practice;
> then he passes his every moment with the Dvaya Mantra which, recited just once, makes for true existence;
> when his confidence is deepened by the compassionate summation [that is the Carama Śloka],
> offered by the One who is the supreme adornment of the Veda,
> the Charioteer at play,
> then a person knows all that's essential;
> whoever is such a person is the leader of our community in this world![92]

The self is known through the Tiru Mantra, and its full existence is realized in the Dvaya Mantra: but this knowledge and this realization are deepened and confirmed by Kṛṣṇa's word in the Carama Śloka – in the whole of it, of course, but even by this first line which we have examined thus far.

[91] P. 163
[92] 46-47/21. See also Chapter 1.

Another passage of note occurs in Chapter 25 in the midst of a lengthy discussion of the balance between the freedom that comes with taking refuge and the continuing obligations with respect to *dharma*; this, as we have already seen, is a major theme for interpreters of the Carama Śloka. Here too Deśika focuses on ethical import, drawing on Rāmānuja's two interpretations of *Gītā* 18.66. First, the verse highlights the right action that the person seeking the Lord must perform, with the right attitude:

> In interpreting *having completely given up all dharmas*, the commentator[93] Rāmānuja first suggests that these words indicate pure and sincere renunciation,[94] in the form of a specific realization [about action and true renunciation]. For the person dedicated to taking refuge as his sole option, this specific realization is sustenance during the time of taking refuge, and it is also a support in what is to be done after refuge, as he acts without connection to any means undertaken for his own purposes.

The Mantra is also consoling, as it dispels the grief of those who have great desire yet little power to achieve what they desire, and for whom instruction on the right thing to do is still not helpful:

> In his second interpretation, Rāmānuja deals with the person of little strength who is unable to tolerate delay. When [such a person] sees that other means are accomplished only over a long period of time and with difficulty, he begins to grieve. To remove this grief, here the Lord enjoins another means that is easy to undertake and needs be done only once. The Lord graciously indicates, "You need not dabble in other means."

In concluding this reading of the Carama Śloka in Chapter 25, Deśika highlights the destitution – lack of means – that prior to refuge seemed fortuitous, but after refuge occurs in obedience to scriptural instruction:

> If we consider the taking of refuge in relation to the state before refuge, competence necessarily entails a lack of any connection to any means (other than God alone). Such a lack of connection might have come about in one way or another.[95] But after taking refuge, it is still necessary to remain firmly established in the condition of not needing anything else; at this point, lack of any connection to other means occurs in obedience to scriptural instruction.[96]

[93] The *Bhāṣyakāra*, Rāmānuja; he is not mentioned by name in the passage, though I have added the name for the sake of clarity.

[94] *sāttvika tyāga*

[95] Literally, "due to the divine," or "fortuitously."

[96] 559-560/315. There are all kinds of reasons why people are spiritually impoverished, unable to complete religious duties successfully; but after surrender to the Lord, one studiously plans to remain bereft of all such competence.

He concedes that *having completely given up all dharmas* may be taken as a statement of fact or as an injunction:

> For those who say that *having completely given up* refers to an existing condition, the point is to indicate (the helpless person) who is competent (for refuge).[97] For those who say it is an injunction, the point is to stipulate that this means, taking refuge, requires nothing else. If (by the former option) *having completely given up* indicates who is competent, then *Me alone* can be meditated on as a further indication that nothing else is required.

Alone, as we saw above, refocuses priority on the Lord as the exclusive and sufficient means and the goal of surrender:

> *Alone* expresses pure renunciation, the claim that agency, etc., function only in dependence on this Other; it expresses the identity of the means and the result [in and as the Lord]; it shows that He takes the place of every means.[98]

This reading of the Carama Śloka, much in keeping with our exegesis of Chapter 29, highlights both its ethical intent in specifying the radical intention that shapes the life of the person who has surrendered to God, and also the intensity of focus cultivated by meditation on the Carama Śloka. At issue are persons who have no recourse except the Lord alone; in Deśika's eyes, the student or reader who understands this is the one ready to heed Kṛṣṇa's command to take refuge.

> *Reflection:*This specificity of audience of course raises for us the question of whether and when the Carama Śloka shifts from being a text we read about, to a text that speaks to us in a powerful, transformative way. There is nothing specifically Śrīvaiṣṇava about Deśika's basic point, that there are in the world some people at least who have no refuge except God alone; in principle, there is no reason for us to exclude Christians from this set of those who hear the Carama Śloka most acutely.

IV. Reading the First Line from a Christian Perspective

In Chapter 1 we already addressed, with respect to the Tiru Mantra, matters basic to each chapter and each Mantra: the potency of the Mantras as sacred utterances rich in theological meaning; the universality and particularity of the truths about God and humans articulated in the Mantras;

[97] That is, competence for this act of taking refuge as a person who in fact has already abandoned all other means.

[98] 560-561/316

the way the Mantras invite us to draw parallels from the New Testament (and potentially later texts of the Christian tradition) even while noticing enduring differences among such texts; and the consequent *possibilities* that are opened for Christian prayer with or at least in light of the Mantras. Here we apply the same procedure to the Carama Śloka, Part 1, considering in turn theological issues, parallel texts, and the possibility of prayer.

1. Theological Insights and Concerns, for a Christian Reader

The Carama Śloka too offers many openings for Christian theological reflections, and only a few of these can be considered here. For instance, we can rather easily identify thematic analogues with Biblical and Christian reflection on faith and works, and we can illustrate this with reference to the insights of Bede Griffiths, Henri Le Saux's[99] successor at Shantivanam. In commenting on *Gītā* 18.66 in his *River of Compassion*, a full-length commentary on the *Gītā*, Griffiths suggests a Pauline parallel that interprets *dharma* in light of Christian views of "the law:"

> "Leave all things behind, and come to me for thy salvation"[100] is literally "give up all *dharmas*." This is exactly what St. Paul meant by the "law." *Dharma* is the law. This is a call to go beyond the law, to enter into a state of grace. Give up the *dharma*, give up the law and any human contrivance or effort, and accept this gift from me. So give up all *dharmas*, turn to me as your only refuge. I will deliver you from all evils. Have no fear, do not be afraid, "I will make thee free from the bondage of sin," he says. The word is *pāpa*, which is the ordinary word for sin.[101]

Griffiths concludes, "It is remarkable how close to Christian revelation this comes."[102] It is certain Christian readers can hardly avoid thinking of St. Paul when reading *Gītā* 18.66, and we may instinctively want to correlate *dharma* and law. In both the Christian and Śrīvaiṣṇava traditions, authors aim to transform human consciousness in light of an articulate and demanding religious law that, in addition to guiding performance, can be strict and unyielding, and revelatory of our ineptitude and ill will. Like Deśika and before him the *Gītā*, St. Paul does not wish to blame the law itself, but rather to note that the law sets a standard we do not and cannot meet. This is a great grief for those who try to live

[99] On Le Saux, see Chapter 2, pp. 69-71.
[100] Thus the translation Griffiths is using.
[101] Griffiths, 322
[102] Griffiths, 322

faithfully in accord with their tradition. As we know from many other passages in Paul's writings he, like Deśika, balances a radical sense of freedom with a continuing commitment to a responsible moral life; breaking with the law and depending entirely on Christ leaves room for a continuation of the ordered moral life, albeit with fresh understanding.[103]

These words of *Galatians* come to mind forcefully in highlighting the transformation that is at stake, and the imperative to live differently:

> For freedom Christ has set us free. Stand firm, therefore, and do not submit again to a yoke of slavery. Listen! I, Paul, am telling you that if you let yourselves be circumcised, Christ will be of no benefit to you. Once again I testify to every man who lets himself be circumcised that he is obliged to obey the entire law. You who want to be justified by the law have cut yourselves off from Christ; you have fallen away from grace. For through the Spirit, by faith, we eagerly wait for the hope of righteousness. For in Christ Jesus neither circumcision nor uncircumcision counts for anything; the only thing that counts is faith working through love.[104]

A perfect heading for this passage might be: Having completely given up all dharmas, to Me alone come for refuge.

However, a caution is required. All this is so even if we ought not push the comparison too far, as if St. Paul's view of Jewish law were a universal principle applying to all systems of religious law. "To be freed from the Law" provides a helpful reading dynamic and sheds fresh light on the Carama Śloka, but that light ought not be distorted by insisting on too close a correlation with St. Paul's theology of Judaism. The Jewish-Christian relationship at work in St. Paul's writing is very different, on historical and theological grounds, from the Christian-Hindu relationship, and it would not be wise to take literally an equation of Dharma and "the Law," nor even of Dharma with the Jewish Law as understood by Jews (before or after Paul).[105]

A second and more basic analogue between Christian theological insight and the Carama Śloka's first line is that both Christians and Śrīvaiṣṇavas believe that God is the kind of God who does speak to us,

[103] The ethical implications of the Carama Śloka become clearer in its second line; see Chapter 4. On ambivalence toward Deśika's cautious reading of Carama Śloka, Part 1, see above, p. 86.

[104] *Galatians* 5: 1-6

[105] How exactly the Christian ought to think of religious law, Jewish or Hindu or Christian, is an underlying question of importance, since how we think of Jewish law – "the Law" – in light of our Pauline heritage may well affect, and possibly distort, how we think of Hindu law.

and in a way that can be radically transformative of our lives. Though God in both traditions is transcendent and beyond our limited concepts and words, this God also accommodates us, in visible form and by words we can understand. Christians too can recognize the challenge presented by the Carama Śloka: to know God, we must be able to stop and listen to God, and for this purpose, to simplify and purify our relationship to the world around us, so that we can hear, and be vulnerable to God's word to us.

But it is reasonable also to ask: does the Carama Śloka speak to Christians? Kṛṣṇa's invitation can be read as addressed not just to a leading representative of the warrior class,[106] but rather to a wide audience of honest people, everyone who grieves acutely at her or his uselessness and inability to find God, and who therefore has no place to go and no resources. And so "the Kṛṣṇa speaking in the *Gītā*" might readily translate, for the Christian reader, into "God speaking to us." Or, perhaps, Christians cannot take the verse as divine speech, and may respect it simply as consolation for those seeking Kṛṣṇa. This is the problem of the specificity and intimacy of *Me alone*. Insofar as Kṛṣṇa's word really means simply *God alone*, then it can easily be taken as speaking to us as well. But if *Me alone* specifically intends Kṛṣṇa and not "God in general" – Śrīvaiṣṇavas are no more pleased with "God in general" than most Christians are – then the idea that we are Kṛṣṇa's audience becomes more problematic: Christians may for the most part not want to be that audience, or find ourselves unable to be among those listening to Kṛṣṇa.

It is still true, however, that the Mantra has a deep truth to it that Christians can recognize, and most of what is implied about Kṛṣṇa, in the *Gītā* and in Deśika's reading of the Carama Śloka, coheres well with a Christian understanding of God. There are seemingly universal

[106] Or, Kṛṣṇa's words might well be taken as meant for certain skilled and erudite Hindu practitioners who are competent to perform orthodox and devotional practices, who err by failing to perform those properly, and who grieve with the acute sensitivity of the tortured consciousness that belongs only to so refined a practitioner. After all, it might be that one cannot give up all *dharmas* unless one is competent to perform them in the first place – having completely given up all *dharmas* is an act of abandonment that means less if one does not already have access to those *dharmas* which are to be given up. One cannot fail to perform properly what one cannot perform at all; one cannot grieve over such failures when success is not even conceivably possible. Similarly, the trials and tribulations of the Law, about which Paul speaks, may not pertain to every person confronted with the challenges and pitfalls of ritual and law, but only to those who have experienced in a certain way the Law given specifically to Israel.

categories operative in defining the person addressed, "having and then surrendering all *dharmas*," "being a sinner," "grieving" at separation from God or the failures of the religious life, "allowing God to make one free." At least by analogy, these might well be the words of Christ, addressed to observant Christians who finally realize that we are not saved by our good works.

If I have recommended that Christian readers take the Carama Śloka to heart and hear its call to the abandoment of all *dharmas* and its urgent invitation to refuge, it can easily also be the case that another respectful Christian reader might honor the Carama Śloka by deciding that it is *not* addressed to Christians, because Christian faith does not enable us to hear this word as a Word addressed to us.

2. Resonances in the Christian Tradition

For deeper resonances that cannot be calculated simply by theology, however, we can further investigate how to read the Carama Śloka's first line along with one or more texts from our Biblical tradition. Since the Carama Śloka offers a comforting message that speaks directly to people who are at least open to spiritual instruction, we might associate it with a Christian text of direct address, such as these lines from the *Gospel according to Matthew*:

> Come to Me, all you that are weary and are heavily burdened,
> and I will give you rest.
> Take My yoke upon you,
> Learn from me, for I am gentle and humble in heart…

And, with more apt reference to the second part of the Carama Śloka that we shall take up in Chapter 4, Christ concludes with a promise:

> You will find rest for your souls.
> For My yoke is easy, and My burden is light.[107]

While Jesus still has great expectations for those who come to him – there is a yoke to be worn – nonetheless that commitment is a new yoke, one that is "easy," a burden that is "light." This passage is simple and direct, and can be taken simply as an invitation to all who are burdened and

[107] *Matthew* 11.28-30. Scholars note that the "burden" may also refer, here as in early rabbinic texts, to the burden of legal observance. If so, the passage might then be understood as directed to those religious persons to whom the Law does pertain in all its obligations, and for whom the Law might actually be experienced as a burden because they have taken it so seriously.

weary, and yet still willing to hear this invitation. Similarly, Kṛṣṇa places great demands on those who listen to him, but the way to rise to those challenges is simply by trusting him completely. And so we have might have a sympathetic pairing of texts such as this:

Come to Me, all you that are weary and are heavily burdened, and I will give you rest. Take My yoke upon you, learn from Me, for I am gentle and humble in heart.	Having completely given up all *dharmas*, to Me alone come for refuge...

We can make further sense of the imbedded personal appeal by Jesus – *learn from Me* – by noticing that in this way Jesus is presenting himself as already sharing the carrying of the burden to which he invites the listener. He is neither detached nor a mere observer, but bears the burden along with whoever accepts his invitation. Like the person of Kṛṣṇa, the person of Jesus matters; since neither the texts nor the speakers are identical, we can also see that Jesus and Kṛṣṇa matter in different ways, even as we hear their words together.

Or we might think of the challenge Jesus places on the man who comes to him seeking the way of perfection, a challenge that highlights all the more intensely the surrender of all possessions that precedes a radical new state:

> Jesus said, "If you would be perfect, go, sell your possessions and give the proceeds to the poor..."[108]

The listener is invited to let go of everything else – even if meticulously giving it to the poor – and then, while not precisely taking refuge with Jesus, beginning to walk with him, sharing in his ministry of complete service to others. Renunciation, intimacy with the Lord, and service are common to both the Carama Śloka and *Matthew* 19.21.

Then our locus for meditation might be this pair of texts:[109]

If you would be perfect, go, sell what you possess and give the proceeds to the poor...	Having completely given up all *dharmas*, to Me alone come for refuge...

108 *Matthew* 19.21

109 In a double reading we can fully realize only after completing our consideration of the Carama Śloka in Chapter 4.

We fill out this comparison in Chapter 4, but for now we have two pairs of texts for reflection:[110]

Abba, Father.	Aum, obeisance to Nārāyaṇa.
If you would be perfect, go, sell your possessions and give the proceeds to the poor...	Having completely given up all *dharmas*, to Me alone come for refuge...

One can read back and forth between these texts, noticing differences in context, background, language, etc., but the primary point is still the power of the personal invitation, now enriched through the proximity of the Carama Śloka to a Gospel invitation of Jesus. Insofar as the texts differ, they can be taken as complementary, each enriching the way the other is read and pondered.

3. Praying with the Carama Śloka's First Invitation?

In reflecting on the Tiru Mantra, the possibility of prayer had to do with the circumstances under which we might find ourselves addressing its words to God, now as our words. Here, as already explained, prayerful listening is the main thing. Before we say or do anything, we need to decide whether to listen, and to determine how this listening might become a religious and potentially liberative act. Praying with this Mantra will not be about words one uses in praying – for these are not words the recitant can make her or his own by reciting them as if in the first person. Rather, it is about prayer as listening; prayer here lies in vulnerability to the spoken word and the call to surrender. While the theological question remains open – What would it mean for a Christian to be confronted and challenged by the Carama Śloka as a word of God? – at a more immediate level, learning to listen can do no harm, and the Śloka occasions for us a potent form of prayer, as we attend most closely to the words of Kṛṣṇa, now vulnerable to them as we should already be to the words of Jesus.

Or we might choose to place the Śloka back in its *Gītā* context, and find it helpful also to contemplate the *Gītā* scene on the battlefield, visualizing Kṛṣṇa and Arjuna in dialogue. With this we could bring to mind also our more familiar visualization of Jesus speaking to the rich man who would be perfect, or to the heavily burdened person who seeks relief. Such visualizations, in which the words of our mantras recover their

[110] For the sake of simplicity, I do not repeat here the double reading with the *Matthew* 11 text.

voice, place, and person, will awaken the spiritual senses we need in order to be all the more deeply touched by what we hear.

V. Looking Ahead

In the Śrīvaiṣṇava tradition, Kṛṣṇa's invitation is not the end of the story; the consequent response from persons hearing the Carama Śloka is an enunciation of words of radical surrender – the words of the Dvaya Mantra.

Chapter 3

THE WAY OF RADICAL FAITH: THE DVAYA MANTRA[1]

Father, into Your hands I commit my spirit.

I approach for refuge the feet of Nārāyaṇa with Śrī; obeisance to Nārāyaṇa with Śrī.

Reflection: Even when the fundamental truth of our orientation to God and of the divine invitation to all human beings become clear, it remains less certain that we can rise to the challenge and respond to God in a way that is faithful to the transcendent perfection of God and to our own deepest identities. We may at a deep level lack faith in our ability to surrender adequately to God, or even to perform adequately the religious actions expected of Christians. But respond we must. Christ shows us the way and enables us to travel with him, in his complete surrender into the hands of his Father, as he hung on the cross near death.

At least indirectly, the Dvaya Mantra is an exemplary expression of this faith and dependence that comprise our best response: the person who has heard the voice of God abandons herself or himself into the hands of God, Nārāyaṇa ever with Śrī, confident that God will bring to completion what God has begun. However different we might imagine the beginnings and ends of the Christian and Śrīvaiṣṇava journeys to be, we can certainly share the sentiment expressed in the Dvaya Mantra, the mantra of surrender.

I. Introduction

Śrīmannārāyaṇacaraṇau śaraṇaṃ prapadye
Śrīmate Nārāyaṇāya namaḥ

Śrī – Śrī, the goddess; *man* [*mat*] – with; *Nārāyaṇa* – Nārāyaṇa; *caraṇau* – feet; *śaraṇam* – refuge; *prapadye* – I approach;
Śrīmate – with Śrī; *Nārāyaṇāya* – for Nārāyaṇa; *namaḥ* – obeisance

[1] Portions of the research in this chapter have also appeared, in a slightly different form, in Clooney, forthcoming 2007b.

I approach for refuge the feet of Nārāyaṇa with Śrī;
obeisance to Nārāyaṇa with Śrī.

Śaṭakōpaṉ's Example

The Dvaya Mantra is properly read against the background of acts of refuge remembered and revered from earlier in the tradition as central and fundamental in defining Śrīvaiṣṇavism at its core. Most famous is the example of Śaṭakōpaṉ from the 9th century. By tradition, the āḻvār was born with a pure and exclusive desire for union with the Lord, and a refusal to settle for anything less than God. His great song cycle of 1102 verses, the *Tiruvāymoḻi*, is taken to be the record of his difficult, tumultuous journey toward God. By tradition, the first six books of ten songs each serve to document the nature of God and self, the āḻvār's desire for God and determination to see God, and his increasing desperation as his ideas, songs, and meditations on renowned temples fail to bring him into direct encounter with God. At the end of the last song of Book VI, Śaṭakōpaṉ, helpless and desperate, takes refuge at the feet of Nārāyaṇa, the Lord of the Tiruveṅkaṭam mountain and temple[2] who is ever with Śrī, and sings these famous words:

"I cannot be apart even for a moment,"
says the Lady in the lotus who dwells on Your chest;
You are unmatched in fame, owner of the three worlds, my ruler,
O Lord of holy Veṅkaṭam
where peerless immortals and crowds of sages delight:
with no other refuge,
this servant has entered right beneath Your feet.[3]

By this verse, Śaṭakōpaṉ both performs his own act of taking refuge and exemplifies the words and feelings underlying refuge. Śaṭakōpaṉ's verse should be kept in mind as we read the Dvaya Mantra. If it is a distillation of the theology, passion, and radical choice underlying the act of surrender, then Śaṭakōpaṉ's verse, and the personal experience underlying it, confirm the truth and efficacy of the Dvaya Mantra. Śaṭakōpaṉ voiced radical surrender in simple Tamil words; the Mantra gives its expression as an utterance available to all. To read the Mantra is to enter the tradition, to begin to experience and enact its values.[4]

[2] Today's Tirupati, one of the most popular temples in India

[3] *Tiruvāymoḻi* 6.10.10

[4] The Śrīvaiṣṇava teachers who commented on Śaṭakōpaṉ's verse were aware of the parallel and symbiosis between the verse and the Dvaya Mantra. Indeed, the greatest of

An early theological illumination of the Dvaya Mantra is the *Śaraṇāgati Gadya* of Rāmānuja,[5] a work composed a century or more after Śaṭakōpaṉ, and more than a century before Vedānta Deśika. In the *Gadya*, Rāmānuja mentions the Dvaya Mantra several times, and the *Gadya* is by tradition taken to be expressive of Rāmānuja's own act of taking refuge – a kind of amplification of the truth, sentiment and practice of the Dvaya Mantra, and as providing the authoritative context in which the Dvaya Mantra found its place in the tradition. We can therefore read the *Gadya* and the Dvaya Mantra in alliance, each authorizing the other.

At the very beginning of the *Gadya*, the speaker takes refuge with the Goddess Śrī:

> She possesses proper form, forms, qualities, glory, lordly power, generous disposition, and a host of innumerable auspicious qualities, unsurpassed and flawless, such as are appropriate and pleasing to the Lord Nārāyaṇa; She is the Lady, Śrī, Goddess, and never apart from Him; She is the flawless divine consort of the God of gods, Mother of the entire world, our Mother, refuge of those who have no refuge: *I who have no other refuge seek Her as my refuge.*[6]

Śrī assents, giving permission and her blessing. Then, at greater length, the speaker seeks refuge with Nārāyaṇa, with these climactic words leading up to a mention of the Dvaya Mantra:

> You are the refuge of the whole world without exception and without consideration of any further qualifications; You dispel the distress of those who offer obeisance to You; You are an ocean of pure affection for those who depend on You; You know always the true nature and condition of all created beings; You are ever engaged in the control and ordering of all beings without exception – the moving and the stationary; You are the one for whom all conscious and non-conscious beings exist, the support of the whole Universe, the Lord of the Universe, my Lord; all Your desires come true, Your will is ever accomplished, You are different from all else, You are the kalpaka tree[7] of those in want, friend in need for those in distress,

these commentators, Naṃpiḷḷai, elaborately spells out the connections between the words of the verse and the words of the Mantra. On the commentarial treatment of *Tiruvāymoḻi* 6.10.10 in relation to the Dvaya Mantra, along with the Tiru Mantra and Carama Śloka, see Clooney 1996, 180-192.

[5] Some scholars dispute the correctness of attributing the *Gadya* to Rāmānuja; it seems to me correct, particularly in this context, to treat it as Rāmānuja's own work.

[6] *Śaraṇāgati Gadya*; Rāmānuja 2002, 38 (Sanskrit)/12 (translation). Throughout, however, I offer my own translation.

[7] The tree that fulfils the wishes of those eating its fruit.

> consort of Śrī; You are Nārāyaṇa, refuge of those without refuge: *I who have no other refuge come for refuge at Your lotus feet.*

And Rāmānuja adds:

> Here the Dvaya Mantra.[8]

This double surrender, to Śrī and to Nārāyaṇa, is condensed in the words of the Dvaya Mantra. All the better, of course, if the recitant preparing to utter the Dvaya Mantra already knows the *Gadya.*

Two other passages in the *Gadya* mention the Dvaya Mantra. First, Rāmānuja says that it is perfectly effective however it is uttered, as it were an expression of the divine compassion enunciated here:

> Since you have uttered the Dvaya Mantra, whatever the manner of your utterance, solely by My compassion you will have entirely eradicated all obstacles to exclusive and single-minded superior devotion, superior knowledge, and supreme devotion for My lotus feet...[9]

It is integral to the ideal Śrīvaiṣṇava way of life, centered at the great Śrīraṅgam temple:

> You are devoid of the slightest trace of sufferings and you are free of obstacles with respect to the self, this world, and the gods; remain happy here at Śrīraṅgam until the body is cast off, always uttering the Dvaya Mantra, meditating on its meaning.[10]

Naṭātūr Ammāḷ[11] was a great teacher of the generation before Deśika. In his *Prapanna Parijāta,* well known to Deśika, he refers several times to the Dvaya Mantra. First of all, he documents that it is known from scripture and tradition:

> This Mantra is declaratory of taking refuge... Having the same meaning as *aum*, and composed of twenty-five characters, it is detailed over and again with its auxiliaries, its seer and so forth.[12]

[8] *Śaraṇāgati Gadya,* 39/15; The meaning may be, "Here the Dvaya Mantra is recited."

[9] *Śaraṇāgati Gadya,* 41/17. Deśika gives only "by My compassion," and I have amplified the quotation. See also Chapter 3. Superior devotion, superior knowledge, and supreme devotion are dynamic gradations of the desire to know and see God; these gradations are practiced and experienced usually from a foundation in devotion, but for the person who desires to see God – now – they give way to the more desperate step of taking refuge. See Clooney 1996, 130-131.

[10] *Śaraṇāgati Gadya,* 42/19.

[11] Naṭātūr Ammāḷ, (Vātsya Varadācārya) was the grandson of Varadaguru, Rāmānuja's nephew and disciple.

[12] That is, with all the formal features required for an orthodox mantra.

It is traditional and orthodox, but Naṭātūr Ammāḷ likewise insists that it is the most inclusive and least burdensome of mantras:

> It is meant for everyone, and need be uttered just once. Elsewhere, in the [*Pañcarātra*] *Śāstra*, it is taught by the Lord. Even those outside the three castes are competent for the Dvaya Mantra.[13]

The Dvaya Mantra is free of the social and religious restrictions potentially woven around the Tiru Mantra with its orthodox *aum*; though less well known than either of the other Mantras, it is potentially the mantra of widest access and easiest use.

1. The Dvaya Mantra in the *Aṣṭaślokī* of Parāśara Bhaṭṭar

Verses 5 and 6 of Parāśara Bhaṭṭar's *Aṣṭaślokī* explicate the Dvaya Mantra. Verse 5 details its content and basic power:

> This Mantra of six words and two clauses[14] is handed down in the Veda, and it protects the one who meditates on its ten meanings:

[Śrī's] leading the way,	*Śrī*
Her eternal union [with Nārāyaṇa],	*mat*
the class of appropriate qualities,	*Nārāyaṇa*
reference to Nārāyaṇa's body,	*caraṇau*
the means,	*śaraṇaṃ*
the part to be done [by the individual],	*prapadye*
and so too, the supreme couple as the goal,	*Śrīmate*
their lordship,	*Nārāyaṇa*
the prayer [for protection],	*Nārāyaṇa-āya*
the destruction of the greater obstacles.	*namaḥ*.[15]

Verse 6 paraphrases the Mantra, its double movement of refuge with Śrī and then refuge with Hari, Nārāyaṇa:

> First I take refuge with this ruling Lady,
> the eternal and inseparable Consort of the Lord of the universe, and
> then I resort to the feet of Hari,
> all of whose qualities are conducive to my taking refuge,
> He is my chosen means:
> for this Lord of my self, joined with Śrī,
> I beg to perform service

[13] *Prapanna Parijāta* 1.9 [4/4-5], 3.3-5 [13-14/17]. Numbering according to Naṭātūr Ammāḷ, [Nadadoor Ammal] 1971. Deśika himself echoes the *Prapanna Parijāta* in his introduction to Chapter 28, referring to the same texts. (718/420)

[14] *Śrīmannārāyaṇacaraṇau* + *śaraṇam* + *prapadye* + *Śrīmate* + *Nārāyaṇāya* + *namaḥ*; and, *Śrīmannārāyaṇacaraṇau śaraṇaṃ prapadye* + *Śrīmate Nārāyaṇāya namaḥ*.

[15] The righthand column is only implicit in Bhaṭṭar's verse.

that is in no way deficient, without interruption, forever,
taking no thought of myself.[16]

The concluding prayer for service – for the Lord, for other devotees – is notable, since service is not explicit to the last words of the Mantra itself, *Obeisance to Nārāyaṇa with Śrī*. Yet it is a consistent teaching of the tradition that taking refuge eventuates in a life of service within the community. Now let us return to Deśika's commentary on the Mantra in Chapter 28 of the *Essence*.

II. Exegeting the Dvaya Mantra

Before his word-by-word exegesis of the Mantra, Deśika makes a series of introductory claims that preview values that will appear in the course of the exegesis. The opening Sanskrit verse praises the Mantra as a guide pointing out the goal, and the strength by which to reach it:

Once heard, the Dvaya Mantra reveals that what had to be done has been done;
repeated, it shows a person whose goal has been accomplished;
after this world's gloom, it arrives like dawn –
such is this Mantra of refuge with the consort of the Lady in the lotus.[17]

The meaning of *dvayam* – "two" or "double" – can be most easily related to the double content communicated by the Mantra, regarding the way and the goal.[18] It is a teaching essential to the Śrīvaiṣṇava tradition that Nārāyaṇa with Śrī are themselves the means to liberation, and that they are also the goal, liberation itself. These truths are essential to the tradition, and must be preserved, guarded, and passed down in the teaching lineage. So it is not surprising to observe that praise of this "king of Mantras" is intertwined with praise for the guru in a long passage Deśika quotes from the *Satyakī Tantra*:

Let a person come to understand this king of mantras
after saluting the guru;
the guru alone is the highest Brahman, the guru alone the highest way,
the guru alone the greatest wisdom, the guru alone the refuge,

[16] See Chapter 1 on the unexpected appearance of service as a key fruit of the Tiru Mantra; p. 60, n. 131.

[17] 717/420

[18] On this general theme in early Śrīvaiṣṇava theology, see Narayanan.

> the guru alone the greatest desire, the guru alone the greatest wealth;
> when you have been taught by the guru,
> that guru will be all the more revered.[19]

The *Tantra* then shifts back to the Mantra itself, as the most accessible and simple of teachings:

> This Mantra requires no favorable circumstances, no auspicious star,
> no dwelling at a holy place, no preparatory rites, no regular recitation, etc.

And finally, the *Tantra* gives instructions about actually learning the Mantra:

> After first reverencing the guru with three full-length prostrations,
> after grasping his feet and with proper courtesy putting them upon one's own head,[20]
> a person should next take hold of this king of mantras,
> like someone who has no wealth and so desires treasure;
> holding onto this king of mantras, let that person come to Me for refuge;
> with this Mantra alone should a person give his self over to Me.
> Giving himself over to Me, he becomes a person who has done all he had to do.[21]

Deśika cites this text in order to emphasize strongly the importance of commitment to the guru by whose grace the Dvaya Mantra is transmitted and made available in every generation. The Mantra and the teacher are thus complementary: the teacher personifies the tradition by his transmission of the Mantra's truths; transmitted, the Dvaya Mantra enlivens the tradition, and provides in brief form what teachers explain in their many words. Together, Mantra and teacher embody tradition, provide its living practice, and insure its vitality and continuity over the generations.

Yet even when guided by tradition and educated in the meaning of the Mantra, it is still of central importance to have great faith in the potency of the Mantra's words:

> It is well known from the scriptures that even a single utterance of this Mantra, preceded by knowledge of the whole of its meaning, saves the good person. Thus Rāmānuja distinguished the potency of this Mantra from that of other mantras.[22]

[19] Literally, the guru will be *gurutara* (*gravior*), more weighty, esteemed.
[20] By touching his feet and then touching one's own head.
[21] 719-720/421
[22] Here Deśika cites the passage from *Śaraṇāgati Gadya* cited above on page 112.

Its power is rooted in the power of the divine names, Nārāyaṇa and Śrī:[23]

> You can see the potency of praising the holy name in various texts:
>
> > The person who without compulsion praises this name
> > is immediately freed from all sins –
> > as if from beasts fearing a lion.[24]
>
> and,
>
> > Hari, the power of Your name in removing sins
> > cannot be countered even by the sins
> > committed by the eater of dog flesh.[25]

By such texts we can easily grasp the power that lies even in a single utterance of this special Mantra that fully illumines the object of refuge, the act of taking of refuge, and its specific result. One finds the reasons for this power in various texts and in tradition.[26]

Respectful of the gracious mystery of the Mantra, Deśika also steers the would-be student and practitioner away from irreverent and distracting questions about a Mantra that is, after all, secret (*rahasya*), even most secret (*rahasyatama*), and beyond the grasp of an inquisitive intellect:

> It is not proper to seek reasons for most secret things of this kind. One should accept scripture and have faith, as is said in the *Mahābhārata* and elsewhere. Consider texts such as this:
>
> > O Goddess, reason is of no use regarding matters hidden among the gods.[27]
> >
> > Whoever desires what is beneficial should act like the deaf and blind.[28]

Deśika is an erudite and vigorous dialectician, but he does not hesitate to insist that reason alone cannot estimate the depths of the Dvaya Mantra. He fears that reasoning, which can travel in many directions for many purposes, is likely to deviate from the authentic and proper teachings and purposes. One needs rather to depend on one's teacher for a proper and efficacious understanding of the Mantra, which is in this sense a secret teaching, never obvious or merely available. The Dvaya Mantra is received, not seized on one's own.

[23] This reflection on the power of the divine name echoes Deśika's meditations on *Nārāyaṇa* with respect to the Tiru Mantra; see Chapter 2.

[24] *Viṣṇu Purāṇa* 6.8.19

[25] *Viṣṇu Smṛti* 109; the "eater of dog flesh" is the untouchable person of very low caste; unfortunately, Deśika simply quotes this text without making clear that the Dvaya Mantra is for that very person, making her or him too a member of the community.

[26] 720-721/422

[27] *devaguhyeṣu*; or, by another reading, *vedaguhyeṣu*, "hidden in the Vedas."

[28] *Mahābhārata, Anuśāsana Parva* 228.60 (721/422).

Reflection: We are reminded here, perhaps more clearly that anywhere else in Deśika's treatment of the Mantras, that true understanding – true commentary and true reading – requires more than intellectual analysis and reasonable assessment. Even when not reading with a teacher – such is my situation, and presumably that of most of my readers – we are still in a position to respond to the expectation that we need to read more deeply and humbly, open to the spiritual power of the Mantra. Faith is required, and of course we must determine what degree of faith in the Mantra is possible for the Christian.

The introductory paragraphs in Chapter 28 conclude by excerpting three verses of Śaṭakōpan̲'s *Tiruvāymoḻi*. First we hear words urging us to surrender to the Lord:

> After contemplating the downfall of people in this world seize the moment,
> be exalted, contemplate the feet of the holy Nārāyaṇa.

And next, words testifying to the āḻvār's own transformation:

> Śaṭakōpan̲ has reached the feet of the cloud-colored one,
> uplifted by His grace...

By way of a climax, we are reminded of Śaṭakōpan̲'s own utterance of surrender:

> With no other refuge,
> this servant has entered right beneath Your feet.[29]

Such verses from this most revered āḻvār enhance the tradition of the Dvaya Mantra; as indicated at the beginning of this chapter, Śaṭakōpan̲ is the living exemplar of the Dvaya Mantra.[30]

Reflection: It is one thing for us as Christian readers to ponder the words of the Mantra on their own, and with Deśika's guidance; it is another to recognize and remind ourselves that these powerful words are utterances revered and cherished within a Tradition that has passed them down for a very long time. The Christian tradition teaches us over and again the importance of teaching and preaching the truth we have received – and not a private or novel truth; and we know from the Eucharist and other central liturgical events that we utter and enact the faith in community and following those who have gone before us. So it is illuminating to realize that the Dvaya Mantra, as we read it and think about it, draws us into the great flow and narrative of the Śrīvaiṣṇava Tradition. Even if we do not prostrate

[29] 726/426; respectively from *Tiruvāymoḻi* 4.1.1, 7.2.11, and 6.10.10. I have cited a bit more of these verses than Deśika actually does.

[30] The citations also remind us of an important stratum in the history of the Dvaya Mantra, since it is in the traditional commentaries on *Tiruvāymoḻi* that we find early and concerted exegesis of the Dvaya Mantra, Tiru Mantra, and Carama Śloka. See Clooney 1996b, 215-217.

ourselves at the feet of a guru, we are drawn to reexamine the attitudes of mind, word, and body we bring to bear in our reception and practice of our faith – and again, to review the attitudes we bring to our study of the great texts of another tradition. In any case, it is striking, perhaps ironic, that religious people most respectful of and deeply committed to their own Tradition are most able, yet sometimes least disposed, to share values with people of another, similarly precious Tradition.

Now let us turn to the Mantra in detail.

The First Line of the Mantra: *I approach for refuge the feet of Nārāyaṇa with Śrī*, Śrīmannārāyaṇacaraṇau śaraṇaṃ prapadye

I approach Nārāyaṇa: *Nārāyaṇaṃ prapadye*

In the following pages, I trace the exegesis of the Dvaya Mantra and its articulation of total surrender, by a "theological (re)construction" that diverges from the simpler word by word analysis I have used for the Tiru Mantra and the Carama Śloka. I first postulate a very simple version of the Mantra and the act of taking refuge, and then build into it the further complexities the words of the Mantra give to us. I do this in order to highlight what is at stake in the Mantra's theology and devotion.[31]

For the simplest expression of surrender, we begin simply with the grammatical subject and verb of the Mantra's first line: *I approach Nārāyaṇa* (*Nārāyaṇaṃ prapadye.*)

In glossing the word *Nārāyaṇa*, Deśika has us recall the exegesis developed extensively in Chapter 27.[32] As we saw in our Chapter 1, that exegesis included reflection on the meanings of *nāra* + *ayana* that express the Lord's role as foundation (*ayana*) for all beings (*nāra*) and, conversely, identified the Lord's place within living beings, as it were finding his own dwelling in beings. There, Deśika recounted the 108 characteristics of the supreme deity who deserves to be called *Nārāyaṇa*;[33] here he lists just twelve qualities that are pertinent to the Dvaya Mantra's representation of Nārāyaṇa as our place of safe refuge:

1. maternal tenderness,
2. lordship,
3. good disposition,
4. accessibility,

[31] But by this graded reconstruction I do not make any claim about the historical genesis of the Mantra.

[32] 737/437

[33] 672-674/389-392

5. omniscience,
6. omnipotence,
7. having all one's intentions come true,
8. being supremely compassionate,
9. (gratefully) recognizing what has been done,[34]
10. steadfastness,
11. being entirely perfect, and
12. supreme generosity.[35]

In this abbreviated version of the Mantra, *I approach* is a simple expression of coming-near; it is only later, after other words in the actual Mantra have been considered, that we will be able to note several nuances in the nature of this action, *I approach*. But in the shortened form thus far considered, the Mantra might be taken as combining a proper and respectful theology of Nārāyaṇa with a simple act of approach and worship.

I approach Nārāyaṇa with Śrī: *Śrīman-Nārāyaṇaṃ prapadye*

But the Dvaya Mantra is all the more interesting because it is much more than the brief version I have just offered; it is complex and, in its multiple words, expectant of fuller exegesis by its readers. A first complication enters when a crucial modifier is added to *Nārāyaṇa*. He is *Śrīmān*, with-Śrī: *I approach Nārāyaṇa with Śrī.*

In theory, Nārāyaṇa is entirely capable of making surrender efficacious, and so it might be taken as simply a pious supplement to observe that Śrī too is present. Yet in Deśika's view, the Dvaya Mantra announces that Nārāyaṇa is always with Śrī, and that she is a full partner in leading those who take refuge to ultimate union.

Like *Nārāyaṇa* here and in the Tiru Mantra, *Śrī* is a word with both general and specific meanings. On the one hand, Śrī is the Goddess, a particular divine person to whom one goes for aid and encouragement. She is the one by whose grace one is able to approach the Lord efficaciously, and, as Deśika insists here, it is with her as well as with Nārāyaṇa that one actually takes refuge. On the other hand, *Śrī* is a word with specific conceptual meanings that can be discovered by tracing it to several possible roots and verbal formations:[36]

> *śrīyate* – She is taken refuge with: "She is taken refuge with by those who seek their personal uplift…"

[34] That is, acknowledging the taking of refuge by the person who approaches him.
[35] 737-741/436-440
[36] 727/427

śrayate – She takes refuge: "...and She then takes refuge with the Lord of all, for the sake of uplifting those people;"[37]
śṛṇoti – She hears: "When we, devout yet sinful, take refuge with Her, begging, 'Grant us access to the feet of the Lord of all," She hears our anguished cry..."
śrāvayati – She makes heard: "...and She then makes sure our petition is heard by the Lord of all, and thus calms our anguish."[38]
śṛṇāti – She removes: "She removes karma and other obstacles thwarting those who are (otherwise) competent for this means (taking refuge);"[39]
śṛīṇāti – She ripens: "By Her qualities of compassion, etc., She ripens the good qualities of those taking refuge, all the way to fruition in service."[40]

These six root meanings bring out dimensions of the person and activity of Śrī; they reflect her mediating role, and her relationship with the person and work of Nārāyaṇa. Even when *Śrī*, like *Nārāyaṇa,* is taken as indicating a specific divine Person known from the Hindu traditions, it still illumines important qualities integral to a proper conceptualization of "divine person," and it would seem evident that anyone with theological sensitivities can appreciate the rich meaning given to "God" and "Goddess" in the Dvaya Mantra as a prayer of surrender.[41]

The *with* (*mat*) – Nārāyaṇa-with-Śrī (*Śrīmannārāyaṇa*) – requires delicate nuance, lest Śrī be merely adjunct to Nārāyaṇa, connected to him in an impermanent relationship – as if, now "with Śrī," but perhaps later, "without Śrī" – or lest it seem that there are two supreme deities, not one. After some technical discussion why the conjunctive *mat* need not suggest two separate beings connected only temporarily, Deśika adds a comment that emphasizes the point of mentioning Śrī so prominently in the Mantra:

> In the present instance, even if there are authoritative texts pointing to an eternal relationship of Nārāyaṇa and Śrī in the context of the means and the context of the goal, this essential relationship should also be illumined by the Mantra itself. Accordingly, in the Mantra's first and second clauses, *with* indicates that Śrī and Nārāyaṇa cannot bear to be apart.[42]

[37] 727/427

[38] 731/430-431

[39] 733/431; "She hears" and "She makes heard" are treated together.

[40] 733/432

[41] Further complications in the relationship of Nārāyaṇa and Śrī are considered in Chapter 23, where Deśika boldly defends the equality and inseparability of Nārāyaṇa and Śrī. See forthcoming d.

[42] At all, even in the Mantra.

The means is the goal, taking refuge is its own reward; this identity is in turn rooted in the love Nārāyaṇa and Śrī have for one another, their inability to be apart. Deśika enlists multiple texts to illustrate the importance of their relationship, with particular reference to Lakṣmaṇa who loyally follows his brother Rāma into the forest, vowing to serve not only Rāma, but also Sītā:

> As it says,
>
> > His brother Lakṣmaṇa steadfastly touched Rāma's feet, and then spoke to Sītā with Rāghava...[43]
>
> and
>
> > Sir, you and Sītā[44] may relax on the mountain heights; I will do everything for you, awake or asleep.[45]

Deśika then turns again to Śaṭakōpaṉ's *Tiruvāymoḻi*:

> > "I cannot be apart even for a moment,"
> > says the Lady in the lotus who dwells on Your chest, [46]
>
> and,
>
> > The holy Lady with her splendid bracelets and You abide together,[47]
>
> and,
>
> > Neither here nor there did I see anything other than the Lord of Śrī.[48]
>
> In this way Śaṭakōpaṉ meditates on the eternal connection expressed in *Śrīmat* in the context of both the means and the result.[49]

Deśika sums up what is at stake: "This meditation is a reason for sinners to take refuge, provided they think upon it without second thoughts."[50] That is, it is most helpful that Śrī be seen to be the mediator (*puruṣakāra*), since her presence encourages the hesitant. Of course, in the Sanskrit, *Śrī* is the first word enunciated in each line of the Mantra, and so even the utterance of the Mantra begins with her.

> *Reflection*: That there is a mediator and the mediator is a person, and that this mediation in no way detracts from the power of God – all of this we should be able to share easily with Śrīvaiṣṇavas. Yet the very idea of Śrī may be a challenge to many. It seems easier for many Christians to think of the God of another religion, and to see how that God shares many features with the God of the Christian tradition, than to reflect upon Goddesses. Even

43 *Rāmāyaṇa, Ayodhyā Kāṇḍa* 31.2. Rāghava is Rāma; I have added "Lakṣmaṇa" and "Rāma" to clarify the quotation.

44 Literally, Vaidehī, she who is from the land of the Videhas.

45 *Rāmāyaṇa, Ayodhyā Kāṇḍa* 31.37. Only the first words are actually quoted.

46 *Tiruvāymoḻi* 6.10.10

47 *Tiruvāymoḻi* 4.9.10

48 *Tiruvāymoḻi* 7.9.11; "Śrī" here is the Tamil word "Tiru."

49 736/435-436

50 736/436

Christians who insist that God is the referent of male and female characteristics – God is our Mother as well as our Father – hesitate to take up the language of the Goddess. Yet the Dvaya Mantra is clear on the importance of Śrī, and her mediating role, as integral to the monotheism of his tradition. No liberal, Deśika still insists on acknowledging her full participation in the work of salvation along with Nārāyaṇa. As we continue reading, it is well for us to observe the implications of her presence in the Mantra, and to assess what may be the limits of our openness to what is clearly central and salutary – and yet so very different – in another tradition.[51]

I approach the feet of Nārāyaṇa with Śrī: *Śrīmannārāyaṇa-caraṇau prapadye*

The Mantra becomes still more complex if we say: *I approach the feet of Nārāyaṇa with Śrī*. What is the difference between approaching Nārāyaṇa with Śrī and approaching the *feet* (*caraṇau*) of Nārāyaṇa with Śrī? Certainly, there was a long tradition among the āḻvārs of devotion to the Lord's feet, and so too more broadly in Indian culture the custom of the veneration of the feet of a king or deity; this veneration signifies humility, dependence, and service. To some extent, the Mantra simply echoes this cultural convention. But here Deśika emphasizes that the mention of the divine feet shows the transcendent, perfect Nārāyaṇa, always with Śrī, to be possessed also of an eternal, perfect, yet material form by which he and Śrī are all the more accessible:

> The word *feet* stands for the whole eternal and auspicious divine form. The most important things to be known are that the Lord of Śrī is higher than everything, *and* that He has an eternal form. As it says,
>
> O Pauṣkara, whoever is certain in his heart
> that the Lord's form is eternal
> and that He is superior to all –
> may the Lord come to that person.[52]
>
> Therefore, when we think of *Nārāyaṇa with Śrī* we should meditate on transcendence joined with accessibility, and eternal form joined with *feet*.[53]

Moreover, these feet are the adequate object of meditation for those incapable of more rarified reflection:

> For those who do not clearly understand the qualities previously mentioned [implicitly in *Nārāyaṇa*] or the proper form of the divine self, it suffices to

[51] On the Christian response to Goddesses, see Clooney 2005b, particularly Chapter 2, which is a reflection on Śrī in the 62 verses of the *Śrī Guṇa Ratna Kośa* ("Auspicious Treasury of Her Qualities") of Parāśara Bhaṭṭar, whose *Aṣṭaślokī* we have been consulting.

[52] *Pauṣkara Saṃhita*.

[53] 742/441.

> know this auspicious divine form. It is made entirely of pure-matter; knowing it ends the constriction of knowledge; it suggests both His transcendence and His accessibility.[54]

That refuge occurs at the Lord's feet marks the concrete and material immediacy of Nārāyaṇa with Śrī, the object of refuge: not only is Nārāyaṇa with Śrī perfect in every way, but he is also a perfect being who is accessible, at whose feet one can always take refuge.[55] In short, that the Dvaya Mantra gives significance to the divine feet opens the way to a true sacramental theology.

I approach for refuge the feet of Nārāyaṇa with Śrī: *Śrīmannārāyaṇacaraṇau śaraṇaṃ prapadye*

But we can move to still another level of complexity, from *I approach the feet of Nārāyaṇa with Śrī* to *I approach for refuge the feet of Nārāyaṇa with Śrī*. *Refuge* may seem doubly redundant, nestled as it is between *feet* – the specified place of refuge – and *I approach*, the verb indicative of the movement toward the Lord. But Deśika (like his predecessors) reads *śaraṇam* as in deliberate juxtaposition to *feet* in order to emphasize that the accessible Lord himself is the refuge, instead of any human action of taking refuge: what matters are the Lord, the Lord's feet, and refuge – all one reality – and not the human activity of taking refuge. *Feet* is thus further specified by *refuge*:

> It may be asked: if the Lord of all – worshipped in accord with all the scriptures and available to all competent persons – is the means to the result, why further specify this means (by adding *refuge*)? We respond: doing so [explicitly] puts the Lord, distinguished by His innate compassion and other qualities, in the place of other means, and makes clear the nature of taking refuge.

But isn't the act of taking refuge the means to salvation? No, because the person seeking refuge

> must depend on the Lord's distinctive nature, His innate compassion, and so forth. For the person who has nothing, the Lord takes the place of

[54] 743/441. "Pure-matter" (*śuddha sattva*) is a special form of matter that is free of the defects of ordinary matter, including *rajas* and *tamas*, the other expected constituents of matter.

[55] Deśika follows tradition in asserting that Nārāyaṇa's material form, indicated by this reference to his feet, is made of a uniquely pure-matter. It is attractive even to the senses, an appropriate imaginable object for meditation, such as leads finally to taking refuge at those divine feet.

> all other means. When a person who has nothing is unable to bear anymore the burden enjoined as means to the desired result, he has the Lord take the place of other means. This is why he says, "Be for me the means, protector!" That is, "If, instead of my bearing the burden of other means on my head, You bear my burden, then the task of bestowing everything I desire is a burden to be borne by You, since You are both compassionate and capable."[56]

Since Nārāyaṇa with Śrī alone are the refuge, the correct division of the line is not

> I approach for refuge / the feet of Nārāyaṇa with Śrī,

as if to suggest that *refuge* is a human act, but rather

> I approach / the refuge, the feet of Nārāyaṇa with Śrī

which makes clear the that the refuge is nothing but Nārāyaṇa with Śrī, accessible in the divine feet.

I approach: *prapadye*

Finally we can make a more substantive comment on the verb, "I approach," "I come near." The true refuge (*śaraṇam*) is not the human act of taking refuge, but rather the "act" of enduring divine presence. But if the Lord is the refuge, then the purpose of the human act indicated by *I approach* (*prapadye*) must be justified, since it does not itself produce the desired liberation. For Deśika, *I approach* should be taken as indicating not so much a human initiative and achievement, but rather the act of faith, total trust in the Lord. He therefore highlights the cognitive dimension of *I approach* by reconsidering the meaning of the Sanskrit verb:

> As for *pra-padye*, the root *pad* expresses movement (*gati*), meaning both "going" and "understanding." Here it indicates the latter, the specific, desired understanding, the faith that is the firm conviction, "He will protect me."[57]

The prefix *pra* intensifies this understanding is a matter of intense insight, faith:

> This faith is essential among the subsidiaries [of taking refuge]. Putting it prominently in front here makes clear the means to be accomplished with its subsidiary components. How? We reply: The prefix *pra* indicates

[56] 750-751/447-448

[57] *Ahirbudhnya Saṃhitā* 37.29; 751-752/449.

> abundance, in the form of abundant faith. This abundant faith arises when one meditates on the mediator [*Śrī*], the relation [*mat*], the qualities [of *Nārāyaṇa*], and so forth, as found respectively in the words *Śrīmat* and *Nārāyaṇa*. This[58] ends all doubts arising due to the abundance of one's transgressions and other such factors.[59]

After citing texts that emphasize great faith, Deśika highlights the relevance of this faith to human surrender before the Lord:

> If this great faith exists, during subsequent reflection doubt never arises. To insure that afterwards doubt not arise, at the very moment of taking refuge great faith is the key subsidiary to the taking of refuge.[60]

In conclusion:

> When we indicate great faith – "I have made a firm resolution regarding the means" – it is a prayer choosing the means, in accord with authoritative texts such as these:
>
> When that which a person most desires can be accomplished by no one else,
> then asking, with great faith, that He alone be that means
> is itself the surrender, the taking of refuge.[61]
>
> and,
>
> "Taking refuge" is what is meant by the prayer,
> "You alone be for me the means."[62]
>
> and so too,
>
> Be my means.[63]

This interpretation shifts attention from human activity to the essential, underlying recognition of the divine person's absolute priority. Nārāyaṇa is the refuge, easily accessible and active in doing all that needs to be done.[64]

58 The faith, and the meditative appreciation of the faith.

59 752/449. Taking refuge is thus a realization; but see also Deśika's interpretation of *come for refuge* in the Carama Śloka, discussed in Chapter 3 – where he denies that taking refuge is *only* a mental act, as if human action is to be totally excluded.

60 752-753/449

61 Cited also in Chapter 24, where it is attributed to Bhārata Muni; I have translated *prapatti* as "surrender," and *śaraṇāgati* as "taking refuge."

62 *Ahirbudhnya Saṃhita* 37.31

63 *Viṣṇu Purāṇa* 3.7.33 (753/450)

64 Echoing claims made elsewhere in the *Essence* about the once-for-all nature of *I approach*, Deśika explains that the present tense of the verb simply signals the vivid moment of the action. It is not to be construed, he says, as indicative of an ongoing, even life-long action, nor as requiring constant repetition. Repetition is possible, but only as a matter of enjoyment, not necessity: "Even if the Mantra is repeated because a person is most eager, finding it a form of enjoyment, this does not detract from the means that

Thus we have Deśika's interpretation of the first line of the Mantra, *I approach for refuge the feet of Nārāyaṇa with Śrī.* Our "reconstruction" highlights the claims pressed upon the reader who takes seriously the simplicity and density of the line's several words. In utterance, of course, the Mantra simply flows without any need to dissect its meanings as we have done. Yet a person who is attentive as well as devout will notice the teachings inscribed in the Mantra, and will affirm its several truths in reciting the Mantra, as understanding overflows into practice.

> *Reflection*: The very idea of taking refuge, finding safety in God alone, is an ideal that every Christian should recognize and honor; we know that we are sinners, that we cannot save ourselves, that even the best resources of our faith do not guarantee that we can reach salvation or find God. Taking refuge is both a truth and an affective state of a somewhat desperate trust in God, and this we can respect, and share. A particular challenge of the Mantra, of course, is that it is not a statement about taking refuge: it is rather a performative word that, when uttered, brings about the reality of which it speaks. As we learn the Dvaya Mantra's first line and as it finds its way into our memories and hearts, *I approach for refuge* may become words that arise on our lips as well, an utterance of a surrender in which we find ourselves participating. With all the qualifications I have considered here and in previous chapters about the possible meaning of *Nārāyaṇa* and *Śrī* for the Christian, we may justly find ourselves in the situation where the words *I approach for refuge* enable us to imagine more immediately and directly our own act of surrender, the grace of refuge that no Christian need ignore or reject. The words are potent. When Rāmānuja insists on their efficacy, "whatever the manner of your utterance," we cannot but recall the power of utterance St. Paul points to when he characterizes the confession of Christ's identity: "No one can say 'Jesus is Lord' except by the Holy Spirit."[65]

The second line of the Mantra: *Obeisance to Nārāyaṇa with Śrī*, Śrīmate Nārāyaṇāya namaḥ

There is nothing particularly complicated about the second line of the Dvaya Mantra, and we can review Deśika's interpretation of it more quickly.

With Śrī: *Śrīmate*

Śrīmate reaffirms that Nārāyaṇa is to be understood inseparably from Śrī:

> When we speak of the object of attainment as endowed with both realms of glory, we also mean the following. Being the One on whom everything

has [once, already] been performed, in accord with the first line. The present tense in the statement regarding the means neither signals (nor forbids) repetition as a form of enjoyment prompted by one's own wishes; as it says, 'He keeps on reciting the Dvaya Mantra, reflecting on its meaning.'" (*Śaraṇāgati Gadya* 20) (756/454).

65 *I Corinthians* 12.3

> is dependent and thus too recipient of the oblation of self, and consequently being also the One to whom all consequent service is due: all this pertains to this special divine Couple, who are together the primary object of attainment. In order to show all this, *with-Śrī* is employed here.[66]

For Nārāyaṇa: ***Nārāyaṇāya***

Nārāyaṇa [in *Nārāyaṇa-āya*], already explained at length with reference to the Tiru Mantra and in the first line of this Mantra, serves in this second line to reaffirm core truths:

> In this context, *Nārāyaṇa* with its specification [*with-Śrī*] has the primary purpose of indicating His characteristics, in accord with authoritative texts. He is Lord, and so forth,[67] as is fitting to His being the goal. As Lord, He is an object of enjoyment that is unsurpassable in all modes, distinguished by endless realms of glory and good qualities.[68]

Even if all this is already known – from the first line of the Dvaya Mantra and from the Tiru Mantra – it still bears repeating in this context:

> Even if the Lord is already implied as correlative to and specified by *with-Śrī*, [explicitly adding] *Nārāyaṇa* brings about a perfectly full experience of His relationships,[69] qualities, and glories, and in turn this gives birth to the distinctive pleasure that inspires every kind of service.[70]

Deśika affords the dative case – the *to* (-āya) in *to Nārāyaṇa* – its full force in a Sanskrit verse about perfect bliss that arises as one recognizes that the Lord, and not one's own activity, is the means to salvation:

> Giving up as unattainable the notion of being saved by oneself or anyone else,
> dismissing the notion of existing either for oneself or anyone else
> because a person exists (only) for that Person –
> then, averse to all other enjoyments and freed of impurity,
> the person who has taken refuge
> savors his own enjoyment in full –
> as dependent on the Lord's enjoyment.[71]

66 757/456

67 That is, possessed of the all powers and good qualities of the true divine Lord.

68 28, 757/455; "realms of glory" refers to the Lord's cosmic and earthly realms of power, in both of which his glory is manifest.

69 That is, the *śeṣi-śeṣa* relationship, between the individual self (which is *śeṣa*, totally dependent) and God (who is *śeṣi*, to whom all belongs and upon whom the self depends entirely)

70 28, 758-759/456-457

71 759/457

Being *for* Nārāyaṇa (and Śrī) was stated already in the Tiru Mantra; here, after the enunciation of the taking of refuge in the first line of the Dvaya Mantra, it is uttered again, now as the statement of a person who has taken the radical risk and is beginning to live that way.

Obeisance: *Namaḥ*[72]

Against this background and assuming the exegesis of *namaḥ* with respect to the Tiru Mantra,[73] Deśika interprets *namaḥ* as meaning not only *obeisance* but also, in accord with tradition, *not mine* (*na mama*). One thus adds an additional word such as [*na*] *bhaveyam*, ["May I (not) be:]"[74]

> To *namaḥ* one must add some verbal formation, such as, "May I not be my own," "May I not be for myself."[75] Accordingly, "May nothing be mine" is a prayer to end all that is undesirable primarily by ending the sense of "mine" with respect to all objects (that might be possessed).[76]

Namaḥ thus marks the definitive cancellation of the self-attention that might recur even in the act of surrender:

> *Namaḥ* indicates the person's lack of connection with self and what belongs to self, and with the protection of self and the results of that protection. The point lies in enjoining an orientation to this [divine] other and in prohibiting an orientation to oneself; this result accrues to both the dative [in *Nārāyaṇāya*] and to the *namaḥ*. During the offering itself, *namaḥ* indicates the prohibition of any agency, etc., that would be independent of this divine other.[77]

Deśika adds that even the ordinary sense of *namaḥ* as expressive of obeisance implies the denial of self and the choice for the Lord. The second line thus implies a series of increasingly intense claims:

> *Nārāyaṇāya namaḥ*: Obeisance to Nārāyaṇa
> *Śrīmate Nārāyaṇāya namaḥ*: Obeisance to Nārāyaṇa with Śrī
> *Śrīmate Nārāyaṇāya bhaveyam, na mama bhaveyam*: May I exist for Nārāyaṇa with Śrī, may I not exist for myself.

> *Reflection:* In our reflection on the Tiru Mantra and in the earlier portion of this chapter, we have already pondered the power of *obeisance* and the

[72] On the several ways of reading *namaḥ* as obeisance and as "not mine," see my comments on *namaḥ* in Chapter 2.

[73] See Chapter 2.

[74] Or *na mama syām*, with the same meaning.

[75] Unusually, Deśika includes here a Tamil translation of the Sanskrit word, hence the apparent repetition in English.

[76] 759-760/457-458

[77] 761/460

negation of self enunciated in *namaḥ*. If we follow the wisdom of the Śrīvaiṣṇava tradition and contemplate the Dvaya Mantra after the Tiru Mantra and (by my reading) after the invitatory first line of the Carama Śloka, then this obeisance, self-negation, is a second moment of praise and reflection on what it means to exist for God alone, after we have made our act of self-dedication to the Lord. Obeisance is not simply a good idea or a theological assertion; it also gives body and voice to a life of total dependence on the Lord. Such is the meaning of these repeated words; if, in our commentary, we read them over and over again, our response will be increasingly awakend to what it means to live entirely for God.

The Whole Dvaya Mantra

Given the fullness of meaning in the first line and the simple affirmation assigned to the second line (*Obeisance to Nārāyaṇa with Śrī*), as a commentator Deśika is concerned to justify on literary and theological grounds the purpose of the second line, in light of the first line and the already familiar Tiru Mantra (*Obeisance to Nārāyaṇa*) as well. Or, the second line might appear to supersede the first line (as might the *Tiru Mantra*), since the act of worship might be taken as tantamount to the act of taking refuge. Since by the tradition of Indian exegesis, mere repetition is a flaw, the two clauses of the Mantra have to have distinct purposes that justify their presence.

Deśika's strategy is evident in an earlier passage in Chapter 28 where, reflecting on *I approach for refuge*, he explains the interrelation of the two clauses. Both seem to be prayers for the same desired result, that Nārāyaṇa with Śrī should replace all other means and results. Yet there is no redundancy: were surrender merely a means to another goal, such as enhanced devotion, it would seem sensible enough to pray also for the speedy arrival of the desired goal that would arrive after the means was performed. But in this case, surrender to Nārāyaṇa and Śrī is not merely instrumental to any anticipated further action or further goal:

> For the person who has nothing and surrenders the entire burden, the act of taking refuge should not be subsidiary to any additional means;[78] to insure this, the object of refuge Himself takes the place of other means *and* gives the result.[79]

So one is simply praying that Nārāyaṇa and Śrī take the place of all other means; this divine initiative is good in itself, and is itself the desired

[78] For this person who has nothing and performs the laying down of the burden, taking refuge is not accessory to some other means.

[79] 753/451

result: the way is the goal. When one begs Nārāyaṇa and Śrī to take the place of all other means and to be the highest goal, we stress in distinct moments of prayer specific aspects of that divine finality. If the first line stresses that Nārāyaṇa and Śrī are the means, the second emphasizes that Nārāyaṇa and Śrī themselves are the goal:

> I make this surrender of the burden of protecting my self, so that You, who stand in the place of other means for me who has nothing, may [at this very moment] give me the specific result [which too is nothing but You].[80]

Deśika drives home the point with further quotations that emphasize complete surrender of self to Nārāyaṇa and Śrī:

> When I offer myself to Nārāyaṇa with Śrī, as it says,
>
> Right now, I am offered – by myself,[81]
>
> then the burden of protection and the result of self-protection belong to the Lord. As it also says,[82]
>
> What is surrendered is what needs protection...[83]
>
> and
>
> I am Your burden.[84]

The person reciting the Dvaya Mantra then belongs entirely to them, and that new state is confirmed in the second line of the Mantra, *obeisance to Nārāyaṇa with Śrī.*

At the chapter's end, Deśika offers three Sanskrit verses in which he again testifies that he is reading the Mantra in accord with the dedicated and compassionate teachers who exemplify what they teach, the power of the Mantra to change lives. I include here just the first:[85]

> Their inner selves won over by detachment,
> the Lord won over by their taking refuge,

[80] 754/451-452. Deśika draws a ritual analogy: "Just as a person offering an oblation says, 'This is for Indra, not for me,' so too here one offers up the very source of the burden, saying, 'I am for Nārāyaṇa with Śrī,' and then one breaks the connection of the action with oneself, by asserting [in the second line], 'This is not mine.' This is the proper sentiment that makes the offering coherent. Accordingly, the first line is about the five aids subsidiary [to the act of taking refuge], while the second expounds that primary reality [toward Whom everything points]." The five subsidiary aids are: 1. choosing what is suitable to pleasing the Lord, 2. rejecting what is not suited to pleasing him, 3. a realization of one's pitifulness and need, 4. great faith (confidence in the power of taking refuge), and 5. choosing a protector who can make refuge possible.

[81] *Stotraratna* 52

[82] 760-761/458-459

[83] *Ahirbudhnya Saṃhitā* 52.36

[84] *Stotraratna* 60; 761/459

[85] The second verse considers several ways of parsing the multiple words of the Mantra. The third cleverly enumerates the complexity, conciseness, and communal power

as teachers won over by compassion,
they teach all this.[86]

This recalls the emphasis on veneration of the guru at the chapter's beginning, a theme key to the whole *Essence*: personal contact with persons who have experienced the truth of the tradition is prerequisite to knowing fully the truth of the Mantra and in a way that changes one's life; in turn, those who have learned in this way are those able to pass on the truth to the next generation.

The closing Tamil verse aptly encapsulates the power of reciting the Mantra, as it makes available the values its expresses:

Joining as one the two parts of this Mantra that are to be recited together,
Tirumāl aids us by His grace and
we take refuge at His feet and so
we come near to this Lord of the Lady in the lotus,
with a flawless intention to serve in every way in that good, bright Land:[87]
how to do all this, we discover right here [in this Mantra].[88]

By contrast, the closing Sanskrit verse indicates more substantively a hierarchy of religious values and means, culminating in this Mantra:

Than Vedānta, no greater scripture;
than Kṛṣṇa the killer of the demon Madhu, no greater reality;
than His devotees, no holier place;
than that which pleases them, no purer dwelling place;
than pure being, no greater health;
than devotion to those who are awakened, no greater cause of awakening;
than liberation, no greater happiness;
than uttering the Dvaya Mantra, no greater means of welfare.[89]

of the Mantra for the community gathered at Śrīraṅgam: "This *one double* Mantra – *triple* in parts / By which the *fourth* state is easily attained / Containing *five* distinct points / Connected with the *six* defined subsidiaries / Great like the *seven* oceans / Explaining the *eight* syllables – Produces the *ninth* rasa / For good people in Śrīraṅgam." (764/463). The commentators decipher the numerical riddle more or less as follows. In the Dvaya Mantra, there is *one* statement uttered in a *double* Mantra divisible into *three* parts. The Mantra offers the *fourth* and final state of liberation beyond all conditioning; it explains the *five* truths (the Lord, conscious beings, the means, the result, the obstacles), and the *six* component parts of taking refuge (that is, the act of refuge and its five subsidiary aids). Its greatness is comprehensive, like that of all *seven* oceans; it also explains the *eight*-syllable (Tiru) Mantra, and it leads to the ultimate *ninth* "taste" (*rasa*), the *śānta rasa* (ultimate contentment) which is the state of those who take refuge with the Lord in Śrīraṅgam, thus finding rest from their strivings.

86 764/462-463

87 The highest place, Heaven (Vaikuṇṭha).

88 764-765/463

89 765/463-464

Even if this verse cannot be taken to indicate some definitive superiority of the Dvaya Mantra over the Tiru Mantra and Carama Śloka – as we have seen, those Mantras too are praised as the best of mantras – the verse nonetheless indicates that nothing outweighs the recitation of the Dvaya Mantra as the religious act most efficacious with respect to human welfare.

> *Reflection*: The Dvaya Mantra encodes important values/truths of the tradition; it also balances simplicity in practice – a single utterance of the Mantra is quite sufficient – with the value of a meticulously clear understanding of each and every word. Deśika himself and careful readers following his example are challenged to read the Mantra meticulously and to the best effect, as a subtly composed confession of total dependence on Śrī and Nārāyaṇa and, by way of the Mantra, the inculcation of attitudes preparatory to the act and utterance of surrender. When one finally utters the Mantra, theology, practice, and transformative insight all come together in the instant of recitation: taking refuge, union, and delight in service occur all at once. If as Christian readers we end up repeating the Dvaya Mantra – in reading, or by way of experiment, aloud – we are at least implicitly affirming all that is of value in the Śrīvaiṣṇava tradition. The words of Rāmānuja cited several times over by Deśika may now apply to us, as the Mantra works to good effect even when we have come from a different place, had different teachers, affirm different truths in a different Faith: "Whatever the manner of your utterance…" Both the act of refuge and the subsequent affirmation that God is the goal as well as the way are then ours as well, truths we would be hard pressed to find reasons to deny.

III. The Dvaya Mantra in the Larger Narrative of Surrender in the *Essence*

As was the case with the Tiru Mantra and Carama Śloka, this intense, close reading of the Dvaya Mantra in Chapter 28 is enhanced by occasional significant reference to the Mantra elsewhere in the *Essence*. As in previous chapters, several examples of this wider reference must suffice, to give us a sense of the "life" of the Mantra in the *Essence* and the Śrīvaiṣṇava community.

First, in Chapter 3, Deśika says that the distinctive Viśiṣṭādvaita (and Śrīvaiṣṇava) teaching that the Lord and all beings are by analogy in a soul-body relationship[90] is a truth already inscribed in the three Mantras. *Aum* and *Nārāyaṇāya* in the Tiru Mantra reveals the truth, showing

[90] A body-soul relationship, in the sense of the total dependence of the one on the other, even if the two remain distinct.

the orientation of all beings to the Lord. The Dvaya Mantra, "the jewel among Mantras," is the Mantra of performance, showing what is crucial in actually taking refuge:[91]

> The Dvaya Mantra's first line illumines the fact there is no other refuge; the second, that there is no other goal; both clauses, that there is no other foundation. The same points are made in the Carama Śloka too, explicitly and implicitly.

Lest the two Mantras seem identical, Deśika continues:

> [In the Carama Śloka] we find specified the means that is to be accomplished if one is to win over the Lord. By the Dvaya Mantra, we learn what needs to be meditated on during the time of performance.

By contrast, the Tiru Mantra shows us the truths which are acted upon in the Dvaya Mantra:

> The Tiru Mantra, like a small mirror illumining large objects, succinctly illumines all the prerequisite truths.[92]

The Tiru Mantra reveals the truth, and the Carama Śloka indicates what is to be done; but it is the Dvaya Mantra that is operative during the act of taking refuge.

We can also understand better the reasons for Deśika's appreciation of the Dvaya Mantra if we look at Chapters 11 and 12, the two chapters expounding the context and performance of the taking refuge.[93]

In Chapter 11,[94] Deśika lists the five aids to the act of refuge: 1. choosing what is suitable to pleasing the Lord, 2. rejecting what is not suitable to pleasing him, 3. a realization of one's pitifulness and need of help, 4. great faith (confidence in the power of taking refuge), and 5. choosing a protector who can make refuge possible. A key goal of Chapter 11 is to bolster confidence that taking refuge is plausible, even if we are daunted by the prospect of standing as a weak and flawed human before a perfect deity. It makes the case by investigating the nature of the divine person to whom surrender is made. In the middle of the chapter,[95] Deśika raises a series of theological problems regarding the plausibility of

[91] Cited already in Chapter 1.

[92] 54/27

[93] Chapter 10 too is essential to understanding the act of taking refuge, since it highlights the two essential characteristics in accord with which a person becomes ready to take refuge: having-no-resources and having-nowhere-to-go-for-refuge.

[94] This chapter is entitled, "The Classification of Subsidiary Aids"

[95] 219-225/121-125

surrender, and sketches the right solution – taking refuge with confidence – by holding up the examples of Sītā and Vibhīṣaṇa. Sītā protects even the demonesses holding her in captivity in Laṅkā, despite the fact that they have been hostile to her. Vibhīṣaṇa, who is entirely vulnerable and without resources after fleeing Laṅkā (and his brother, King Rāvaṇa) risks everything by taking refuge at the feet of Rāma. Both examples demonstrate the power of refuge in improbable circumstances, and so encourage the reader to believe that she or he too can confidently approach Nārāyaṇa (Rāma) with Śrī (Sītā). In the course of each example, Deśika documents the five subsidiary aids, but then also correlates them to the Dvaya Mantra, which speaks the possibility and plausibility of surrender to the perfect God:

Choosing what is suitable		Śrī
Rejecting what is unsuitable		Nārāyaṇa[96]
Great faith	faith in the mediator	pra-
	faith in its proper form	-pad[97]
pitifulness		śaraṇam
Choosing the protector		śaraṇaṃ prapadye[98]

Thus, the Mantra, which is necessary to the performance of taking refuge, also creates the requisite psychological and spiritual conditions in which refuge comes to be seen as a plausible undertaking. Ideally, the devout practitioner learns the theology, remembers the stories of Sītā and Vibhīṣaṇa, and grows firm in the truth of the former and spirit of the latter by reciting the Dvaya Mantra over and over.

In Chapter 12,[99] we find a discussion of refuge as an act articulated in accord with the Dvaya Mantra and ordinarily performed with an utterance of the Mantra. The chapter begins with this verse:

> When something is desired but hard to gain
> by oneself or in some other way,
> then one lays down that burden with a plea (for help) –

[96] 219/121

[97] *pra-* and *pad*, the prefix and root of the word *prapadye* (I approach) in the mantra.

[98] 222/124; "I approach for refuge."

[99] Entitled, "Taking Refuge, with Its Subsidiary Aids"

> that is what they[100] call "taking refuge,"
> and this they recognize as the defining insight:
> "After this, irrespective of our effort,
> by Your own self my goal must be achieved."[101]

Effectiveness in taking refuge depends on the Lord, not on human effort. Much of Chapter 12 is about the act of taking refuge, surrendering the burden:

> In implementing the specific reflection enjoined where it says,
>
> > Let him give himself over to Me,[102]
>
> I no longer belong to myself. Accordingly, the Lord, who is free and to whom all belongs, offers protection to me, even as His personal goal. I am entirely dependent, I exist for His sake, I am fit for no one else, dependent on no one else. As it says,
>
> > Even my own self is not mine,[103]
>
> and so I do not belong to myself. I cannot even say that there is anything that belongs to me unconditionally. As it says,
>
> > This embodied one is dependent on another, like a lump of clay,
> > impotent with respect to its own protection:
> > what basis then does it have for protecting others?[104]
>
> I am not suited to protect myself and those things said to be mine, as if a person who is free and the primary recipient of the fruits [of his action]. My self and all that is mine are His, as the discerning Uparicaravasu understood when he said,
>
> > My self, kingdom, wealth, wife, vehicles – all these are for the Lord.[105]

This radical change in perspective is the faith theologically and practically voiced in the Dvaya Mantra:

> Thus, in the first line of the Dvaya Mantra that deals with the means, surrender to the Lord of the burden of one's own protection is accompanied by the realization that one exists entirely for Him. All this is to be understood from the verb [*I approach*] in its proximity to the word *refuge*. This understanding gives rise to the act of choosing a protector, an act preceded by great faith.[106]

[100] "They," the wise teachers of the tradition.

[101] 231/126

[102] *Satyakī Tantra*

[103] *Mahābhārata, Śānti Parva* 25.19

[104] *Itihāsa Samuccaya* 17.63

[105] 232-234/128-129; *Mahābhārata, Śānti Parva* 343.24. Uparicaravasu was a king who, cursed, gave up all his possessions, family, and own self, and found God; he then received it all back again.

[106] 237/131.

Taking refuge, even with its subsidiary aids, occurs as a single event,[107] a carefully prepared single moment, with a single utterance of the Mantra:

> This enactment, with its five subsidiary helps, is the laying down of the burden of protecting oneself, an act which is the origin of giving up both one's own proper form and also the results [of one's action]. This is accompanied by the utterance of the Dvaya Mantra, preceded by meditation on choosing what is suitable[108] acts of reverence for the succession of gurus, and so forth. And this too is in turn preceded by giving up the idea of being a doer, giving up the idea of "mine," giving up the result, and giving up all means to obtaining that result.[109]

Deśika makes clear the rationale for taking refuge, the faith and love voiced in the climactic moment that includes recitation of the Dvaya Mantra:

> The Lord is the means to this result. Because of His innate love,[110] He has been the primal cause for all these things, beginning with giving us our body and senses, up to and including this utterance of the Dvaya Mantra. His is a specific intent preceded by graciousness; He is the immediate cause, the means for persons who have no other means.[111]

Taking refuge is a heartfelt, intense act, as Deśika indicates in repeating the words of his esteemed teacher, Naṭātūr Ammāḷ:

> I have been wandering about this world from time without beginning, doing what does not please You, my God. From this day forward, I must do what pleases You, and I must cease what displeases You. But my hands are empty, I cannot attain You, my God; I see that You alone are the means. You must be my means! Hereafter, in the removal of what is not desirable

[107] He offers a further elaboration, including an analogy with the arrow: "And so, although the six subsidiary aids may be considered as distinct from one another in reflection on this Mantra, together they constitute a single mental act, just as ordinarily the various [word] meanings occurring in a sentence coalesce into the single meaning of that sentence... Therefore, in accord with the scriptures, the performance of the primary with its subsidiaries occurs all at once. An archer's shooting of an arrow to hit a target is constituted of several separate actions, and yet it is to be done all in one moment. It is known from revelation that surrendering the burden of protecting the self is like that." (237/131)

[108] And, presumably, the other four aids subsidiary to taking refuge.

[109] 238/132. Taking refuge is also heartfelt and intense, as the prayer of Naṭātūr Ammāḷ, cited earlier in this chapter, exemplifies. Although Naṭātūr Ammāḷ's words are not expressly those of the Dvaya Mantra and do not match it point for point – Śrī, for instance, is not mentioned at all – the prayer is taken to echo the Dvaya Mantra.

[110] *sahaja sauhārda*, "innate good-heartedness."

[111] 239/133

> or in the attainment of what is desirable – could anything be a burden to me?[112]

These words, it seems clear, are Naṭātūr Ammāḷ's formulation of the Dvaya Mantra – just as Rāmānuja found his own words for it in the *Śaraṇāgati Gadya*.

I briefly note four other passages, from Chapters 13, 14, 15, and 27. The power of the Mantra even in completing the promise of the Carama Śloka – *Do not grieve* – is indicated in Chapter 13,[113] where the utterance of the Dvaya Mantra, and what precedes and follows it, described:

> Rāmānuja summarized his reflection on the state of being one who has done all that had to be done when he said in the *Śaraṇāgati Gadya*,
>
> > Therefore without doubting that you know Me, see Me, and gain Me, you should therefore rejoice.[114]
>
> The meaning is as follows: Because of the Lord's punishment that is due to our transgressing His commands from time without beginning, we are in this world. But now, due to the Lord's compassion, which is ever seeking a pretext (for helping us), we have received the glance of a noble teacher, and so we enact taking refuge, reciting along with the teacher's recitation of the Dvaya Mantra.[115] After that, there is nothing lacking in our propitiation of the One with whom we have taken refuge. This consort of Śrī, upon whom all depends, extinguishes all the causes for punishment. For His own sake, He purifies His perfected devotees; for His own sake, He protects them. Therefore, have faith and be free of any burden.[116]

In the Dvaya Mantra is thus encoded an entire tradition of theology and devotion, such as should persuade the student and reader to become active participants in the tradition by learning the Dvaya Mantra and reciting it with a teacher, with a strong sense of belonging to the tradition and community, and with an ever clearer understanding of its meanings.

As we saw in Chapter 1, Chapter 14 lists signs indicative of the fact that one is firmly established with respect to the truth of reality (*tattva*), the means (*upāya*), and in one's focus on the final goal (*puruṣārtha*).

[112] 239/133

[113] "On the Person Who Has Done What Had to be Done"

[114] *Śaraṇāgati Gadya*, 42/20

[115] In the *Sārabodhinī* comment on this passage, Sri Srirangasankopa Yatindramahadesika says that the *act of taking refuge* in question here is *ukti-prapatti*, enacted through the utterance of the Dvaya Mantra, evidently following along with one's teacher.

[116] 250-251/138-139. Deśika ends with a reference to the final words of the Carama Śloka: "Knowing this, one becomes bereft of burden. This is the correct meaning of the words spoken by the one with whom one takes refuge, 'Do not grieve.'"

To the previously described Tiru Mantra, we can now add the Dvaya Mantra, as illustrative of the means:

Chapter 27	Chapter 28
tattva (truth)	*upāya (means)*
knowing the self, detached serenity with respect to bodily flaws and criticisms by others	knowing that only the Lord is one's resource, protector
compassion toward those who criticize	no longer fearing death but welcoming it as pleasing
remembrance of the help being given even by those who criticize	clarity in dependence on the protector
seeing that criticisms are really from the Lord who controls all	expending no effort in the work of self-protection
rejoicing that by these criticisms, karma is being expended	realizing that gaining the desirable and removing the undesirable are in God's hands

What is declared as true in the Tiru Mantra, is further nuanced as psychologically effective in the Dvaya Mantra.

In Chapter 15, Deśika describes how the person who has taken refuge should think, speak, and act. While the major portion of the chapter seems geared to the Carama Śloka, Deśika characterizes wrong and right speech respectively as "boasting of one's own excellence" and "reciting the Dvaya Mantra:"

> In order that our realization of pitifulness[117] not be dissipated, the most important thing *not* to say are words in praise of oneself; lest we repudiate firm establishment in the means, the main thing to say is the Dvaya Mantra: "Always uttering the Dvaya Mantra."[118]

Repetition of this Mantra is a remedy to pride, serving to purify and clarify one's intentions. It is the Mantra of spiritual healing.

Finally, in Chapter 27, Deśika explains that while the Tiru Mantra is instructive primarily regarding the most basic divine and human realities

[117] And thus of a profound need for God

[118] 290/158. The quotation is, as seen earlier in this chapter, from the *Śaraṇāgati Gadya*, 42/19.

and their interrelationship, this knowledge is insufficient for a full appropriation of the spiritual life. For this, the Dvaya Mantra is needed:

> Our predecessors have graciously said, "*Born* in the Tiru Mantra and *grown up* in the Dvaya Mantra, he becomes one *established solely* in the Dvaya Mantra."

That is:

> To be *born* here means that he leaves that state prior to when knowledge is born; as it says,
>
> Until then I was not born; after that birth, I do not forget.[119]
>
> That is, by his own desire, he belongs to no other, is dependent on no other, and on that basis has no other goal, no other refuge.
>
> To be *grown* means that due to distinct knowledge of this distinct topic[120] – what must be accomplished in accord with one's distinctive competence – one grasps the means.
>
> To be *established solely* in the Dvaya Mantra means that by meditation on the Dvaya Mantra he breaks his connection to other means and other goals, and is established firmly in the means and goal it indicates. In this way, the Tiru Mantra joined with the Dvaya Mantra shows the proper form, the means, and the human goal.[121]

The Tiru Mantra is powerful in its communication of knowledge, but for the way of living the truth and persisting in it, one turns to the Dvaya Mantra. Reciting it marks a definitive change in life; repeating it shapes a way of life.

IV. Reading the Dvaya Mantra from a Christian Perspective

1. Theological Insights and Concerns, for a Christian Reader

It will be obvious that the theological implications of the Dvaya Mantra – this most theologically interesting of mantras – are considerable; in it there are myriad theological insights that can be brought into interesting and fruitful proximity with Christian theological insights. Theologians of both traditions, who have taken the time to read each other's texts, have much to talk about.

Unlike in the preceding two chapters, we do not have here the comments of an Henri Le Saux (regarding *Abba, Father*) or of a Bede

119 *Tirucanda Viruttam* 64

120 That is, the Lord, who is revealed in the Dvaya Mantra to be the Means and Goal.

121 679/398-399. Oddly, the Carama Śloka seems not to be mentioned here.

Griffiths (regarding *Gītā* 18.66) to show us the way. The Dvaya Mantra seems thus far not to have been contemplated in a Christian context; perhaps it is too "interior" to the Śrīvaiṣṇava tradition for ready attention, and perhaps too richly complex for easy summation and simple parallels. Carefully read with a guide like Deśika, however, the Dvaya Mantra yields insights into divine initiative, human action, and the positive practice of religion and duty. Many of these insights can be appreciated and even appropriated by Christians.

We can quickly summarize some of the specifically theological dimensions of the Mantra:

1. Like the Tiru Mantra, the Dvaya Mantra offers insight into the nature of God (*Nārāyaṇa*) – particularly with respect to the practical concerns of those seeking liberation;
2. universal divine salvific action is specified through complex intermediate agencies, including the presence and work of a divine Person (*Śrīmat*);
3. divine transcendence is made accessible through sacramental immediacy (*caraṇau*);
4. God alone is our protection, our place of safety (*śaraṇam*);
5. taking refuge is a realization and response rooted in recognizing how we are and how God is (*prapadye*);
6. worship involves revising one's perspective on the world, such that everything is recast in terms of God, not self (*Śrīmate Nārāyaṇāya namaḥ*);
7. as a Mantra – by analogy, a prayer, words of spiritual practice – the Dvaya Mantra explains surrender to God and yet too enables people actually to surrender. Utterance comes first, as it were, paving the way for a theology that is rooted in religious practice: *lex orandi, lex credendi.*

Like the Tiru Mantra and the Carama Śloka, the Dvaya Mantra usefully encodes doctrine. It is a mnemonic inscribing theological themes such as I have suggested. Anyone can memorize and utter this Mantra, and by its utterance at least implicitly affirm its full theological and practical meaning, thus facilitating a larger and longer term commitment.

The issues of universality and particularity that arose in each of our preceding chapters, with respect to the identity of Nārāyaṇa and Kṛṣṇa, arises here again: is the Dvaya Mantra only for those who worship

"Nārāyaṇa with Śrī"? As we have seen (here and in Chapter 1), "Nārāyaṇa" carries with it a long list of universalizable meanings and implied attributes, but it still also has particular, specific reference: this is Nārāyaṇa, consort of Śrī, who has acted in specific ways, loved the world through specific deeds, become embodied as Rāma and Kṛṣṇa, and remains accessible in temples in south India and elsewhere. Similarly, *Śrī* can indicate the divine glory and power, introducing a kind of "Trinitarian" distinction within the Godhead, and giving personal form to the graciousness of God; yet too, she is also the Goddess who is the consort of Nārāyaṇa. So here again we encounter a gradation in specificity analogous to the move from speech about "God" and "the Christian God," possessed of various attributes appropriate to divine perfection, such as omniscience and omnipotence, divine wisdom, speech, and self-presentation, to a more specific confession of "the God and Father of our Lord Jesus Christ, Jesus who died for us on the cross and sent His Spirit upon us." But even if the most specific and precious truths of a tradition seem inaccessible, and even if these are as it were seamlessly woven together with the more general truths, nevertheless we do have choices to make about how much of the meaning of the Dvaya Mantra to appropriate, and how much to leave untouched, as it were inaccessible to Christian appropriation.

Since the Dvaya Mantra is a performative utterance – its words declare the speaker's surrender to God as this surrender takes place – understanding and appreciating it also bring us closer to enacting the surrender it articulates. The challenge of our commentary is therefore pushed to yet another level, as we have not only to understand and agree or not, but also decide to what extent we are implicitly or consciously making the Mantra's words our own words. To engage in the full surrender intended by the Mantra as a Śrīvaiṣṇava confession of faith will of course appear a daunting level of involvement – even if we should admit that *any* act of total surrender to God is a daunting possibility.

But again, cautious optimism is legitimate. Should it turn out that at their best both the Catholic Christian and the Śrīvaiṣṇava Hindu share a desire for this transformative, radical act of surrender, desire the grace to act accordingly, and offer profound words expressive of this surrender, then this is a spiritual convergence of great importance, seemingly of greater importance than any of the differences that will still remain regarding God's identity and how we are to think about and picture Her/Him. If we feel the pull of the Mantra and yet decline to make its words the words of our own surrender, nonetheless we have progressed greatly in interreligious empathy, to the edge of participation.[122]

2. Resonances in the Christian Tradition

As in the previous chapters, here too we can also seek meditative scriptural parallels for our Mantra, finding in recitation and meditation a different kind of access to what the Dvaya Mantra means. If we see surrender to God as key to the Mantra, an obvious parallel to the Dvaya Mantra might be, for instance, any of the vow formulas used in different communities of religious men and women in the Christian context. For example, we have the Jesuit vow formula, addressed to God, in the presence of Jesus, Mary, and the entire heavenly assembly:

> Almighty and eternal God, I understand how unworthy I am in your divine sight. Yet I am strengthened by your infinite compassion and mercy and am moved by the desire to serve you. I vow to your divine majesty, before the most holy virgin Mary and the entire heavenly court, perpetual poverty, chastity, and obedience in the Society of Jesus. I promise that I will enter this same Society to spend my life in it forever. I understand all these things according to the Constitutions of the Society of Jesus. Therefore by your boundless goodness and mercy and through the blood of Jesus Christ, I humbly ask that you judge this total commitment of myself acceptable; and, as you have freely given me the desire to make this offering, so also give me the abundant grace to fulfill it.[123]

Or, staying with New Testament texts, as I prefer in the limited context of this book, we can seek out words of surrender, such as the following. First, we have Mary's words of radical trust:[124]

> Be it done unto me according to your word.[125]

Or, in the midst of the ministry of Jesus, the words of Peter:

> So Jesus asked the twelve, "Do you also wish to go away?" Simon Peter answered him, "*Lord, to whom can we go? You have the words of eternal life.* We have come to believe and know that you are the Holy One of God."[126]

[122] See Clooney, forthcoming a., Chapter 4.

[123] To this profession is added the following information: "City… in the chapel of…, on (day, month, year). (Signatures of the one making and the one receiving the vows)." The novice pronouncing the vows also adds his own name in the first line of the vow fomula. The formula is found in *Practica Quaedam* 51, p. 14.

[124] Including several texts already noted in previous chapters.

[125] *Luke* 1.37

[126] *John* 6.67-68

Or, as in Chapter 1 with respect to the Tiru Mantra, the words of Jesus in the Garden:

> And he said, "*Abba, Father*, all things are possible for you. Remove this cup from me. *Yet not what I will, but what you will.*"[127]

Finally, and perhaps most potently, we might select this basic and profound utterance of Jesus himself, at his most dire moment:

> Father, into your hands I commit my spirit.[128]

I have settled on this last passage for reflection along with the Dvaya Mantra in part because of what I have learned in a related project, in which I have read the *Essence* along with the *Treatise on the Love of God* of St. Francis de Sales. This classic of spirituality also builds with increasing force to complete surrender to God. In the climactic pages of the key Book IX of the *Treatise*, de Sales identifies the Lucan text I have just cited as expressive of Jesus' quintessential surrender to God, Jesus' most articulate and decisive expression:[129]

> For though he cries out: *My God, my God, why have You forsaken me?*[130] yet this was to let us understand the reality of the anguish and bitternesses of his soul, and not to violate the most holy indifference in which he was. This he showed very soon afterwards, concluding his whole life and his passion with those incomparable words: *Father, into Your hands I commend my spirit.*[131]

All that needs be said about surrender to God as an ideal and existential state, however deep and expansive the theological meanings might be, is already inscribed in these words of surrender. Such words of Jesus serve as a Mantra very near to the Dvaya Mantra. And so we might have:

Father, into Your hands I commend my spirit.	I approach for refuge the feet of Nārāyaṇa with Śrī, obeisance to Nārāyaṇa with Śrī.

Reading these texts together, differences remain evident: only by way of grace does the Christian reader take as her own the words of Jesus, whereas the Dvaya Mantra's word are everyone's words; the existential situations of the now paired Śrīvaiṣṇava and Christian Mantras are surely different, even if the person reciting the Dvaya Mantra too is on the edge of despair; and some complex reflection is required in pondering whether the Holy

[127] *Mark* 14.36
[128] *Luke* 23.46
[129] See Clooney, forthcoming a, Chapter 4.
[130] *Matthew* 27.46

Spirit, though not mentioned, plays a role like that of Śrī, in the prayer of Jesus. Nevertheless, in commentarial close reading this kind of textual proximity does come to the fore, and even as we resist equating the two texts, we can find in a shared, double reading of them the possibility of a deeper appreciation of each in the light of the other and, in ourselves as vulnerable readers, a growing sense of the intensity of the surrender to which both texts call those who dare to read them and utter them aloud.

3. Praying with the Dvaya Mantra?

We can move quickly then from reflection on texts of prayer placed and reflected on together, to the possibility of Christian prayer with a mantra, now the Dvaya Mantra. The Tiru Mantra is dedicated to the exposition of the truths of the tradition, and the Carama Śloka in its first line voices a divine invitation to take refuge, addressed to the person who is beginning to realize the truth of the Tiru Mantra. The Tiru Mantra expresses a declaration about how reality is, and the Carama Śloka requires that we listen to the voice of God. But the Dvaya Mantra is comprised of performative words that give voice to – and then make occur – a radical life decision: those who would utter the Dvaya Mantra, "whatever the manner of your utterance" as Rāmānuja put it,[132] are choosing to engage (or not) in radical surrender to Nārāyaṇa with Śrī, mindful of the particular identity of these deities, but yet too of the universal divine qualities manifest in them as the Śrīvaiṣṇava tradition has understood them.

In the passion and intensity of this Mantra we find the utterance of a radical choice, an assent that reaches where reason alone cannot reach, where doctrinal differences do not entirely determine significance, and where even the most important of religious differences do not necessarily predict any single ending to the process of spiritual learning and the prayer that should follow from such learning. The dynamic possibility of the Dvaya Mantra is caught in the act, as experienced in the existential situation of extreme need and extreme desire, of having to depend entirely on Nārāyaṇa and Śrī. It is, therefore, a prayer that demands great commitment, in addition to openness to the ideas of the Śrīvaiṣṇava tradition. Dare we pray with these words?

As in theology, so too in practice: because the Dvaya Mantra is rich in meaning and can be appropriated in various degrees of its fullness, it

[131] IX.15, 804/406. Mackey translation, slightly modified.

[132] In his *Śaraṇāgati Gadya*. See page 112 above.

would seem that the Christian can pray with the Dvaya Mantra, even if not quite in the same way as a Śrīvaiṣṇava. We allow some of its meanings to create fragile new possibilities even as we also draw the line at the edge of an intensity of prayer that is still not possible, but nevertheless nearer, because we have read, understood, and come to respect what we have learned. While a Christian utterance of the Dvaya Mantra may remain incomplete, it nonetheless becomes for the Christian a real prayer that merits utterance. With the Dvaya Mantra on our minds, perhaps on our lips, we surrender to God, as it were borrowing for the moment the insight and energy of this Mantra – even while admitting that the words of Jesus will always mean more to us, more deeply and absolutely. In this unsettled but richly promising environment, we no longer have to exclude or distance ourselves from the Dvaya Mantra, a prayer rooted in the tradition of Deśika, Naṭātūr Ammāḷ, Rāmānuja, and Śaṭakōpaṉ; in some way, it is now our prayer too, "whatever the manner of that utterance".

Drawing on our choices from Chapters 2 and 3, we now have a still richer site for prayer:

Abba, Father.	Obeisance to Nārāyaṇa.
If you would be perfect, go, sell what you possess and give to the poor...	Having completely given up all *dharmas*, to Me alone come for refuge...
Father, into Your hands I commit my spirit.	I approach for refuge the feet of Nārāyaṇa with Śrī; obeisance to Nārāyaṇa with Śrī.

V. Looking Ahead

The conversation with God that the Mantras propose to us is nearly done: in the Tiru Mantra, we find the already true, given fact of the orientation of reality to God, and the Mantra is a free affirmation of that reality; in the first part of the Carama Śloka, we see and hear the divine invitation to the recitant of the Tiru Mantra to respond by an act of complete trust, refuge at the Lord's feet; and the Dvaya Mantra is the recitant's response, the taking of refuge along with a reaffirmation of the obeisance already uttered in the Tiru Mantra. And yet there is more, a final divine word to this person, a final divine response that is the further promise of liberation and the ending of grief. This is the message of the latter portion of the Carama Śloka: *I will free you from all your sins. Do not grieve.*

Chapter 4

TO LIVE IN FREEDOM: THE CARAMA ŚLOKA'S SECOND LINE

...you will have treasure in heaven; and come, follow Me.

...from all sins I will make you free.
Do not grieve.

Reflection: Even the ideal confession and act of surrender to God, the quintessential human response, does not end the story. God always has the last word, the word that brings about the full transformation of the human condition. For Christians, in the end God speaks in order to make us free, promising us a life already in the kingdom of God, a life of discipleship with Christ, and in receipt of the Spirit. The second line of the Carama Śloka – "The Last Verse" – too is a final word on what God will do, in liberating humans for freedom and from fear and grief. Hearing Kṛṣṇa's words then is still deeper practice in learning to listen, an occasion for seeing again what we expect if we are truly listening to God.

I. Introduction

...ahaṃ tvā sarvapāpebhyo mokṣayiṣyāmi | mā śucaḥ
...*aham* – I; *tvā* – you; *sarvapāpebhyo* – from all sins; *mokṣayiṣyāmi* – I will set free; *mā* – do not; *śucaḥ* – grieve

...From all sins I will make you free. Do not grieve.

In light of the Dvaya Mantra and the act of surrender enacted in accord with it, we can now return to the Carama Śloka in order to appreciate its second line, what I am reading as a final and definitive divine response to the taking of refuge.[1] The person who hears this divine response, after

[1] Again, my reading is a variant with respect to the Śrīvaiṣṇava tradition, which usually reads the entire Carama Śloka after the Dvaya Mantra.

uttering and coming to depend on the Dvaya Mantra, is drawn into a new state of freedom from sin, fear and grief. Accordingly, we will also notice in a special way Deśika's emphasis on the ethical implications of this final word regarding how people are to live after radical surrender, in the new freedom given by God.[2]

1. The Carama Śloka's Second Line as Verse 18.66b of the *Bhagavad Gītā*

But we first must recall the basic meaning of the second line of the *Gītā* 18.66 – as a *Gītā* verse – thus completing the review begun at the beginning of Chapter 2.

From all sins I will make you free. Do not grieve. This second line too is in direct address: Kṛṣṇa (I, *aham*) speaks to Arjuna (you, *tvā*). Perhaps this familiarity and directness remind us of the particularity of the speaker and hearer and, most importantly, the direct, uninterrupted communication of the one with the other.[3] Here too, the line informs us in two ways: first, it tells us what God will do: *From all sins I will make you free.* Second, it tells us how the human hearing these words and receiving this grace ought to be, feel, and act: *Do not grieve.*

In response to the divine invitation in the first line of 18.66, Arjuna becomes ready for a refuge that is also a release from *sin* (*pāpa*). It is frequently noted that Hindus do not share precisely a Biblical or Christian notion of sin; we know that "sin" should not be casually introduced into Hindu texts. But the *Gītā*'s use of *pāpa* is rich enough in nuance that it includes much of what Christians mean by sin. The word refers to the obstacles, flaws, faults that interrupt the movement toward God, actions arising from ignorance, and the delusion furthered by those actions. These flaws are spiritual and moral, to be sure, yet in certain ways also material, liable to taint and pollution. Included too is the bondage of lesser goods, merit (*puṇya*) that is as binding as sin (*pāpa*).

Kṛṣṇa's liberative act is a *freeing-from*: *mokṣayiṣyāmi*, from your sins I will make you free. Only in 18.66 in the *Gītā* is this verb used as a transitive finite verb; liberation itself, however nuanced it may be epistemologically, in terms of self-knowledge, and within the broader Indian debates about liberation (*mokṣa*), is something Kṛṣṇa does. When he promises to make Arjuna free, he shifts to his own domain that freedom

[2] See Clooney in Cornille 2006.

[3] Signaled clearly in the Sanskrit, as the *aham* and the *tvā* – I, you – stand next to one another.

which had previously been viewed as the responsibility and inner potential of the ascetic or meditator. Agency has clearly shifted to the Lord, who intends to bring about the needed liberation from sins. After taking refuge with the Lord, there is nothing to do but to allow God to act as God promises to act – and yet again, thereafter to act accordingly.

The command at the end of this second line, *Do not grieve* (*mā śucaḥ*), may be taken as an allusion to the grief that paralyzed Arjuna at the *Gītā*'s beginning and that is now finally banished. But it is also a grief that now includes the human situation as viewed in light of the entirety of the *Gītā*. Grief is a paralyzing condition rooted in confusion about self, action, and duty; it disables the person who should be doing his or her dharmic work for the sake of the world. But, by the liberative power of Kṛṣṇa, all obstacles are removed, and with them grief about the human condition. Our sorrow turned into joy, we begin to live a more subtle state of spiritual freedom.

2. The Carama Śloka's Second Line in the *Aṣṭaślokī* of Parāśara Bhaṭṭar

Turning then to an exegesis of this second line as part of the Carama Śloka and to be read in that distinctive context, let us begin by recalling Parāśara Bhaṭṭar's seventh and eighth verses in the *Aṣṭaślokī*, the former of which we have already commented on in Chapter 2. Verse 7 is Kṛṣṇa's word:

> You have completely given up all that *dharma*
> which had been expounded by Me for the sake of reaching Me;
> anguished, now make the determination
> that I alone am your refuge, your way to attaining Me;

The second part of Verse 7 most clearly paraphrases the divine initiative so prominent in the second line of the Carama Śloka:

> for I, full of all knowledge and all else too,
> will make you, thus determined,
> free of all obstacles to attaining Me.
> So be without grief.

As a still further response that echoes the Dvaya Mantra in addressing Kṛṣṇa, Verse 8 signals the listener's acceptance of his word and an urgent request that Kṛṣṇa do as he promises:

> "I have realized my dependence on You;
> I have no ability to perform those means, rites, etc.,
> nor to give them up, nor even to take refuge –

Grief then marks the difficult situation in which the speaker finds himself:

> "so I am indeed afflicted with sorrow;

But even in this dire situation, the speaker is already transformed, and so a prayer and testimony of faith follow, concluding the verse and the *Aṣṭaślokī*:

> "but I have this knowledge[4] –
> so now be the destroyer of all my sins;"
> speaking thus, I am steadfast,
> remembering Your last word, O Charioteer.

These words both acknowledge and expect the act of Kṛṣṇa, the liberation from sin and grief he promises.

Our emphasis in this chapter is this latter dynamic, Deśika's view of the human response to the liberative act of Kṛṣṇa and, even more particularly, the way of life presumed to ensue upon the liberative transformation of the person who has surrendered to the Lord. For if, as we saw in Chapter 2, Deśika is concerned about the maintenance of social order in light of Kṛṣṇa's call to radical surrender, he is also concerned about the positive, integral way of life that ensues upon divine action. All of this is the topic of the second line.

II. Exegeting the Second Line of the Carama Śloka

I: *aham*

Deśika discovers several nuances in the *I* (*aham*) at the beginning of the second line. At issue is the fact that *I will make you free* (*mokṣayiṣyāmi*) is grammatically first-person, and so the first person pronoun is not needed. *I* must therefore have some particular purpose:

> Since the verb *I will make you free* (*mokṣayiṣyāmi*) already expresses the first person, the additional *I* (*aham*), by its implied meanings, has the purpose of emphasizing His power to achieve what is impossible and the like, all of which contribute to His act of freeing from all sins... The primary force of the word *I* is His innate compassion, etc.; auxiliary to this is that special grace which is at the root of taking refuge; out in front stands His freedom, such as removes all obstacles without any particular instigation.[5]

[4] Of the Lord as means to liberation.

[5] 875-876/529

The image is that of an army with primary, secondary, and vanguard forces. The divine *I* is singularly suited to the event of taking refuge – for in that *I* is manifest transformative power, compassion, grace, and the freedom to bring about refuge even when the person in question has not merited this divine favor in any particular way.

you: *tvā*

Explicating the *you* (*tvā*) even more simply and to the point, Deśika rehearses the orientation of the self to God, already well-established with reference to the Tiru Mantra and the self's inability to reach God except by divine guidance, as is known from the Dvaya Mantra. By Kṛṣṇa's instruction, the listener's consciousness is gradually transformed:

> In accord with a series of teachings beginning with these words,
> Never was there a time when I was not,
> nor you, nor these rulers of the earth,
> nor hereafter a time when we will not exist...[6]
> you become able to distinguish the three realities, the non-conscious, conscious, and the Lord; you come to know that human goals such as lordship, etc., are subject to flaws such as being puny, unstable, etc. All this becomes clear, and on that basis you begin to desire that highest human goal which is union with Me. In order then to end your connection to other, hard to accomplish means, you surrender your burden to Me who am the goal and who can end all obstacles. You thus become a person who has done all that needs to be done, and at this point you have no interest in doing other things that would be required to gain other results of any sort.[7]

That is, the *you* does not indicate every sinner in every situation; rather, it identifies the sinner who has taken refuge, who is realizing the truth about human reality and beginning to change, and who is thus open to receiving without obstacle the full liberative grace of the Lord.

From all sins: *sarva-pāpebhyo*

Within the context of the difference and yet close relationship between the *I* and the *you,* Deśika is primarily concerned to balance the irresistible divine intention to make the devout person definitively free, with the nearly inevitable human proclivity to continue sinning even after taking refuge.[8]

[6] *Gītā* 2.12. Deśika quotes only the first words.

[7] 876-877/529-530

[8] The deliberation on sin and the delicate balance between surrender of all responsibility to the Lord and enduring responsibility for sins committed after taking refuge occurs in *Essence* 18. See Clooney forthcoming c.

Sin before and after the taking of refuge is an issue that must be attended to. Deśika is succinct in explaining what sin (*pāpa*) is:

> *Sin* indicates the means to acquire things that are known from scripture to be "not beneficial," and this is the acquisition of what is not suitable and letting go of what is suitable.[9]

Sin is also taken to be comprehensive of both demerit (*pāpa*) and merit (*puṇya*) too:

> In this context *sin* also indicates worldly merits, with fruits deemed undesirable from the perspective of the person who desires liberation...[10] The word *sin* thus expresses the cause of bondage that takes the form of either merit or sin; the plural [*sins*] indicates the infinity of such *pāpa*.[11]

And finally, *all* [*from all sins*] serves

> to connect the mass of sin back to what are both the cause and effect of that karma which blocks attaining [the Lord]: ignorance, deep contrary tendencies, the contrary desire, and even the connection with material nature in its gross and subtle forms.[12]

In previous chapters we have already seen that Deśika prizes the paradoxically continuing freedom of the person who has surrendered responsibility to the Lord. As we have already seen in Chapter 2, this is a major point regarding the first imperative in the Carama Śloka – *to Me alone come for refuge* – since such an imperative makes sense only if there is in the human person a capacity and a freedom in accord with which one can decide to take refuge or not. Here too, in explaining what liberation from sin is all about,[13] Deśika goes out of his way to stress the need of the person who has taken refuge to continue choosing to refrain from sinful activity, lest unfavorable results accrue. Although God is most tolerant, he does not delight in sin:

> It has been said,
>
> The faults of the person who has taken refuge are
> like the dirt on the body of one loved most dearly, or slime on a body of a calf.[14]

[9] 877/530; "suitable" with respect to pleasing and reaching the Lord, and "unsuitable" in the same regard.

[10] 877/530. This is a reference to the first two of the five aids subsidiary to taking refuge. See Chapter 3, pp. 130,133.

[11] 878/531

[12] 878/531

[13] As in *Essence* 18

[14] Unidentified.

> But this means only that the Lord does not abandon evil people who take refuge – even if He does still chastise them. Were it to mean that deliberate sin is enjoyable to the Lord, then the person taking refuge would have to commit sins as often as possible.[15]

While those who have taken refuge are not in danger of falling into hells and thereafter suffering a doleful return to this world, since liberation and no more rebirth are certain; but the Lord still intervenes with instructive punishments that are not mortal wounds, just as a king may lightly punish his son or others of his own inner circle:

> The Lord's forgiveness is special, in that "the loss of an eye" can be counted a light punishment, similar to how a king might punish the transgression of the prince or others (in the royal family or palace). Visible misfortunes and the misfortune of hell are fitting punishments for sins, but specific statements indicate that the person taking refuge will not suffer the misfortunes of hell. But such statements do not exempt that person from misfortunes in this life. This is clear if one pays attention carefully: punishment does take place. Reasoning that contradicts (scriptural) statements in this regard leads nowhere.[16]

So why do the evil prosper? Actually, they do not; they miss out on more subtle spiritual pleasures and benefits, and suffer the sure judgment of the good and the wise:

> It is unconvincing to point out that some sinners, even after taking refuge, do not show remorse and do not repeat the act of taking refuge,[17] yet seem not even to suffer visible misfortunes such as blindness, the so-called lesser punishments. But they still suffer the three modes of afflictions,[18] varying in accord with the seriousness of the transgression, plus other afflictions: dullness in expected understanding,[19] interruptions and diminishments in their delight in experiencing the Lord here, interruptions in the delight of serving the Lord and the Lord's people, offences and the like with respect to the Lord and the Lord's people.[20] They also suffer censure, expulsion, and so forth, at the hands of the learned; their specific good works are destroyed, they lack respect from virtuous people, and become sorrowful when what

[15] 881-882/533

[16] 882/533-534

[17] It is a matter of debate among Śrīvaiṣṇavas whether a "second," "repeat" act of refuge is possible; Deśika is the leading proponent of the view that the repetition of the act of refuge is possible, even if the first act is sufficient, final, and irreversible. See *Essence* 18.

[18] Viraraghavacharya indicates that the three pertain to the self (*ādhyātmika*), to life in this world (*ādhibhautika*), and to divine matters (*ādhidaivika*).

[19] Wisdom such as would be expected after taking refuge.

[20] Perhaps, "inadvertent offenses"

> they wish for is destroyed. These and other such smaller misfortunes are commonly seen among such people.[21]

In a lovely Tamil verse that concludes the section on sin, Kṛṣṇa is shown again to be intervening personally in human lives, and particularly in the lives of devotees – who, as the verse's concluding question shows, remain free, able to decide their own destinies:

> With no obstacles blocking His intentions,
> the Lord instills all manner of intentions into those denying Him – yet blocks them too;
> now He has changed my intention regarding this world,
> He has drawn me into refuge,
> He has ended the wrath caused by deeds rooted in my past intentions,
> He has appeared before me, offering me liberation –
> "By your best intention,
> will the right moment for saying yes be today or tomorrow?"
> He asks, with a smile.[22]

Even after the divine action of taking over a person's burden, the Lord waits, to see when this person will become willing to allow this divine action to transform her or his life; even in sin, a person is free to accept grace and the freedom that comes with it.

I will make you free: *ahaṃ tvā mokṣayiṣyāmi*

In treating *I will make you free*, Deśika's exegesis predictably aims not only to emphasize the effectiveness of that divine act, but also to make clear the continuing relevance of human responsibility even after God has taken the initiative and changed everything. This is clear, when he glosses *mokṣayiṣyāmi* as "I will make you free *when you wish*,"[23] and it was clear in the verse just cited: "Will the right moment for saying yes be today or tomorrow?" The divine liberative act could take place anytime, now or in the past, but Deśika interprets the future tense as indicating that the divine liberative act will be conditioned on human cooperation with the divine initiative. He explains how the change in the Lord's attitude toward a person transforms the person and frees up her or his basic capacities:

> In this context, *freeing from all sins* means that the Lord leaves off His intent to punish, which had arisen because, from time without beginning, we had

21 882-883/533-534
22 885/536
23 886/536

done what is contrary.[24] By ending this punishment, He also ends the ignorance and other results produced by His punishment. The Lord's ending of His anger is specifically what is meant by the words,

> He should always do all works in dependence on Me;
> by My grace, he reaches the eternal, imperishable place.[25]

And so, the ending of this individual's ignorance and so forth also entails the expansion of his knowledge and so forth.[26]

Even if taking refuge is definitive immediately upon the act of self-surrender performed just once, the liberative experience can be described in stages, as taking refuge with the gracious Lord gradually overtakes and disperses residual karma:

> Things opposed to the means come to an end due to fitting causes.[27] Merit and demerit[28] capable of blocking attainment of the Lord, other than karma that is already working itself out, end without a trace when the means (refuge) is undertaken. Later unintentional sins that occur due to defects in time, place, etc., do not stick at all. Deliberate transgressions – aside from those committed in emergency[29] circumstances – are ended by specific reparations in accord with the agent's competence, and by specific light punishments imposed to instruct the person. A portion of the active karma becomes ripe in a convenient time[30] and then comes to an end due to (her or his) experience of just a portion of the karma, and due to intervening expiations. The remainder [of the karma] ends simply due to the greatness of the means.[31]

Subsequent deeds too have no lingering effects:

> This person is then no longer connected to the various subsequent merits that arise with double effects.[32] Various merits prior and subsequent [to taking refuge] that are conformable to the meditator's knowledge come to an end, since their result has appeared. As for subsequent intentionally gained merits that are not conformable to meditative knowledge, their

24 Contrary to the Lord's good purposes.

25 *Gītā* 18.56; "by My grace" are the only words Deśika cites.

26 887/537

27 Ramadesikacaryar mentions various fortuitous happenings that have good effects: finding a teacher, receiving the teacher's instruction, etc.

28 *Puṇya* and *pāpa*

29 These, as exceptional, have no bad effect.

30 Effects of karma that are already working themselves out will do so in ways convenient to the person involved, and not, as is usually the case, in ways convenient and inconvenient.

31 887-888/537-538

32 With the continuing after-effects (*bhāvanās*) related to both life in the world and to the merging knowledge of Brahman, the highest Reality.

> results are constricted.[33] Prior and posterior merits that are apt to meditative knowledge will have opportunity or not depending on the results of other acts that are in effect helpful or not;[34] they linger but without giving their results, and cease entirely at the last moment of life.[35]

Clearly, these passages are very technical, and would require more elaborate exegesis in light of the traditional commentaries to become clear; and still more details of this sort follow regarding the mechanics of the distribution of karma. But it is important to recognize that Deśika's meticulous analysis is driven by his realist concern for the truth of the Lord's claim – *I will make you free* – as effective in a world where karma is taken to be real and materially and spiritually effective in people's lives; it is not helpful merely to imagine that karma is banished by divine promises, unless attention is also paid to how karma's different powers are attenuated in appropriately distinct ways within the temporal experience of the person who is liberated.[36]

He is also concerned to see the positive side of this liberation from sins, as a liberation of the self from unnatural constraints:

> The words *From all sins I will make you free* speak of the removal of the entire torrent of hindrances that take the form of causes and effects; that is, a self-evident, perfectly realized experience of the Lord is made manifest.[37]

Once constrictive and obscuring sins have been removed, then knowledge, the will to good, and the ability and desire to serve selflessly, all become evident in a manifestation of what was actually real and true even though obscured by karmic effects. The Lord's liberative power restores human beings' underlying and original connaturality with God. The Carama Śloka's promise, then, is taken to be powerfully transformative, yet also in keeping with the innate, innermost reality of human nature.

> *Reflection:* That God is just and merciful, forgiving sin while not entirely protecting the sinner from the effects of her or his deeds is a familiar enough

33 Lest these minor worldly benefits be distracting.

34 Other karmic results that are also playing out, that may or may not interfere with the merits related to meditation.

35 888/538-539 Deśika adds, "All this is explained in *Uttara Mīmāṃsā Sūtras* 4.1.14."

36 The discussion of karmic residues and their dispersal occurs in pages 888-891/539-542. Deśika also assesses that alternative, competing state of liberation known as *kaivalya* ("total apartness"), and shows its limitation and undesirability. (893-898/542-547)

37 891-892/542. The self is thus freed from constrictions that gainsay even the possibility of the experience of God. Deśika goes on (892/543) to elaborate the nature of this expansion of experience that is a "removal of constrictions" and a "restoration" of the original wholesome state of knowledge.

Christian belief. That God in the end triumphs over sin is also Christian faith, and the mystery of salvation as a heavenly but also this-worldly reality is rooted deeply in the Christian faith. That the Carama Śloka's second line should detail the real effectives of divine grace is therefore something we can rather easily acknowledge and affirm. Even the extended definition of sin to include also the good deeds which tend to enhance our egos and trap us in more immediate rewards should also make good sense to the Christian. Even if the promise of a state beyond both good and evil effects may raise fears about a non-Christian stoic indifference, etc., such concerns have little to do with Śrīvaiṣṇava piety, which is simply stating that even material and human goods must not be allowed to stand in the way of God's greater plan for us. Most of us, too, can share Deśika's concern about the continuation of human responsibility in light of divine action: however complete and irreversible divine salvific action may be, humans are still responsible and we may, in the short run, experience the bad effects of the bad things we do. That so much theological and spiritual common ground should be discovered in the words, *From all sins I will set you free*, is a striking fruit of our study, an event in itself worthy of further reflection.

Do not grieve: *mā śucaḥ*

Presupposing his lengthy discussion of the injunctive force of *take refuge* (*vraja*) in the first line of the Carama Śloka,[38] Deśika does not say much about the injunctive force of the directive, *Do not grieve* (*mā śucaḥ*). We can presume, though, that here too the force of injunction marks the particular claim Kṛṣṇa makes on those who have thus far followed the teaching and practice of the three Mantras: "If you understand all that I have been saying, then it is you who should no longer grieve."

What Deśika does stress is that in light of the promised liberation, the issue is not that a grief must be repressed, but rather the lack of reasons for grieving:

> Therefore, for the person immersed in this means [who is the Lord], all causes of sorrow come to an end; the point of saying *Do not grieve* is to confirm this faith.[39]

Like Rāmānuja in his *Gītā* commentary, Deśika explains that the grief at issue here is no longer grief at the prospect of bloodshed and destruction, such as tormented Arjuna at the *Gītā*'s beginning, but rather grief at the prospect of painstaking and arduous practices that tradition and habit seem to require of those wishing to reach Kṛṣṇa – a grief recognizing that we know the goal, we still cannot reach it in the forseeable future.

[38] See Chapter 3.
[39] 901/550

This grief is dispelled by the realization that one simply has to put all this aside, by taking refuge with Kṛṣṇa.

Deśika also admits the fact of a more ordinary, even harrowing sorrow at the difficulties of this life, and pain at separation from God:

> The person infused with a specific grief is the one competent for taking refuge. Thus:
>
> I am terrified, Lord of the gods, in this fearsome world of sorrow![40]
> Protect me, lotus-eyed Lord, for I know no other refuge.[41]
>
> and
>
> Frightened at the words, "Embrace this copper image, O sinner,"
> I have come and reached Your feet.[42]

By the first quotation, Deśika points to an existential terror experienced by life in the world. The second invokes Tirumaṅkai Āḻvār's portrayal of a promiscuous person who, upon reaching the house of Death, hears the frightening invitation, "Come, embrace this molten copper statue of a woman:" finally, here in hell, live out the lust that drove you during your sinful life. But for the person who instead seeks the Lord, an additional and more particular kind of grief,[43] which is also a kind of fear, is at stake:

> What is it to say that the person competent for refuge is terrified?[44] When a person sees that he has not gained a previously favored goal, he is grieved; when he sees powerful obstacles contrary to what he wants, he becomes afraid. When we see mention of either "the terminating of what is not suitable" (to pleasing the Lord) or "the acquiring of what is suitable" (to pleasing the Lord), both are intended. So too here, when either fear or grief is mentioned with reference to one's competence, both are at work in the person seeking liberation.[45]

It is possible to grieve when we see the good slipping from our grasp, while at the same time fearing acutely the alternative, life without the Lord, trapped amidst lesser goods, evils of our own making.

And while the Lord's liberative act definitively frees the person taking refuge from all sorrow, Deśika is aware that the person who has taken

40 "In this *saṃsāra* that carries with it fear."

41 *Jitānte Stotra* 1.8

42 *Periya Tirumoḻi* 1.6.4; 905-906/554

43 Respectively, *bhaya* (fear and danger) and *śoka* (grief).

44 Terrified, *bhīta*; this might imply that only the cognate *bhaya* (fear) is intended, but in fact both fear and grief are at issue.

45 906/554

refuge may still be particularly anguished by a desire to die and be with the Lord – and thus still in tumult while alive, *because* alive. The true abolition of grief and fear comes with the experienced realization – and not mere knowledge – that the Lord is the sure means and the sure goal for all those who surrender to the Lord:

> The ending of grief mentioned here is without restrictions. That is, by knowledge of the specific means and by its performance, the causes of grief of every kind are entirely terminated. Were it just knowledge that is gained from the Lord's teaching, knowledge [of taking-refuge] that does not eventuate in performance [of taking refuge], that would be without benefit.[46]

Deśika quotes a verse that makes clear the difference between mouthing words and understanding their meaning:

> The song does not instruct the singer
> even if he sings it many times;
> things follow their own nature,
> like the kuliṅga bird
> which does not act to its own benefit.[47]

The bird sings of prudence and caution, but acts rashly, to its own destruction.[48] Similarly, the life of person who merely recites the words of surrender without feeling their impact is little affected. Understanding, feeling, and doing are all deeply interconnected:

> So here the point is that the complete ending of grief is the fruit of both the knowledge and performance [of taking refuge]. Therefore, what is ended here is all the grief that arises before, during, and after performance.[49]

Ever thorough, Deśika goes on to list ten kinds of grief meant to be banished by Kṛṣṇa's *Do not grieve*:[50]

Grief regarding competence for taking refuge:

1. The characteristics of taking refuge are the desire for the goal, faith in the one who enables us to reach the goal, the lack of resources and knowledge and so forth. These are unrestricted by

[46] 910/558

[47] 910/558. *Mahābhārata, Sabhā Parva* 42.21. Deśika does not cite the last line.

[48] Ayyangar, in a note in his translation (p. 558), indicates that the cry of the kuliṅga bird sounds like *mā sahasaṃ kuru*, "Do not act rashly" – advice the bird does not follow when it attempts to snatch flesh from the mouth of the lion.

[49] 910/558

[50] What follows is my paraphrase. Ramadesikacaryar divides the list into a list of ten; 911-913.

birth status, religious class, stage of life and so forth. There is no reason to grieve because one lacks competence for them.

Grief regarding the means of taking refuge:

2. This specific means, taking refuge, with its accessories need be performed only once; this is easy and effective. There is no reason to grieve over potential difficulty or delay.
3. The Lord can be won over by this means; He is the accessible and most compassionate goal of refuge. One need not grieve because (the perfect, transcendent) God is the objective means.

Grief regarding what is to be done after taking refuge:

4. After taking refuge, none of the things one might do is a necessary accessory to taking refuge, so deficiency in such activities does not detract from the sure efficacy of taking refuge.
5. Even sins after taking refuge can be canceled by an intention to this effect at the time of taking refuge, or by an additional act of taking refuge.
6. Even if a person does deliberately commit sins after taking refuge, the Lord arranges expiation and repentance by sending relatively smaller sufferings.

Grief regarding the accomplishment of the results:

7. Even if a person desperate for God had desired release[51] as the fruit of taking refuge immediately yet does not obtain that release, she or he should not grieve over the body, even if it seems like hell.[52]
8. If one is content with the idea that the body ends at this life's end, there is no reason to grieve about deeds occurring during the interim (after taking refuge and before death); taking refuge's good effect is undiminished.
9. The person who has taken refuge need not worry about the prospect of another birth.[53]
10. Since his sins are gone, this person need not worry about the experience of self, etc., such as might threaten to delay the highest goal.

[51] From the body, for union with God.

[52] On the problem of a life longer than desired, see *Essence* 18, and Clooney, forthcoming c.

[53] Since further births will not occur.

Deśika concludes the list with a paraphrase of the divine promise implied by *Do not grieve*:

> You have become the recipient of My grace, such that every manner of cause for grief comes to an end. It is grief that now marks a lack of discernment, just as lack of grief had been the distinguishing mark of your previous state, when you were still the receptacle of My punishment. Grief at this point would not be fitting to this specific, unique means, taking refuge, nor to My power, for I am the objective means who has assumed the burden of protecting you. Nor would it be fitting to your condition as one who has accomplished everything, for you have placed your entire burden on Me.[54]

All of this is surely consoling, marking the apex of spiritual advancement as also the ending of grief; it marks a very high ideal that is easily reached by those willing to let go: grief must end and joy take its place, a deep change in disposition that cannot be manufactured by good effort or good theology; rather, one must have experienced a change in one's life.

> *Reflection*: A key test of our faith lies in our ability to rejoice – to appropriate deeply and personally, with emotional force, the truth of the good news we hear. It is important to allow the truths of the Faith and the reality of divine action to become so real that we assent, undergo affective transformation, and begin to live in accord with the fact of salvation – being already saved – that now characterizes our lives. It is a Christian imperative to let our inner selves be so pervaded by the new reality of what God has done for us in Christ that we are able to feel differently, rejoicing at a deep level in the new reality of Christ: *Therefore I tell you, do not worry about your life, what you will eat or what you will drink, or about your body, what you will wear. Is not life more than food, and the body more than clothing?*[55] and, *Take courage; I have overcome the world.*[56] Or, as St. Paul commands his readers, *Rejoice in the Lord always. I will say it again: Rejoice!*[57]

Kṛṣṇa's command, *Do not grieve,* seems designed to touch similarly those listening to the Carama Śloka, to experience the divinely effected freedom by a transformed feeling toward life, a new ability to live what is given to us, yet without fear and anxiety. Yet for us to profit from hearing the Carama Śloka, simple comprehension of its second line, or even approval of it, cannot suffice, any more than reading about joy and courage in the New Testament means that we automatically become joyful and carefree. We have to allow the words to touch us deeply enough that we at least begin to feel what it means to feel differently, neither grieving or being anxious, and instead rejoicing. If this deeper affective connection is possible, then there seems to be no reason why the Christian should not be touched by

[54] 913/561-562

the Carama Śloka in this way too. But this is a big "if," for it is not evident that all or many Christian readers will want to open themselves to being touched so deeply by Kṛṣṇa's words; many may feel that they should not thus become vulnerable. But at least, at this point, we should be in a position to understand the difference between knowing about the Carama Śloka and feeling the effect of its powerful words.

Deśika's Summation

As we saw in our consideration of the first part of the Carama Śloka in Chapter 2,[58] Deśika offers a summary near the end of *Essence* 29,[59] in which he takes up each component part in sequence, identifying explicit and implied meanings of the individual words. Here is the remainder of that summary, picking up with his seventh insight. Deśika highlights the implicit theology and anthropology underlying the divine-human interrelationship:[60]

7. *I* (*aham*) indicates the protector who is supremely compassionate, easy to please, independent, requiring no instigation, hard to stop, dependent on no one else, seeking opportunities to protect;
8. *you* (*tvā*) indicates that the person who has taken refuge has done all that needs be done; there is no need to do anything else regarding the means taken up or its results; this person is most pleasing to the Lord;

Sin is assessed pragmatically as an obstacle to what one truly desires:

9. *sins* (*pāpebhyo*) in the plural indicates that there is an abundance of sins, obstacles in the past, present, and future. "All sins" (*sarvapāpebhyo*) indicates obstacles of every type;

God acts, indubitably, but the future tense – *I will* – suggests that human response remains essential:

10. the Lord's intention to make free (*mokṣayiṣyāmi*) ends all sins, but the time of their ending has to do with the choice of the person taking refuge; *I will make you free* also indicates the nature of the ending of obstacles (as the Lord's work);

55 *Matthew* 6.25
56 *John* 16.33
57 *Philippians* 4.4
58 Chapter 2, pp. 97-98
59 913-914/562-563
60 Again in my own paraphrase.

Again, as would be expected in a ritually sensitive tradition, the promise of the verse can be articulated in terms of specific results, which Deśika goes out of his way to introduce into the verse:

11. *do not grieve* (*mā śucaḥ*) reminds us that beforehand there was an abundance of reasons for grief, while afterwards there is no grieving at all; that there need not be any doubt in any moment of reflection; that grief truly is ended; that there is no more fear or danger; that now there is a special delight; that one looks forward to the falling away of the body; that one deeply enjoys offering flawless service.

And to complete the second chart begun in Chapter 2,[61] here is the remainder of the even more succinct summary offered by Deśika:

4. tvā	Having thus implemented the means [by taking refuge], you have done all that is to be done, you have reached Me and are utterly pleasing to Me;
5. aham	I am most compassionate, most pleased, free and without any [external] prompting, engaged in My own purposes, aided simply by My own intention in accomplishing all that I have promised;
6. sarvapāpebhyo	sins are of many kinds, endless, hard to get beyond, posing obstacles of every kind;
7. mokṣayiṣyāmi	by experiencing union with Me and My self and what is Mine, you are set free [from those sins] and gain a flood of perfect experience, enjoyment like Mine, and the opportunity for service in every time, place, and condition;
8. mā śucaḥ	so you no longer have any reason to grieve.

The chapter's concluding Tamil verse describes true refuge:

Free of those *dharmas* that had to be minded so dutifully before,
we come near in haste
to the feet of the Cowherd adorned with fragrant basil,
our true refuge;
our pile of sins[62] is cut off and no longer overwhelms us:
by His captivating word of grace
our Great One has ended our darkness.[63]

61 Chapter 3, pages 98-99.
62 "Deeds" as "sins," yet surely including self-righteous good deeds as well.
63 915/564

The concluding Sanskrit verse likewise expresses gratitude for the teaching tradition; Deśika stresses the rare proficiency of those who know and teach the truth of this rare Carama Śloka:

> This kauṣṭubha jewel from the Milk Ocean of Vyāsa's tradition[64]
> this best verse
> is so close to Hari's heart, and
> some few have recognized its meaning
> as a reliable guide to the paths of the world and the Veda too,
> and at their words
> – steps up the stairway to the palace of liberation –
> Vaiśampāyana and Śaunaka[65] and other excellent seers nod in assent.[66]

For Deśika, the Carama Śloka marks a real encounter between the intent and will of God and the intent and will of a human actor. He appreciates the psychological and emotive condition of humans who are both highly capable and greatly in need. The first line of the Carama Śloka stresses the challenge Kṛṣṇa places before the listener, while the second confirms the priority of divine action and then, with *Do not grieve*, the elusive further state in which humans by grace come to feel as well as think differently. Kṛṣṇa's command must be heard in a way that is clear and forceful but that also takes into account and allows for the transformation of affective consciousness.

III. The Second Line in the Rest of the *Essence*

But to live in freedom and without grief is no easy thing; therein lies the challenge posed to those who listen attentively to the words *From all your sins I will set you free; do not grieve.* Outside Chapter 29, Deśika gives further attention to the change of heart and life that is at stake. In particular, while *Essence* 13-19 form an ongoing discourse that is not formally linked to any particular Mantra, the concerns of these chapters – the life after taking refuge, the balance between freedom and obligation, service within the community, the problem of ongoing

64 By tradition, the kauṣṭubha jewel arose during the churning of the ocean in primordial times, and thereafter adorns the chest of Nārāyaṇa. Similarly, this Carama Śloka arises from the ocean of the *Mahābhārata* (in the *Gītā*, which is part of the epic) attributed to Vyāsa.

65 Respected ancient seers

66 916/564-565

inappropriate behavior – are most sensibly thought of as exploring the ethical implications of the Mantras, particularly the Carama Śloka.

In *Essence* 13,[67] Deśika focuses on the new outlook on life of the person who has taken refuge, just as he had previously focused on the desperation of the person who, before refuge, was dissatisfied enough that she or he began heading in the right direction. Deśika glosses the Carama Śloka as a guide to this ethical theme in the *Essence*:

> The Lord is free, His every intention comes true, He gives the result, and He is the one who says, *Do not grieve*. Accordingly, seeing our new condition – we have laid down our burden – we should now be without burden. Moreover, this Lord of all who has been accepted as our means, in accord with *Take refuge in Me alone*, has also resolved to give the result, saying, *From all sins I will make you free*. He is capable of completing the work of salvation, and on that basis deserves our complete trust. When we see that He is the means, we should become free from doubt about the accomplishment of the result, and we should be without fear. We should break off even the slenderest connection with other goals and other means, banishing the slightest trace of attachment. Like the poor man who has gotten a great treasure with little effort, we should rejoice at the supreme goal of life we are obtaining.[68]

As we saw already in Chapter 3, the Dvaya Mantra brings about a new life of joy for the person finding refuge in the Lord. Understanding the Dvaya Mantra and the divine action in response to it, one is relieved of fear – and this is the point of the final words of the Carama Śloka:

> Knowing [that the burden is now solely the Lord's), onc becomes bereft of every burden. This is the definitive meaning of the words spoken by Him with whom one takes refuge, *Do not grieve.*[69]

Deśika further calculates the shift from grief-before to no-grief-after charted by the Carama Śloka:

> One of the qualifications for taking refuge is that one has been grieving beforehand; had a person no grief beforehand, he would have been lacking a necessary qualification. By the principle "No cause, no effect," his means would not have been completed. Similarly if, after reflecting on himself as one who has taken refuge, he were still to grieve because of weak faith regarding the words of his protector then, by the principle "No effect, no complete cause," it would follow that his performance of the means is incomplete, and its fruit delayed because it still wants completion of the

67 "The Person Who Has Done What Had to Be Done"

68 246/136-7

69 251/139

> means. But the person who was previously full of grief and who is now free from grief, in accord with the prohibition, *Do not grieve*, can be recognized as the one who has properly performed taking refuge.[70]

The Mantra is, accordingly, only for people who grieve at their sad plight, and yet are also able to let that grief come to an end, in total reliance on the Lord.

And now too we can finally complete our chart (begun in Chapters 1 and 3)[71] drawn from *Essence* 14, wherein Deśika lists the signs indicative of the fact that one is firmly established with respect to the truth of reality (*tattva*), the means (*upāya*), and in one's focus on the final goal (*puruṣārtha*), respectively geared to the Tiru Mantra, Dvaya Mantra, and Carama Śloka. Here then is the complete chart, given only partially in the preceding chapters:

Chapter 27	Chapter 28	Chapter 29
tattva (truth)	*upāya (means)*	*puruṣārtha (goal)*
knowing the self, detached serenity with respect to bodily flaws and criticisms by others	knowing that only the Lord is one's resource, protector	feeling no anxiety regarding the body and karmic debts
compassion toward those who criticize	no longer fearing death but welcoming it as pleasing	
remembrance of the help being given even by those who criticize	clarity in dependence on the protector	feeling no joy or sorrow at ordinary gains and loss, delight only in service of the Lord
seeing that criticisms are really from the Lord who controls all	expending no effort in the work of self-protection	
rejoicing that by these criticisms, karma is being expended	knowing that gaining the desirable and removing the undesirable are in God's hands	eagerness only for gaining the Lord

70 251/139

71 Chapter 1, p. 62, and Chapter 3, p. 138.

In each case, the qualities mentioned describe a person who is tranquil and equanimous, regardless of what else might happen.

In light of these two fundamental chapters describing the person who has taken refuge, *Essence* 15-18 characterize how such a person is to act, with attention to the liberty of and constraint on such a person, regarding what she or he can do and should avoid. In *Essence* 15, for instance, in the course of delineating the duties of people who have taken refuge, Deśika describes these persons:[72]

1. They have gained clarity and love in the proper way, that is, spiritual knowledge from proper teachers;
2. They have gained purified knowledge;
3. They approach[73] those who are established in these truths;
4. In their actions they have resolutely done what must be done in accord with their religious class, stage of life, birth status, and personal qualities, etc.;
5. They reflect on the greatness of others and on their own lowliness, and thus avoid pitfalls lying before them;
6. They have realized their own pitifulness;
7. Immersing themselves in the mysteries of the *avatāras*, etc.,[74] they understand clearly the teachings that are most pleasing and most salutary, just like mother's milk;
8. They will not let go of that experience of service that arises in following the divine commands and in performing permitted activities in keeping with their new state – building a dam against rising waters;[75]
9. They have immersed their senses in appropriate experiences of pure food, service, etc., and they have changed their attitude toward unworthy objects;
10. They rejoice in doing their duty like those who have become healthy and enjoy milk, no longer just drinking it to alleviate bile;
11. They meditate on the excellence of the One beyond word and mind who nonetheless depends on those who take refuge with Him, and in this way cure the confusion in their minds;

[72] What follows is my paraphrase.

[73] In order to learn.

[74] That is, the divine descents, and other acts of divine presence and activity in the world.

[75] That is, anticipating the dangers of worldly existence.

12. They act in ways appropriate to the accessibility and transcendence of the divine relationship with humans;[76]
13. They deem their activity as unlike anything but how a newly-wed bride cherishes her wedding-thread, etc.;
14. They keep faith [in their teachers] and remain grateful, meditating on the service, etc., they receive due to their teachers;
15. They understand clearly the Lord's innate compassion, and are grateful toward Him.[77]

While these indications are not explicitly linked to the Carama Śloka (nor to any of the Mantras), nonetheless they describe the balanced life of freedom and responsibility after refuge that Deśika takes to be the true point of the Śloka: renunciation, refuge, freedom, life without grief. Similarly, Chapters 16 (on service in the community),[78] 17 (on the continuing obligation of the orthodox life), 18 (on faults and sins after taking refuge, and what is to be done about them),[79] and 19 (on dwelling in holy places and in community) further and more richly describe this life of new freedom and fearlessness.

All is God's, but the hearer still has things to do, in accord with her or his status and time of life, etc. In Deśika's view, the Carama Śloka poses a radical claim, but a radicality that does not indulge what he considers the temptation entirely to discard *dharmas* – the very stuff of tradition – as if irrelevant or impious, or as if insight without context can really change how we live. In his view, the Śloka addresses a person capable of action and, without excusing that person from acting properly, asks her or him to place behavior on the new foundation of recognized dependence on the Lord. This "post-surrender ethics" describes a truly spiritual state and a life of perfect fearlessness and freedom – yet as can actually be lived, because the Carama Śloka predicts how God has brought freedom and the ending of grief into the realm of human experience.

Reflection: It may be that for many readers, reflection on the ethical implications of the Carama Śloka is the place to begin, not end. Most of the virtues professed here can easily be recognized and honored in the Christ-

[76] Reverencing the Lord who is present in temples, for example, while yet worshipping him in his transcendence.

[77] From 275/150 to 289/158; the divisions are not entirely certain.

[78] On service in the community as mutual love and love of God through love of neighbor, see Clooney 1987, and Clooney forthcoming a, Chapter 5.

[79] See Clooney forthcoming c.

ian community as well, and we can likewise recognize that the "proof" of our faith lies in how we live our lives, not just in extraordinary circumstances, but also in smaller, everyday choices. If, for some readers, the benefit of this commentary lies simply in insights into how better to live the Christian life by noticing the virtues inculcated by the Carama Śloka, much will have been achieved, whether or not we decide immediately how it is that we do in fact learn how better to live by heeding the Carama Śloka.

IV. Reading the Second Line from a Christian Perspective

1. Theological Insights and Concerns, for a Christian Reader

Our earlier reflections in Chapters 2-4, respectively on the Tiru Mantra, the first part of the Carama Śloka, and the Dvaya Mantra, all opened up not only theological issues but also matters of ethical import. Who we are, in God's eyes (or, before Nārāyaṇa with Śrī), has very much to do with how we live; radical trust in God changes our calculation of what we need and seek in life, and thus how we are to make our choices before God.

Here too there is great room for agreement: the priority of divine liberative action; the power of God to forgive sins and cancel their effects; the sovereign intention of God also to wait upon human freedom, and even to "respect" human shortcomings and sins; the patience of God in accommodating the shortcomings and errors of even the most devout and earnest of Christians; the transformation of consciousness intended by God; the experience of a life without anxiety; the inevitable move from "freedom-from" to "freedom-for;" the enactment of new freedom in a life of selfless service of God and community. Even if the first line of the Carama Śloka leaves room for disagreement regarding how radical will be the social change occasioned by the "complete abandonment of all *dharma*s," this second line of the Śloka – in both the indication of divine initiative and in the command for the dispelling of grief – seems so very easily consonant with Christian notions of divine action and the corresponding transformation of human living. Both Śrīvaiṣṇavas and Christians should be able to hear the divine promise and, in response, live similarly liberated lives that are marked by joy, not sorrow. There seems to be little here that a Christian cannot assent to. On the contrary, most of Deśika's insights into the Carama Śloka should be readily affirmed by the Christian.

It takes no great insight then to see that we can take up now the next verses of the *Galatians* 5 passage already introduced in Chapter 2. There we saw Bede Griffiths comparing with *Gītā* 18.66 St. Paul's ideas on law and the new life of freedom.[80] If the stress in Chapter 2 was on the call to freedom rooted in radical surrender to God, then here, in light of the ethical emphasis in the second line of the Carama Śloka, we can notice Paul's insistence on the disciplining of freedom by commandment, a life that is truly free, yet lived in responsibility to the community:

> For you were called to freedom, brothers and sisters; only do not use your freedom as an opportunity for self-indulgence, but through love become slaves to one another. For the whole law is summed up in a single commandment, *You shall love your neighbour as yourself.* If, however, you bite and devour one another, take care that you are not consumed by one another.
>
> Live by the Spirit, I say, and do not gratify the desires of the flesh. For what the flesh desires is opposed to the Spirit, and what the Spirit desires is opposed to the flesh; for these are opposed to each other, to prevent you from doing what you want. But if you are led by the Spirit, you are not subject to the law.

As a result, two ways of life can be starkly contrasted:

> Now the works of the flesh are obvious: fornication, impurity, licentiousness, idolatry, sorcery, enmities, strife, jealousy, anger, quarrels, dissensions, factions, envy, drunkenness, carousing, and things like these. I am warning you, as I warned you before: those who do such things will not inherit the kingdom of God.
>
> By contrast, the fruit of the Spirit is love, joy, peace, patience, kindness, generosity, faithfulness, gentleness, and self-control. There is no law against such things. And those who belong to Christ Jesus have crucified the flesh with its passions and desires. If we live by the Spirit, let us also be guided by the Spirit. Let us not become conceited, competing against one another, envying one another.[81]

Deśika would easily recognize the contrasts in virtue and behavior proposed by St. Paul. Indeed, the entire passage is deeply complementary with the Carama Śloka as understood by Deśika, with respect to the life to be lived after taking refuge. In both, at stake is learning, by grace, to live a responsible moral life rooted in radical freedom. We find ourselves invited to reconsider the balance between the stable, ongoing force of religious tradition, and the radical change of life indicated by a turn to the deeper truth of divine action, such as we find in the salvific death of Christ: yet, at this point, tradition, the mysteries of divine action in the world, and living rightly on a daily basis all converge because none of us can simply

[80] Pp. 102-103
[81] *Galatians* 5.13-26

bring about radical surrender or even right living: all this is something God must do to us and in us. It is God alone who saves, our role being to accept God's action. So we can all profit from hearing the Carama Śloka, which so clearly proposes this divine initiation, taking it to heart, and allowing ourselves to be surprised by the joy that follows: *Do not grieve.*

2. Resonances in the Christian Tradition

To continue our practice of reading the Carama Śloka with Biblical texts, and also to see how a Christian's account of the new life of freedom can be illumined by the Carama Śloka, we can first return to our comparison from Chapter 2, now filling out the quotations with the entirety of the Carama Śloka and *Matthew* 19, this time focusing on the second clauses of each, texts that mark the fullness incumbent upon surrender to God in a complementary fashion:

If you would be perfect, go, sell what you possess and give the proceeds to the poor.	Having completely given up all *dharmas*, to Me alone come for refuge.
You will have treasure in heaven; and come, follow Me.	*From all sins I will make you free. Do not grieve.*

The person who has given up everything and followed the Lord now has received the treasure; he or she is made free, and passes beyond fear and grief. Once we have appropriated the invitation and challenge posed by Kṛṣṇa, or by Christ, we learn to live without grief, and as if already possessed of treasures in heaven; we learn to be disciples, dedicated to lives of unending service. Given our treasure, freed from all sins, we walk with Christ, our grief ended. Ideally, it becomes difficult to know where the lessons of one text end and those of the next begin.

We can also allow St. Paul's words, already cited, to enhance for ourselves the ethical possibilities latent in the Carama Śloka:

The fruit of the Spirit is love, joy, peace, patience, kindness, generosity, faithfulness, gentleness, and self-control. There is no law against such things. And those who belong to Christ Jesus have crucified the flesh with its passions and desires.	Having completely given up all *dharmas*, to Me alone come for refuge.
If we live by the Spirit, let us also be guided by the Spirit. Let us not become conceited, competing against one another, envying one another.	From all sins I will make you free. Do not grieve.

If we re-read the Carama Śloka in light of *Galatians*, we can find in the Śloka a passage from the old life to a new liberated life. Surrendering all *dharmas* and taking refuge gains a new, still more radical edge by contemplating this act in light of our crucifixion with Christ Jesus. Living in freedom and living without grief gain for the Christian greater specificity when we see this new life as guided by the Spirit, an enjoyment of the fruits of the Spirit. And we are reminded that in both contexts, the new life is a life for the community; liberation is never a confirmation in selfishness, both St. Paul and the Carama Śloka tell us.

If we wish rather to emphasize the ending of grief and the arrival of joy, two passages from *John* come to mind. First, we hear Jesus invites his disciples to realize that his conquest of the world radically changes their attitudes toward its ongoing sorrows and difficulties:

> In the world you face persecution. But *take courage; I have overcome the world!*[82]

Another text makes the promise and call to joy even more explicit:

> As the Father has loved me, so I have loved you; abide in my love. If you keep my commandments, you will abide in my love, just as I have kept my Father's commandments and abide in his love. *I have said these things to you so that my joy may be in you, and that your joy may be complete.*[83]

Our possible double reading would then be the following:

...From all sins I will make you free. Do not grieve.	I have said these things to you so that my joy may be in you, and that your joy may be complete.

3. Praying with the Carama Śloka's Second Invitation?

Here too, as with the first line of the Carama Śloka, prayer is primarily a matter of listening. The word that has been uttered is the divine word, not a human word: *I will make you free, do not grieve.* The requirement here too is to find ourselves addressed by this promise and injunction. These are words that draw our attention beyond the world as it is now, but they should also have import for the present moment, as liberation, properly understood, occurs even in this life, as grief and fear cease to be expected

[82] *John* 16.33

[83] *John* 15.9-11. The next verse voices a call to service that nicely echoes the Śrīvaiṣṇava view that surrender to God eventuates in a life of service: "This is my commandment, that you love one another as I have loved you." (*John* 15:12)

characteristics of life. Hearing the Carama Śloka becomes prayer in the midst of ordinary life. This is a prayer that is not without cost, and the cost here is to let go of the familiar and sometimes comfortable baggage of sin, fear, and grief. To receive this second line of the Carama Śloka prayerfully is therefore to become vulnerable to changing one's life, to live as if all these promises are true; it is prayer as letting go, letting the word we hear take over our lives. While again it seems unlikely that the Christian can hear Kṛṣṇa's promises with the simplicity and clarity of the Śrīvaiṣṇava – for we do not have a settled, clear way to listen to Kṛṣṇa – we can still listen carefully and take to heart the message of a new way of living; and in this freedom and fearlessness is grounded a true habit of prayer.

Or, drawing together examples now from the preceding chapters as well, we have a wider, more complete template for further reflection and prayer, such as this one:

Aum, obeisance to Nārāyaṇa.	Abba, Father.
Having completely given up all *dharmas*, to Me alone come for refuge...	If you would be perfect, go, sell what you possess and give to the poor...
I approach for refuge the feet of Nārāyaṇa with Śrī; obeisance to Nārāyaṇa with Śrī.	Father, into Your hands I commit My spirit.
...From all sins I will make you free. Do not grieve.	...and you will have treasure in heaven; and come, follow Me.

V. Looking Ahead

With the completion of our explication of the second line of the Carama Śloka, the commentarial work of *The Truth, the Way, the Life* is largely done. I have ventured, in this and the preceding chapters, to introduce the three holy Mantras to a new audience, in accord with the insights of one great Śrīvaiṣṇava teacher, Vedānta Deśika, but for an unanticipated, Christian audience. Although none of this adds up to a full explication of the Mantras as they are explained in the great commentaries of the Śrīvaiṣṇava tradition, this reading is still a real beginning in learning and deeper understanding, so as to educate, deepen, enhance, and transform how we think, act, and pray as Christians. In our last chapter, I offer some concluding reflections on the meaning of this project and where it leads.

CHAPTER 5

AFTER COMMENTARY

The Truth, the Way, the Life: Christian Commentary on the Three Holy Mantras of the Śrīvaiṣṇava Hindus has not been intended to be anything more than a commentary on the three Mantras, a close reading by a Christian reader, for a Christian audience. As I suggested in my Introduction, it remains pre-systematic and pre-dogmatic and does not attempt firm conclusions about the Mantras and their content, nor about Śrīvaiṣṇavism and Christianity. While I have tried to raise relevant and difficult questions along the way, it has been less urgent for me to try to answer all such questions. While I have been – as commentator, and personally – favorably disposed to the texts I have explained, I do not ask my readers simply to embrace my attitudes. My hope is that readers will take seriously the Mantras, Deśika's insights, and my explanations, and recognize the vast array of possibilities opened in this way, such as require at the very least thoughtful and particular responses to particular points that have been raised; and I believe that I have provided the resources by which individuals can make their own assessments, even if some will rightly wish to undertake further study of the Mantras and Deśika's *Essence* on their own. While every academic project has its explicit and implicit presuppositions, and some readers may wish to expose the attitude toward non-Christian religions implied by my commentary, I have not intended to promote covertly or build the case for any definite theology of religions, or of the Christian and Śrīvaiṣṇava religions. This is so even if, as I have been reading them, they might appear to have very much in common, and to a degree that begs to be recognized as of great theological and spiritual import.

Yet it seems possible to say a bit more on the hopes I have for commentarial practice as a religious reading of the great texts of another tradition, as a way to learn from such a tradition without prematurely or too grandly committing to some theory about religions and Christian faith. Given the detail and labor of the preceding chapters, it seems justified to predict a path of reflection we might take from here. Accordingly, I close with some reflections on where we now stand.[1]

In particular, the theme for this concluding chapter is how the three Mantras and a careful study of them in accord with Śrīvaiṣṇava tradition as understood by Vedānta Deśika might affect Christian identity as theologically understood and spiritually enacted, and engaging this tradition in this way exemplifies a more advantageous approach to interreligious learning than would a preoccupation with coming to judgment upon the religion studied or, conversely, with determining to rule out the significance of interreligious commentary.

In the following sections, I take up once more the issue of commentary as a point of departure for further intellectual inquiry. I then review briefly what the three Mantras teach us and what they imply for ethics and the theology of religions; and, finally, I reflect once more on where this commentary might take us with respect to our spiritual practice and prayer.

I. On Reading and Writing from the Perspective of Commentary

Commentary is hard work, and a wise and useful commentary is not easily accomplished even within one's own religious tradition; it is all the more difficult across religious boundaries, where at the beginning one lacks the familiarity and sensitivity to read well, and where at the end too one is still reading as it were belatedly, with partial comprehension and necessarily incomplete appropriation. The reading leading up to this book has only imperfectly been carried out through study of selected texts over a period of just a few years, primarily on my own and without the benefit of reading regularly with a Śrīvaiṣṇava teacher (because I was living in Boston, did not have the time, and could not, in any case, become a properly devout disciple of a Śrīvaiṣṇava teacher). And yet too, this is a considerably more engaged and participatory reading than many an academic work; I have passed over a number of important academic questions – related to history, social context, the meanings of cited texts in their older or original contexts, Deśika's implied conversation partners – and been more comfortable than many a scholar in adopting the

[1] Parts of this chapter appear, in modified form, in Clooney forthcoming b.

sympathies of an insider in my study of another tradition. And so, as I indicated in my Introduction, a study such as this must be sober too in conceding drawbacks: as a Western and Christian commentator on the Mantras, I should not readily expect that either the religious or scholarly communities involved will wholeheartedly applaud the results of my effort to produce an honestly Christian yet humbly commentarial reading of the three Mantras.

Yet this reading practice has produced results. I have read the Mantras through the great commentary of a key Śrīvaiṣṇava teacher who sought to subsume the entire tradition into his commentary; nothing written in the preceding chapters would have been possible had I not been reading with Vedānta Deśika. He, and the tradition/s he represents, have been invaluable in my project of venturing to learn the Mantras. In acknowledging in my dedication to teachers of the Śrīvaiṣṇava tradition from Deśika to great 20th century commentators such as Uttamur Viraraghavachariar, I have ventured to put myself, ever so delicately, near to (even if never really part of) that commentarial tradition, as a commentator from the outside who nonetheless has something to say because his work has been constantly attuned to and dependent on authoritative commentary from within the tradition itself. Or so I think: all this is, of course, my own estimation of my own work, and I must await the reaction of scholars, particularly in the Śrīvaiṣṇava community, and a wider body of readers in the Catholic Christian community, regarding the value of this commentary, and even of the very idea of making the three Mantras available to a wide audience.

My hope for the reader is that what might have begun merely in curiosity or out of interest in this new book series opens, should open, into a more complex engagement, along the lines of the "religious reading" I discussed in my Introduction. The study of another religious tradition also becomes a self-reflective inquiry, while the work of reading and learning about the Mantras cannot be separated from the possibility of a real even if imperfect participation in the realities to which they give voice. Reading the Mantras, and then reading them along with Deśika, should ideally transform the Christian reader who follows the process where it leads. Theologizing and writing *after* commentary is a project *from* commentary; while it can remain thoroughly, deeply Christian, it is nevertheless pervaded by the ideas and words, images and affective states, of Śrīvaiṣṇavas who have submitted themselves to learning from the three Mantras over the centuries and today as well.

II. Theological Openings

It should also be clear now that through focused, careful reading, certain theological truths become evident and impinge upon us; these truths, the more they are clearly understood, engage us and require further reflection that is worked out in detail and not merely theorized on a general level. That commentary can and should raise theological questions is perhaps a commonplace claim within a tradition, but it is important to insist that interreligious reading also has substantive theological implications within one's home tradition, even if those implications are not neatly systematized for easy consumption by those who do not take the time to engage in the same reading. A Christian who is willing to read should be able to engage most of the theological possibilities enunciated in commentary on the Mantras, taking them seriously, simply as claims worthy of consideration. Here in summary form are some of the truths inscribed in the Mantras and observed in our previous chapters:

1. All beings are by their very nature oriented to God, in a dependence that is necessary but also (for humans) freely chosen and enacted in worship and service;
2. God, though transcendent, can in some way be known, named, addressed;
3. there is mediation between God and humans, and the transcendent Person is made accessible in sacramental forms, such as the divine feet;
4. there can be a personal mediator between the transcendent God and all living beings, without prejudice to the intimacy of the divine-human relationship;
5. God invites surrender, and promises liberation to those who trust entirely in Him;
6. since God is accessible, we may in response approach God for protection, union, and salvation;
7. God is our righteousness; it is not even our holiest actions, but only God who saves;
8. in taking refuge with God, humans accept the divine invitation, glorify God, and begin to live out the truths and values at the heart of the Mantras;
9. worship – obeisance – is the beginning and end of theological and spiritual reflection.

All of these doctrinal claims, discerned by Śrīvaiṣṇava Hindus such as Deśika as at least implicit in the three Mantras, could and should be explored in much greater depth. Issues of great theological import thus come to the fore and are open to debate; but given the nature of these claims, and the likelihood of their generating all kinds of subsidiary questions and more refined positions, they are very unlikely to neatly divide Hindus and Christians as two sides in a single consistent argument. We should expect to find ourselves agreeing with Śrīvaiṣṇavas on some of these points, while Christians will disagree among ourselves on some of them too. Honest theological debate, at this level of specificity, will in general have less to do with interreligious dialogue and more to do with how theologians, irrespective of religious belonging, articulate positions on such points.

Of course, some issues require more cautious reconsideration. God, in the Christian understanding, may be possessed of nearly all the attributes implicit in *Nārāyaṇa* as the divine name; but it is considerably more demanding to say that Nārāyaṇa is the divine Person upon whom all depends. It is one thing to say that there is a divine mediator; it is another to insist that the mediator's name is Śrī, and that she shares fully with Nārāyaṇa the desire to liberate all beings and the power to effect that liberation. This new difficulty should be no surprise to Christians, since much of what we as Christians say about God and mediations of the divine presence can easily gain respect in interreligious circles; obstacles arise when we add that the mediator's name is Jesus. We may also find greater complexities as we look more closely into specific theological issues, such as Śrīvaiṣṇava and Christian notions of grace and salvation, or the presupposed understandings of human and divine nature; both in the context of fidelity to the Mantras and then more generally, it would be unrealistic to expect all Christians, or all Śrīvaiṣṇavas, or a large majority of both traditions, to agree on exactly how to define grace, salvation, or human nature. And yet, as I have suggested in earlier chapters, the fact of varied levels of difficulty and complexity suggests not that interreligious learning is impossible, but only that we have to be all the more discerning in recognizing how far we agree, on which points, with which believers in the other and our own tradition.

We therefore need to differentiate our response to the Mantras, and this requires that we recognize different dimensions of meaning. For the Christian, there are both more accessible and more difficult lessons to be learned from the Mantras. Many of these insights, even if *theologically* challenging, do not necessarily raise insurmountable or even important interreligious issues; it will instead be easy for the Christian to affirm what the Mantra and the Essence teach us. But there are also harder and more challenging insights that pose specific interreligious questions; these are related to the specificity of Śrīvaiṣṇava Hindu faith as seen from a Christian perspective. The more difficult insights may be options for Christians, or not. Here is a sample tabulation of such insights:

Tiru Mantra: Aum, obeisance to Nārāyaṇa:

> More accessible truths: The Tiru Mantra calls us to worship, in the context of a necessary ontological and thereafter freely chosen dependence on God; the Mantra illumines for us fundamental attributes of God and self.
> More difficult truths: Obeisance, and not a more active stance is the key human attitude, and most expressive of proper self-understanding; the Tiru Mantra reminds us that *Nārāyaṇa* is the name of the personal God for whom all exists; *aum* is a specific orthodox sacred syllable that is not available to all speakers and readers but rather marks and confirms a traditional social order based in caste.

Carama Śloka 1: Having completely given up all *dharmas*, take refuge with Me alone...:

> More accessible truths: The Carama Śloka's first line is a divine invitation to trust in God and not in ourselves; God alone is our salvation.
> More difficult truths: The Carama Śloka's first line offers radical freedom from all social constraints and traditional duties and responsibilities, hinting at the possibility of a simple abandonment of orthodox tradition as an obstacle to trust in God; the Śloka also announces Kṛṣṇa alone as our refuge, and it is his voice that speaks to us in the Mantra.

Dvaya Mantra: I approach for refuge the feet of Nārāyaṇa with Śrī; obeisance to Nārāyaṇa with Śrī:

> More accessible truths: The Dvaya Mantra emphasizes the primacy of grace and divine action, the sacramental accessibility of the supreme God, the foundations of salvation in divine and not human action, and in a human recognition of the need to depend on God; as the words by which surrender is enacted, the Mantra teaches us the possibility and prime importance of actually surrendering to God.
> More difficult truths: The Dvaya Mantra calls us to take refuge with Lord Nārāyaṇa, and with the Goddess Śrī who is eternally with Nārāyaṇa and who facilitates the taking of refuge with them in particular; it is to this divine couple, thus named, that all praise belongs; the Mantra also narrows, almost to the point of nothingness, the human contribution to human liberation, since God alone is our refuge, and even our approach to God is but an act of faith.

Carama Śloka 2: I will make you free from all sins; do not grieve.

More accessible truths: The Carama Śloka's second line voices the divine promise to liberate us from our sins; it proposes a life beyond grief and fear for those who live by faith in God and not in self-reliance.

More difficult truths: Does the Carama Śloka's second line raise any real difficulties for a Christian reader?

A value basic to this reckoning, even if it is pursued somewhat artificially at first, is that by it we can see more clearly the complexity of the Mantras, and accordingly put aside the expectation that we can dispose of the Mantras by a single judgment, be it positive or negative. Our response will in (large) part still be governed by our own prior judgments about the meaning of the Mantras. As we see the complexities involved, we differentiate our response to the Mantras into moments of wholehearted acceptance (e.g., the value of taking refuge with God, allowing God alone to be our salvation), or qualified embrace (e.g., the value of total dependence on God), or likely non-acceptance (e.g., naming Nārāyaṇa with Śrī as the Persons to whom we pray). Once we have begun to understand the tradition of interpretation, and engage it more readily in some parts, more slowly and with hesitation in others, we ourselves become intelligent, albeit novice interpreters of the Mantras, learning from them sensibly and by degrees.

Differences in meaning will of course be readily found: *Abba, Father* points to the same reality of utter dependence as does the Tiru Mantra, but with a different concreteness and perhaps greater intimacy; while *Abba* and *Aum* are both sacred syllables, they do not after all have the same meaning. The divine invitations to surrender in the first line of the Carama Śloka and in Jesus' challenge to the man who comes to him – *if you want to be perfect...* – are similarly radical, but the challenge to surrender all *dharmas* is probably different from the challenge to give up all possessions; were these renunciations taken to be symbolic of the need to turn exclusively to God, however, they might converge more easily. So too, Arjuna and Kṛṣṇa have already known one another, long before the Carama Śloka and even before the *Bhagavad Gītā*, while the man accosting Jesus seems to be a stranger to him. The Dvaya Mantra is a first person confession of surrender and praise, seemingly in response to the invitation of the Carama Śloka and meant for anyone who wishes to utter the words, while Jesus' prayer is uttered in an already-desperate situation, as the Father, so long familiar, now seems terribly absent; it is only by grace that Christians can make Jesus's words their own. The Carama Śloka's second line and Jesus' promise of rest and joy make clear that both traditions have clear and hopeful ideas about the state of the person who trusts entirely in God, but we need not jump to the conclusion that they portray the same manner of joy achieved in the same way. The results differ too, if we put the Carama Śloka back in the context of the *Gītā*. Arjuna is asked, with and after the Carama Śloka (as *Bhagavad Gītā* 18.66), to go forth and fight, without sadness, while the rich man addressed by Jesus (*Matthew* 19.21) turns away – sad, not sufficiently motivated by the words he hears.

Such differences, and many others like them, are worth further investigation, but they do not obliterate similarities nor render useless the cultivation of the Mantras and their Biblical counterparts as read and pondered together. There might be, but need not be, any competition in this. We need not conflate them by claiming that they are saying the same thing, nor preserve the Christian tradition's purity by uneasily denying resemblances. And where differences do seem nearly insurmountable, we can still move forward simply by choosing to take up others among the myriad possible points of connection made evident in the commentarial practice.[2] Proximity enhances intensity, and with intensification, all their meanings become sharper and clearer, even as the possibilities of a single meaning and single conclusion seem all the more unlikely because now we see clearly what is involved.

But this learning is not merely an intellectual exercise. Once we have read and begun to learn, our learning will be rich also in imaginative and affective implications. Because we understand, we are now involved, regardless of decisions we make about what to do with our learning and the opportunities it offers us. With an intellectually and spiritually rich tradition like that of the Mantras, no plausible reason is likely to arise for total disengagement, as if one might imagine, after study of the Mantras, to return to a Christian theology entirely bereft of the Mantras and their theological and spiritual implications.

III. From Commentary to a Theology of Religions?

Before moving to the realm of the ethical and spiritual implications of the Mantras, it is appropriate to notice for a moment the shift that is now

[2] The flexibility of interreligious reading too, compared with the difficulty of doctrinal exchange, suggests that in other dialogues, such as Muslim-Christian, more reading of each other's sacred texts, with traditional commentaries, is a promising way to proceed.

possible in our reflection on the significance of other religions in the theology of religions discipline. Here too – and so late in this book – I do not wish to burden the commentarial project with undue weight by suddenly discovering grounds for a new or revised theory about Christ and the religions or Catholicism and Śrīvaiṣṇavism, or even about Śrī and Nārāyaṇa in relation to the God of our Lord Jesus Christ. Commentary does not so easily and swiftly turn to, into, systematic reflection replete with definitive claims and judgments about religions in general. Given how little interreligious commentary has been done – notable exceptions aside, and with due gratitude to this series for its important contribution – we should not rush from the close up work of commentary to the loftier perspectives of a theology of religions. Yet, in a Christian commentary on the three Mantras, we can find starting points for fruitful reflection on the Christian (Roman Catholic) and Hindu (Śrīvaiṣṇava) religions in relation to one another, and something can be said about where we now stand with respect to the theology of religions and Christian views of non-Christian religions.

The comparativist who has been a careful commentator should be intellectually informed and affectively enriched. As better informed, she or he will have to come to terms with the religious tradition of this other text without the burden of an abrupt positive-negative decision, but rather through recourse to an array of interconnected smaller responses attuned to specific smaller points with the religious tradition. An understanding of religions rooted in commentarial practice will persist in responding to various religions primarily in further small-scale experiments in reading, writing, and assessment on particular points. As we learn many and multi-faceted dimensions of the Śrīvaiṣṇava tradition of the Mantras, there will emerge no single judgment about how Christians are to think of Śrīvaiṣṇavas, their faith, their Mantras. Of course, this small scale and meticulous approach is time-consuming, slow-moving, and even exhausting, and some among us may fear that the big questions of the theology of religions will retire to an ever-receding horizon, never actually to be decided. It is not that faith itself will decline into agnosticism or relativism, but only that the very idea of a large-scale and conclusive judgment will appear increasingly implausible, or at least less interesting than the progress made through more detailed work. But in reality, neither the theology of religions nor commentarial theology is likely to cease, so we can best hope that both commentarial study and the theology of religions will flourish in cooperation and tension with one another, each reminding the other that neither close reading nor large scale theoretical reflection is the only way forward.

But still: what is, or might be, a theology of religions rooted in this book's project of commentary on the three Mantras? It will have to be a theology grounded in this project, in the claims made in the Śrīvaiṣṇava tradition about the divine persons, the human condition and problem, and the primacy of grace with respect to divine initiative and human acceptance. A theology of religions rooted in commentary on the three Mantras will have to acknowledge such claims as inscribed in the Mantras and not simply as natural signs of divine initiative somehow present in the world, but rather more specifically as indications of conscious, chosen, cultivated Śrīvaiṣṇava reflection on the divine nature, human condition, and divine action in the world. Given the sophistication of Deśika's reading of the Mantras, and the Mantras' own internal complexity, a theology of religions attendant upon the Mantras will therefore have to recognize that these Śrīvaiṣṇava resources cannot simply be treated as objects for Christian theological reflection, as if only we have achieved self-conscious, multi-dimensional reflection on matters of faith. Rather, this will be a theology of religions that moves away from judgments-about-religions to an understanding that is profoundly dialogical, self-critical as well as critical, and enacted in actual peer theological conversation with the Śrīvaiṣṇava tradition and its contemporary proponents. This durable theology of religions will therefore be constructed from the ground up, in reflection on specific points in their dialectical relationship to Christian faith, theology, and commentary. If this approach seems tantamount to an acknowledgment of the intrinsic value of this other tradition, such may be the implication of commentary on a holy text of another tradition. This acknowledgment can be made, however, without a further insistence that the two traditions are equal in inspiration, revelation, the presence of God – questions that can be left open, until more interreligious commentarial work has been done by more theologians, over a much longer period of time.

But at least the following can be said, regarding what the Christian is to think about the fact of so complete and rich a theology as arises in and from the three Mantras. A theology of religions cognizant of the Mantras and their tradition seems necessarily to take seriously the possibility – or rather, probability – that, from a Christian perspective, God intends there to be the three Mantras as enduring spiritual realities that speak of the truth, the way, and the life, Mantras possessed of a wisdom that does not disappear or appear as mere shadow to the light of

Christian revelation. It is not easy to find the right terminology for a Christian assessment of the revelatory status of the Mantras, an assessment that is neither too little for Śrīvaiṣṇavas nor too much for Christians. But it does seem evident that denying to the Mantras their power in encompassing an entire religious world, and then too in impinging deeply on our Christian religious world, would be a denial of what the commentarial process in fact has taught us.

IV. Ethical Openings

After theology, ways of living too are at stake, since the Mantras expect audible utterance and visible performance; they are intended to have a deep effect on the lives of those who take them to heart in surrendering to God. Here the issues may be nuanced as follows.[3]

Commentary itself is all about formative values and ethical formation, for it requires a longer term commitment to texts that are themselves produced by authors who had themselves often enough been transformed by their own long-term commitment to tradition, and to writing patiently in a commentarial mode. All of this confirms Hadot's and Griffiths' expectations, introduced in my Introduction, regarding the commitment to spiritual exercises that comes to the fore if reading is to proceed as a properly spiritual exercise. At issue then is a (spiritual) ethics.

As for the specific ethical import of the Mantras, Śrīvaiṣṇavas believe that the fact that we are innately, ontologically oriented to God should visibly affect how we live; this orientation is also a freely chosen state, in which we decide to live for God and (by extension) for one another, and thus reform the ordinary behavior by which most people live. If we reflect on the characterization of the devotee's life sketched in the Mantras, we inevitably raise questions about how we ourselves are to act. So we can also trace the ethical and spiritual dynamics opened by the Mantras, extending the list begun above with these ethical values – and choices – that Christians share as well:

10. Self-abandonment to divine love means a radical abandonment of all prior habits and dependencies, even those of religious value;

[3] On some ethical dimensions of caste as debated in the Śrīvaiṣṇava tradition by Vedānta Deśika and others, see Clooney 2002b and 2005a. On the tension between teaching a text fairly and fostering a critique from a justice angle, see my brief reflection on the topic, Clooney 2003.

or, from another vantage point, renunciation indicates a change in attitude that prompts us to use and let go of things insofar as they lead toward or away from God;

11. God alone saves, yet humans are still free and even required to act; therefore, with the knowledge that God has accomplished all, we are to act in freedom; the imperative is real, but the choice is ours;
12. we are called to a life of joy, the ending of sorrow and fear, detachment from good and bad karma; and, by a complementary interpretation (in the Christian tradition as well) freedom also indicates mutual responsibility, a way of living that is both pertinent to ordinary life but, when truly free, somehow "apart from the world;"
13. the spiritual values inscribed in the Mantras – particularly the sense of sinfulness, total helplessness and dependence, the fact of grief and the ending of grief – can be valued and cultivated by anyone journeying the spiritual path, and that accordingly map a different way of living, a new ethic.

After these general points, we might also look more deeply into some of the specific ethical perspectives opened by and staked out with reference to the Mantras, in relation to the life of the person who has taken refuge with God and who thereafter balances freedom and enduring responsibility to orthodoxy. With respect to the Tiru Mantra, Deśika elaborates and defends the view that our ontological orientation to God is fundamental and given, but also that thereafter we are in a position to choose, or even to refuse to choose, to recognize this orientation. God is our righteousness, but this divine primacy is mediated in ways accessible to human understanding and volition – and therefore requiring human assent and engagement: God saves us, but we are never merely spectators at the event. But we can ask whether it is possible to live a life entirely oriented to God and not to self. We can also ask whether this can be good for a human being. A spirituality of submission and individual sanctification might seem to foster uncritical submission to divine authority and human mediators of that authority, and an overly narrow concern for personal rather than communal sanctification. And in turn this might well seem to postpone or even foreclose initiatives to change the world for the better.[4]

Deśika, though in many ways a daring thinker, defends a conservative view of society. More cautious even than many other Śrīvaiṣṇavas,[5] he

[4] Of course, the very notion of changing the world for the better is deeply engrained in the Western Christian consciousness.

defends the idea that the *aum* of the Tiru Mantra is reserved for upper caste males; lower caste men, and women, might be limited to saying only *Obeisance to Nārāyaṇa*. Or, since the Tiru Mantra is in Sanskrit, it might be read as the possession of an educated elite, even if – aside from *aum* – the stricter "Sanskrit" of the Mantra (*Aum, obeisance to Nārāyaṇa*) might just as well be the more accommodating "Tamil" (*Obeisance to Nārāyaṇa*). To take up this matter for argument's sake – is the full Tiru Mantra for everyone, or for upper caste males? – would be taking sides in a perfectly respectable and important debate among Śrīvaiṣṇavas. If well informed and respectful, we could do this, although we would have to be careful we did not exploit the debate for theological and ethical reasons extrinsic to the matter of the Mantra itself.[6]

With respect to the Carama Śloka's first line, we might find ourselves able to assent to the Mantra in all its radicality, while questioning the traditional and more moderate interpretation of it. For we have seen how Deśika admits the abandonment of all *dharmas* in the Carama Śloka, but argues that this does *not* indicate a move toward a radically egalitarian society freed from traditional duties and customary expectations. He insists that surrendering all responsibility to God is compatible with an obligation to the duties of life, and with enduring respect for the more arduous but still efficacious modes of religious practice others may choose to follow. As Christians committed to Christian ideals, we may be disposed to disagree with Deśika's caution, and prefer the more radical possibilities inherent in the Mantra and Kṛṣṇa's own words. But if so, we will have to review our Christian expectations about Christian radicalism in order to see how to bring that perspective properly to bear on Deśika's different expectations with respect to the Carama Śloka. And, of course, we will have to review how our Christian churches have been accustomed to fold Gospel radicalism into more ordinary ways of structuring and living Christian life.

With respect to the Dvaya Mantra, there is even less to imagine disagreeing with, regarding ethical implications.[7] In the action of taking refuge,

5 Including for instance, the teachers of the *teṅkalai* school (see Chapter 1).

6 That is, it would be inappropriate to pick up the debate over *aum* without due regard for the Mantra and its tradition, and merely for the sake of criticizing Hindu views of caste from a Christian perspective. Such a critique might be offered, but unless well informed, it would have little to do with the Tiru Mantra.

7 Unless, at some fundamental level, worship of Nārāyaṇa and Śrī has very different ethical implications than worship of the God of the Christian tradition. But this will have to be worked out in detail. For some comparative comments on the matter of Christian and Śrīvaiṣṇava ethics, see Clooney 1987, 2002b and forthcoming c.

and in a radical emphasis on God-as-refuge, we can find grounds for asking about a right balance between divine and human activity. If the Lord alone is refuge, we might rightly define the human enactment of refuge (expressed in the *I approach*) as narrowly as possible, even as a primarily mental insight into divine power and human weakness. But some room still needs to be left for human responsibility and action. Deśika himself asserts this, so those who insist on a more balanced view of grace and responsibility will simply be taking his side in a possible argument.

With respect to the Carama Śloka's second line, particularly as interpreted by Deśika as illumining life after refuge, the problem – for any of us – is how we are to live now a life that is truly free, already liberated, given how prone we are to live in a safer, compromised fashion. We might also be concerned about more particular issues. For instance, if liberation from all sins is read in the Śrīvaiṣṇava tradition as liberation from merit (*puṇya*) as well as demerit (*pāpa*), some Christians (Roman Catholics, for instance) will have to think twice about how to interpret this ethic that seems to treat even good works as a problem; but here too, Deśika's double insistence – works are a problem, but can and must be performed for the glory and pleasure of God – makes easier a nuanced Christian accommodation of the Carama Śloka's challenge. While the ending of fear and anxiety seems an unexceptionable value, we can also wonder whether some grief is not a good idea, particularly with respect to the problems of our contemporary world; and we may fear that too much equanimity will lead to complacency in the face of the evils around us. Yet, while the Carama Śloka, along with a great portion of the Indian traditions, argues for this equanimity and balance, the *Gītā* context of the Śloka does not foster passivity: rather, Arjuna rises and returns to his duty, the battle that lies before him.

Such questions deserve reflection, and as duly considered may lead to still further questions. But here too there is no reason to imagine that even legitimate ethical concerns will be any more disruptive of interreligious learning than the kind of questioning that occurs inside a community. I can see no reason to expect some fatal flaw in the ethics of the Mantras, such as would prove that the Christian has nothing to learn from them. What they do teach us, rather, is that debates about how to live religiously are not the private property of any particular tradition; even in light of basic features that may distinguish traditions from one another, study of the Mantras suggests that we will have more in common than divides us, as we deliberate on how to live out the life to which God has called us, in setting us free.

V. The Mantras and Experiments in Scriptural Intertextuality

As we study the Mantras reflectively, we can find ourselves in the position of searching out and pondering possible "mantras" of our own tradition, texts at least parallel to the Mantras in meaning and affect. In each of the preceding four chapters, I experimented with such choices, placing just a few New Testament texts next to and in conversation with the three Mantras. Choices such as these emerged:

Aum, obeisance to Nārāyaṇa.	Abba, Father.
Having completely given up all *dharmas*, to Me alone come for refuge....	If you want to be perfect, go, sell your possessions and give the proceeds to the poor...
I approach for refuge the feet of Nārāyaṇa with Śrī, obeisance to Nārāyaṇa with Śrī.	Father, into Thy hands I commend My spirit.
...From all sins I will make you free. Do not grieve.	... and you will have treasure in heaven. Then come, follow Me.

Placed together, neither separated nor confused, these Mantras and these words of Jesus affect the meaning of one another and so too the reader's reception of either and then both texts, even as one or the other column is always first and privileged for this or that reader. In this way, we can locate and draw upon these potent Mantras through the construction of possible affinities, opening some fundamental and fruitful intertextual dynamics, yet without too hastily committing to doctrinal similarities. Such pairs of texts can be read together with cognizance of the scriptural and theological worldviews they encode and out of which they emerge; yet too, in the myriad possibilities generated by their juxtaposition in reading, we are not immediately burdened with the more formal and constricted choices the doctrines of communities impose upon those considering them. Just as commentators ceaselessly cite older texts to illumine the text at hand, and by doing so both clarify meanings and yet too open up new possibilities as the cited texts enter a creative relationship with the text being explained, so too in this interreligious context, interreligious citation and the consequent double reading provide possibilities even beyond the specific expectations already identified by the commentator. Patiently and intelligently studied together, these texts read together mark off a new common ground, a site for richer and deeper insight, interacting and creating new possibilities for reading, reflection, and prayer.

Differences obviously remain and dissonances can easily be discovered, and the intertextual process does not require sameness of meaning or even form. No Biblical prayer, however often repeated as – as if – a mantra, can have the same weight and density as an Indian mantra or bear the specific array of meanings that these three holy Mantras bear. The immeasurable power of New Testament words never translates into an equivalent to what one of the Mantras says to us; conversely, the three Biblical texts cited above have a deep resonance in the Christian tradition of devotion to Jesus that naturally will lack any certain parallel in the Śrīvaiṣṇava tradition. Ideally though, as readers study such parallels and construct their own, we all become unable to return to the state of knowing only our own holy texts read only in light of our own tradition.

VI. Praying with the Mantras: A Brief Reprise

It would also miss the point of the Mantras were we to dwell for too long on theological and ethical meanings or even on issues of reading inter-religiously. To fully understand the implications of the Mantras, we must not postpone endlessly our appreciation of the more specifically religious, experiential, and prayerful dimensions of the Mantras. Their spiritual insights – particularly the sense of sinfulness, total helplessness and dependence, the recognition of grief and hope for its ending, the value of receiving and trusting a divine word – indicate values and states that can surely be cultivated by the Christian who journeys along a Christian spiritual path, desiring an encounter with God as intense and intimate as that voiced in the three Mantras. It is at this more refined level that a comparative mystical theology finds its place, in the subtler affective shifts that occur in reading across religious boundaries. That is to say, we must return to the topic of prayer.

We can certainly pray with our New Testament texts, after we have brought them into dialogue with the Mantras. The newly recollected New Testament texts – perhaps even posited here as Christian Mantras – gain a new layer of signification and can be used with greater intensity because they are now newly received and newly illumined by Hindu counterparts which, once known to us, change us as readers and how we read more familiar texts. For most of us, perhaps, this will suffice: close attention to texts of prayer from another tradition enables us to return with new insight and depth of attention to texts of prayer in our own tradition.

But it may also be that the boundaries do not remain so neat. Reading the Mantras and New Testament texts together, as a part of a regular practice of religious reading, is a fruitful endeavor that is or can be very much like praying. Even if we simply, slowly repeat the words together over a period of time – as I have been doing (in English, in Greek and Sanskrit) over the past several years – we have in hand rich, complex material not only for reflection, but also for the prayer that rises from attentive reflection to deep and powerful religious words. The New Testament texts may remain our guide and venue, but with them come the Mantras with their intellectual and spiritual meanings. Just as it was and is impossible for a Christian to come to this Hindu reading process without all kinds of memories of the Christian tradition, now, in a very economical and concise fashion, close reading makes it impossible to take up read the Christian prayer without memory of the Hindu counterpart.

There seems to me to be no reason why a Christian cannot still venture to appropriate the piety, theology, and practice of the three Mantras, as well as the insights and theology of Deśika's *Essence*, for the sake of a deeply Christocentric manner of prayer. It is not that this careful reading and learning lead to a necessarily relativistic or even pluralistic theology. Indeed, a relativistic outcome would be ironic, given the highly confessional and focused perspective of both Christian and Śrīvaiṣṇava prayer. Rather, my hope is that a richer, gracious, reflective reality of and in faith is now seen in the perspective of Christ, heard through the prayerful exchanges that constitute the Mantras.[8]

But can we pray simply with the Mantras? In the processes I have been describing, we pray as Christians with a widened understanding and possibly with hearts moving in two directions at once. With our deepened and enhanced dispositions, we can certainly utter the Mantras[9] with a certain reverence and understanding, even if incompletely and with reservations such as I have been highlighting at the end of each chapter, and in the earlier part of this chapter. Our repetition of the Mantras may

[8] In none of this, of course, is there any obvious reason why Śrīvaiṣṇavas should feel obliged to accept a Christocentric reading of the Mantra tradition. Rather, I would hope that a Śrīvaiṣṇava re-reading of the Mantras in light of other faith perspectives, performed in a properly Śrīvaiṣṇava way, might be seen by Śrīvaiṣṇavas as a worthwhile intellectual and spiritual practice; and, of course, Śrīvaiṣṇavas might wish to comment on Biblical and Christian texts.

[9] The Mantras, or words like them from another tradition that we have learned through close reading; at this point, the Mantras are simply our best example, but there is no reason the practice cannot be extended to other texts as well.

then be something more than reading, even if not fully prayer in a fully Christian sense – our limit resting not on the Mantras, but rather on the truth of who we ourselves are and what we can do. In this new situation, we read and repeat the Mantras as if our own prayers, the meaning of this practice neither more nor less than appears appropriate to us.

To understand more fully these possibilities, the first step – or next step – is again simply to repeat the Mantras in their pairs, reflecting on their meaning and on the experience of repeating them, perhaps even in the sequence I suggest here, as they complement and lead into one another, back and forth:

1. Aum, obeisance to Nārāyaṇa.	2. Abba, Father.
4. Having completely given up all *dharmas*, to Me alone come for refuge....	3. If you want to be perfect, go, sell your possessions and give the proceeds to the poor...
5. I approach for refuge the feet of Nārāyaṇa with Śrī; obeisance to Nārāyaṇa with Śrī.	6. Father, into Thy hands I commend My spirit.
8. ...From all sins I will make you free. Do not grieve.	7. ... and you will have treasure in heaven. Then come, follow Me.

And after this practice, however long it might take to discern God's presence in it, as the one whom we worship, to whom we listen, and to whom we surrender, we might venture again the ostensibly simpler but, for a Christian, perhaps more daunting further practice of just the Mantras:

Aum, obeisance to Nārāyaṇa.
Having completely given up all *dharmas*, to Me alone come for refuge....
I approach for refuge the feet of Nārāyaṇa with Śrī; obeisance to Nārāyaṇa with Śrī.
...From all sins I will make you free. Do not grieve.

Should commentaries such as I have in mind and attempted here become more common and flourish in new schools of commentarial practice that extend across religious boundaries, then the number of those with richly complicated lives will increase, as the commented text and the commentary – as reading, as writing – instigate further reflection on who we are and how we pray, with what uttered and implicit words. If a book like this wins readers who are Śrīvaiṣṇavas, and in such a way that they do not turn away too quickly because this treatment of the Mantras is new, foreign, and imperfect, then such readers too will have new vantage points for theological and spiritual reflection, still within the Śrīvaiṣṇava tradition but with insights and words from a Christian perspective. When this occurs, we all will have much more to talk and pray about, with the Mantras in a new light, with old and revered words, and with new words voiced nowhere else before.[10]

[10] I have been speaking primarily from a Christian perspective, and about the challenges and options before us. In closing, I reaffirm my hope that members of the Śrīvaiṣṇava community will speak to the issues I have raised and indeed engage in an analogous commentarial practice, finding ways to include Christian scriptural and commentarial texts in Śrīvaiṣṇava reading, prayer, and theology. If some at least undertake learning Biblical texts and study them with commentarial patience, and learn to pray with greater mindfulness of the Christian tradition, then there may arise a fully reciprocal conversation owned by praying Christians and praying Śrīvaiṣṇavas. This prayerful conversation will draw members of both communities into a secondary but real community beholden to both traditions, reducible to neither. But however interesting such larger possibilities are, we need to begin with careful reading and commentary, and see where our minds and hearts lead us, rather than turning aside to other kinds of reflection not rooted in careful reading and commentary. On the question of the individual and communal dimensions of dialogue with respect to tradition, see Clooney 1992 and forthcoming e.

BIBLIOGRAPHY

Śrī Vedānta Deśika

Śrīmad Rahasyatrayasāra. Edited and annotated by Ramadesikacaryar Swami. Srirangam: Srimad Andavan Sri Pundarikapuram Swami Asramam, 2000.

Śrīmad Rahasyatrayasāra with the Cetlur Commentary by Tiruvahindrapuram Cetlur Narasimhacary Svami (Chennai: Rahasyatrayasara Pracarana Sabha, 1920)

Śrīmad Rahasyatrayasāra with the *Sārāsvādinī* of Vedanta Ramanuja (cc. 1-12) and Gopala Desika (cc. 13-32) and the *Sāraprakāśikā* of Srinivasa (cc. 1-32). Edited by Srisaila Venkataranganatha Mahadesikar and Raghunatha Tatayaryadasar (Kumbakonam, 1903-1911).

Śrīmad Rahasyatrayasāra with the *Sāravistaram* of Uttamur T. Viraraghavacharya. 2 volumes. Madras: Ubhayavedanta Granthamalai, 1980.

Śrīmad Rahasyatrayasāra with the *Śrīsārabodhinī* of Sri Srirangasankopa Yatindramahadesika. Ahobila: Ahobila Math, 1954.

Śrīmad Rahasyatrayasāra. Translated by M. R. Rajagopala Ayyangar. Kumbakonam: Agnihotram Ramanuja Thathachariar, 1956.

Śrīsampradāyapariśuddhi, in *Cillarai Rahasyaṅkaḷ.* Srirangam: Srimad Andavan Poundarikapuram Swamy Ashramam, 1978. Edited with annotations by Srirama Desikacarya Swami

The Minor Rahasyas of Sri Vedānta Deśika. Translated by A. Srinivasaraghavan. Sri Vishishtadvaita Pracharini Sabha, 1993.

Śrīmadrahasyatrayasārattil Swāmi Deśikaṉ aruḷi cceytulla Ślokaṅkaḷum Pācuraṅkaḷum. Chennai: Sri Poundarikapuram Swami Asrama Veliyitu, 2000.

Virodha Parihāra in *Cillarai Rahasyaṅkaḷ.* Volume 3 of 3 Volumes. Edited by S. Parthasarathi. Srirangam: Paundarikapuram Srimat Andavan Asramam, 1995.

Other Sources

Harvey P. ALPER, editor. *Mantra.* Albany, N.Y.: State University of New York Press, 1989.

Nadadoor AMMAL. *Prapanna Parijāta.* In Sanskrit with English Translation. Madras: Visishtadvaita Pracharini Sabha, 1971.

Parāśara BHAṬṬAR. *Aṣṭaślokī of Sri Parāśara Bhaṭṭārya.* Edited by T. Bheemacharya and S. N. Shastri. Indore: Bharati Publications, 1971.

Dennis J. BILLY. *The Way of a Pilgrim: Complete Text and Reader's Guide.* Liguori, Missouri: Liguori Press, 2000.

Francis X. CLOONEY, S.J. "In Joyful Recognition: A Hindu Formulation of the Relationship between God and the Community, and Its Significance for Christian Theology," *Journal of Ecumenical Studies* 25.3 (1987), 358-369.

—, *Thinking Ritually: Retrieving the Pūrva Mīmāṃsā of Jaimini.* Vienna: University of Vienna. De Nobili Research Series 17, 1990.

—, "Extending the Canon: Some Implications of a Hindu Argument about Scripture," *Harvard Theological Review* 85:2 (1992) 197-215.

—, "In Ten Thousand Places, In Every Blade of Grass: Uneventful but True Confessions about Finding God in India, and Here Too," *Studies in the Spirituality of Jesuits.* 1996a. 28.3 (May).

—, *Theology after Vedānta: An Experiment in Comparative Theology.* Albany: State University of New York Press, 1993.

—, *Seeing through Texts: Doing Theology among the Srivaisnavas of South India.* Albany: State University of New York Press, 1996b.

—, *Hindu Wisdom for All God's Children.* Maryknoll: Orbis Books, 1998.

—, *Hindu God, Christian God: How Reason Helps Break Down the Barriers between Religions.* New York: Oxford University Press, 2001.

—, "Theology and Sacred Scripture Reconsidered in the Light of a Hindu Text," in *Theology and Sacred Scripture.* Edited by Carol J. Dempsey, OP, and William Loewe. Maryknoll: Orbis Books, 2002a, 211-236.

—, "Fierce Words: Repositionings of Caste and Devotion in Traditional Śrīvaiṣṇava Hindu Ethics," *Journal of Religious Ethics* 30.3 (Fall 2002b), 399-419.

—, "When Researching and Teaching, Where and with Whom is My Heart?" *Conversations in Jesuit Higher Education* 24 (Fall 2003), pp. 46-48.

—, "The Constraint of Theory by Practice: Three Controversial Examples," *The Companion to Religious Ethics*, edited by William Schweiker. Blackwell Publishing, 2005a, 78-85.

—, *Divine Mother, Blessed Mother: Hindu Goddesses and the Virgin Mary.* New York: Oxford University Press, 2005b.

—, "Forms of Philosophizing: The Case of Chapter 7 of Vedānta Desika's *Śrīmad Rahasya Traya Sāra,*" *Satya Nilayam* 8 (August 2005c), 21-33.

—, "From Person to Person: A Study of Tradition in the *Guruparaṃparāsāra* of Vedānta Deśika's *Śrīmad Rahasyatrayasāra,*" *Boundaries, Dynamics and Construction of Traditions in South Asia*, edited by Federico Squarcini. Florence: University of Florence, 2006a, 203-224.

—, "Surrender to God Alone: the Meaning of Bhagavad Gītā 18:16 in Light of Śrīvaiṣṇava and Christian Tradition," in *Song Divine: Christian Commentaries on the Bhagavad Gita.* Edited by Catherine Cornille. Leuven: Peeters Publishing, 2006b, pp. 191-207.

—, "Rāmānuja and the Meaning of Krishna's Descent and Embodiment on This Earth," in *Krishna.* Edited by Edwin F. Bryant. New York: Oxford University Press, 2007a, pp. 329-356.

—, "Exegesis, Theology, and Spirituality: Reading the Dvaya Mantra according to Vedānta Deśika," *International Journal of Hindu Studies.* 11.1 (2007b), 27-62.

—, "Divine Absence and the Purification of Desire: A Hindu Saint's Experience of a God Who Keeps his Distance," *Science and Religions: Knowing the Unknowable about God and the Universe*. Edited by John Bowker. London: I.B. Tauris, 2008.

—, *Beyond Compare: St. Francis de Sales and Sri Vedānta Desika on Loving Surrender to God*. Washington, DC: Georgetown University Press. Forthcoming a.

—, "Christian Readers, Hindu Words: Toward Christian Commentary on Hindu Prayer. 2006 Bellarmine Lecture, *Theology Digest*. Forthcoming b.

—, "For Your Own Good: Suffering and Evil in God's Plan according to One Hindu Theologian," *Deliver Us From Evil: Boston University Studies in Philosophy and Religion*. Edited by M. David Eckel. Forthcoming c.

—, "Only for Those with Heart: The Symbiosis of the Theological and Spiritual in a Hindu Defense of the Godness," *Studies in Spirituality* (Nijmegen). Forthcoming d.

—, "Tradition and Dialogue: Reflections on Ravi Gupta's "Walking a Theological Tightrope," *ISKCON Studies* 1.1. Forthcoming e.

Catherine CORNILLE. *Song Divine: Christian Commentaries on the Bhagavat Gītā*. Leuven: Peeters Publishing, 2006.

Harold COWARD and David GOA, *Mantra: Hearing the Divine in India* Chambersburg, PA: Anima Books, 1991.

Mary Rose D'ANGELO, "Mark and Q: Abba and 'Father' in Context," *Harvard Theological Review* 85.2 (1992), 149-174.

Henri DE LUBAC. *Medieval Exegesis: the Four Senses of Scripture*. Translated by Mark Sebanc. Grand Rapids: W. B. Eerdmans, 1998.

Stephen FOWL. *Engaging Scripture: a Model for Theological Interpretation*. Malden: Blackwell Publishers, 1998.

Jan GONDA, "The Indian Mantra," *Oriens* 16 (1963), 244-297.

A. GOVINDACARYA. *The Holy Lives of the Azhvars or The Dravida Saints*. Bombay: Ananthacharya Indological Research Institute, 1982.

Joseph A. GRASSI, "'Abba,' Father (Mark 14:36): Another Approach," *Journal of the American Academy of Religion* 50.3 (1982), 449-458.

Bede GRIFFITHS. *River of Compassion: A Christian Commentary on the Bhagavad Gītā*. Continuum Publishing Company, 1995 [1987].

Paul GRIFFITHS. *Religious Reading*. New York: Oxford University Press, 1999.

Sanjukta GUPTA. *Lakṣmī Tantra: A Pāñcarātra Text*. Translated by Sanjukta Gupta. Delhi: Motilal Banarsidass Publishers, 2000.

Steven P. HOPKINS. *Singing the Body of God: The Hymns of Vedāntadeśika in Their South Indian Tradition*. New York: Oxford University Press, 2002.

Robert E. HUME. *The Thirteen Principal Upanishads translated from the Sanskrit*. Delhi: Oxford University Press, 1993.

N. JAGADEESAN. *History of Sri Vaishnavism in the Tamil Country (Post-Ramanuja)*. Madurai: Koodal Publishers, 1977.

Jean LECLERQ. *The Love of Learning and the Desire for God: A Study of Monastic Culture*. Translatedy by Catharine Misrahi. 3rd edition. New York: Fordham University Press, 1982.

Michael MCGHEE. *Transformations of Mind: Philosophy as Spiritual Practice*. Cambridge: New York: Cambridge University Press, 2000.

Patricia Y. MUMME, *The Mumukṣuppaṭi of Piḷḷai Lokācārya with Manavāḷamāmuni's Commentary.* Bombay: Ananthacharya Indological Research Institute, 1987.

—, *The Śrīvaiṣṇava Theological Dispute: Manavāḷamāmuni and Vedānta Deśika.* Madras: New Era Publications, 1988.

The New Oxford Annotated Bible with the Apocrypha. Edited by Michael Coogan, Mark Z. Brettler, Carol A. Newsom, and Pheme Perkins. New York: Oxford University Press, 2007.

André PADOUX, "Mantra," in the *Blackwell Companion to Hinduism*, edited by Gavin Flood. Malden: Blackwell Publishing, 2003, pp. 478-492.

Mangalam R. PARAMESWARAN. *Studies in Śrīvaiṣṇavism.* Winnipeg: Larkuma, 2005.

Laurie L. PATTON. *Bringing the Gods to Mind: Mantra and Ritual in Early Indian Sacrifice.* Berkeley: University of California Press, 2005.

Periyavāccāṉ PIḶḶAI. *Parantappaṭi,* in *Eṭṭu Rahasyaṅkaḷ.* Edited by Krsnaswami Ayyangar. Trichi: n.d.

Practica Quaedam: Norms for Correspondence with Father General and Other Concrete Business items. Rome: General Curia, 1997.

Sri RAMANUJA. *Sree Gadhyathrayam.* Translated by M.R. Rajagopalan Ayyengar. Chennai: Sri Nrsimhapriya Trust, 2002.

—, *The Śrī Bhāṣya. The Vedānta-Sūtras with the Commentary of Rāmānuja.* Translated by G. Thibaut. Delhi: Motilal Banarsidass, 1976 [1904].

Anbil RAMASWAMY. *Hinduism Rediscovered: A Contemporary Study of Hindu Thought.* Kuwait: the The Tiruvenkatam Group, 2004.

N. S. Anantha RANGACHARYA. *Essence of Śrīmad Rahasyatraya Sāram of Sriman Nigamanta Maha Desikar.* Bangalore: Sri Rama Printers. 2004.

Francis DE SALES. *Treatise on the Love of God.* Translated by Henry Benedict Mackey, OSB. Rockford: Tan Books and Publishers [1884] 1997.

Henri Le SAUX. *Prayer.* Philadelphia: The Westminster Press, 1973 [1967].

Satyavrata SINGH. *Vedānta Deśika: His Life, Works and Philosophy.* Varanasi: Chowkambha Sanskrit Series, 1958.

A. SRINIVASARAGHAVAN. *The Life and Work of Sri Nigamanta Maha Desika.* Madras: K.R. Ramaseshan, n.d.

Aaron STALNAKER. *Overcoming Evil: Spiritual Exercises in Xunzi and Augustine.* Washington: Georgetown University Press, 2006.

Krister STENDAHL, "The Bible as a Classic and the Bible as Holy Scripture," *Journal of Biblical Literature* 103.1 (1984) 3-10.

Tiru VALLUVAR. *The Tirukkural with Translations in English by G. U. Pope, W. H. Drew, John Lazarus, and F. W. Ellis.* Madras: Suth India Saiva Siddhanta Works Publishing Society, 1981.

David TRACY, *The Analogical Imagination.* New York: Crossroads, 1981.

K.K.A. VENTAKACHARI. *Śrīvaiṣṇavism: An Insight.* Mumbai: Ananthacharya Indological Research Institute, 2006.

Swami VIMALANANDA. *Mahānārāyaṇa Upaniṣad.* Madras: Sri Ramakrishna Math, 1957.

R. C. ZAEHNER. *The Bhagavad-Gita.* Oxford: Oxford University Press, 1968.

INDEX OF NAMES, TERMS, TEXTS

For words appearing frequently, only select introductory or key citations are given

INDEX OF BIBLICAL REFERENCES

PRINTED ON PERMANENT PAPER • IMPRIME SUR PAPIER PERMANENT • GEDRUKT OP DUURZAAM PAPIER - ISO 9706
N.V. PEETERS S.A., WAROTSTRAAT 50, B-3020 HERENT